KT-178-250

medi

MANUAL

studio and outside broadcast camerawork

media

MANUAL

16mm Film Cutting
John Burder

Basic Betacam Camerawork, Third Edition
Peter Ward

Basic Film Technique
Ken Daley

Basic Studio Directing
Rod Fairweather

Basic TV Reporting, Second Edition
Ivor Yorke

Basic TV Technology, Second Edition
Robert L. Hartwig

The Continuity Supervisor, Fourth Edition
Avril Rowlands

Creating Special Effects For TV And Video, Third Edition
Bernard Wilkie

Digital Video Camerawork
Peter Ward

Effective TV Production, Third Edition
Gerald Millerson

Film Technology In Post Production
Dominic Case

Grammar Of The Edit
Roy Thompson

Grammar Of The Shot
Roy Thompson

Lighting For Video, Third Edition
Gerald Millerson

Local Radio Journalism, Second Edition
Paul Chantler and Sim Harris

Motion Picture Camera and Lighting Equipment
David W. Samuelson

Motion Picture Camera Techniques
David W. Samuelson

Multi-Camera Camerawork
Peter Ward

Nonlinear Editing
Patrick Morris

Single Camera Video Production, Second Edition
Robert B. Musburger

Sound Recording And Reproduction, Third Edition
Glyn Alkin

Sound Techniques For Video And TV, Second Edition
Glyn Alkin

The Use Of Microphones, Fourth Edition
Alec Nisbett

Video Camera Techniques, Second Edition
Gerald Millerson

The Video Studio, Third Edition
Alan Bermingham et al.

TV Technical Operations
Peter Ward

THE LIBRARY
GUILDFORD COLLEGE
of Further and Higher Education

media

MANUAL

studio and outside broadcast camerawork:

a guide to multi-camerawork production

second edition

peter ward

Focal Press

OXFORD   AUCKLAND   BOSTON   JOHANNESBURG   MELBOURNE   NEW DELHI

to7052. 141 589

7-77 WAR

Focal Press
An imprint of Butterworth Heinemann
Linacre House, Jordan Hill, Oxford OX2 8DP
A division of Reed Educational and Professional Publishing Ltd

 A member of the Reed Elsevier plc group

First published as *Multi-Camera Camerawork* 1997
Second edition published as *Studio and Outside Broadcast Camerawork: A Guide to Multi-camerawork Production* 2001

© Peter Ward 2001

All rights reserved. No part of this publication may be reproduced in
any material form (including photocopying or storing in any medium by
electronic means and whether or not transiently or incidentally to some
other use of this publication) without the written permission of the
copyright holder except in accordance with the provisions of the Copyright,
Designs and Patents Act 1988 or under the terms of a licence issued by the
Copyright Licensing Agency Ltd, 90 Tottenham Court Rd, London,
England W1P 0LP. Applications for the copyright holder's written
permission to reproduce any part of this publication should be addressed
to the publishers

British Library Cataloguing in Publication Data
Ward, Peter, 1936–
   Studio and outside broadcast camerawork
   1. Video recording
   I. Title
   778.5'9

Library of Congress Cataloguing in Publication Data
Ward, Peter.
   Studio and outside broadcast camerawork/Peter Ward.
   p.cm.
   ISBN 0-240-51649-4
   1. Television cameras.   2. Television – Production and direction.   I. Title.
   TR882.5 .W37 2001
778.59–dc21   2001033577

ISBN 0 240 51649 4

Typeset by Avocet Typeset, Brill, Aylesbury, Bucks
Printed and bound in Great Britain by Biddles Ltd
www.biddles .co.uk

FOR EVERY TITLE THAT WE PUBLISH, BUTTERWORTH-HEINEMANN
WILL PAY FOR BTCV TO PLANT AND CARE FOR A TREE.

Contents

ACKNOWLEDGEMENTS 9

INTRODUCTION 10
STUDIO AND OUTSIDE
  BROADCAST CAMERAWORK 12
INVISIBLE TECHNIQUE 14
TELEVISION TECHNIQUE 16

TECHNOLOGY
THE TELEVISION SIGNAL 18
COLOUR TEMPERATURE 20
OPERATIONAL ASPECTS
  OF THE CAMERA 22
FULL FACILITY CAMERA 24
THE ZOOM LENS (1) 26
THE ZOOM LENS (2) 28
THE ZOOM LENS (3) 30
CAMERA MOUNTINGS 32
THE STUDIO FLOOR 34
CONTROL ROOMS 36
OUTSIDE BROADCAST
  FACILITIES 38

PRODUCTION METHODS
CONTROL ROOM STAFF 40
STUDIO FLOOR STAFF 42
THE PLANNING PROCESS 44
CAMERA COVERAGE
  FORMATS 46

RIGGING AND SAFETY
SAFETY 48
RIGGING A STUDIO 50
FLOOR MONITORS 52
SLUNG MONITORS 54
RIGGING CAMERAS 56
DE-RIGGING A CAMERA 58
BALANCING A LIGHTWEIGHT
  HEAD 60
OUTSIDE BROADCAST
  RIGGING 62

WORKING AMONG THE
  PUBLIC 64
WORKING AT HEIGHT 66
ADVERSE WEATHER 68
OUTSIDE BROADCAST
  HAZARDS 70

BASIC SKILLS
CABLES AND MONITORS (1) 72
CABLES AND MONITORS (2) 74
CAMERA REHEARSAL 76
REHEARSE/RECORD 78
TRACKING 80
OPERATING A CAMERA
  FOR THE FIRST TIME 82

OPERATIONAL SKILLS
PEDESTAL DESIGN 84
PRE-REHEARSAL CHECKLIST 86
PEDESTAL TECHNIQUE (1) 88
PEDESTAL TECHNIQUE (2) 90
PEDESTAL TECHNIQUE (3) 92
REPOSITIONING THE PED 94
TRACKING ON A PEDESTAL 96
CRABBING 98
CRANING 100
FOCUS 102
ZOOM FOCUS 104
PANNING AND TILTING 106
ZOOMING 108
PIVOT POINTS 112

PICTURE MAKING SKILLS
PICTURE MAKING 114
POSITIONING THE LENS 116
STRUCTURAL SKELETON
  OF A SHOT 118
PERSPECTIVE OF MASS 120
PERSPECTIVE OF LINE 122
CAMERA DISTANCE 124
CAMERA MOVEMENT 126

INVISIBLE MOVEMENT 128
CAMERA MOVEMENT –
    PANNING 130
STATIC AND MOVING
    OBJECTS 132
CONTAINING MOVEMENT 134
THE DEVELOPMENT SHOT 136
TRACKING AND ZOOMING 138
WIDE ANGLE/NARROW
    ANGLE 140
INTERNAL SPACE 142
SPACE AND ATMOSPHERE 144
TRACKING LINES 146
CAMERA HEIGHT 148
CAMERA POSITION AND
    LIGHTING 150

INTERCUTTING
CHANGE OF SHOT 152
INVISIBLE CUTS 154
INTERCUTTING 156
CROSS-SHOOTING 158
INTERVIEW/DISCUSSION 160

WORKING IN A CREW
WORKING IN A CAMERA
    CREW 162
THE VIEWFINDER 164
WORKING WITH TALKBACK 166
NEW TO TALKBACK 168
VISUAL MEMORY/CAMERA
    CARDS 170
CAMERA CARD NOTES 174
WORKING TO CUE LIGHTS 176
CUE LIGHT CONTROL 178
WORKING ON A CRANE 180
REMOTE CONTROL 182
SAFETY AND CRANE WORK 184
ASSESSING A SHOT 186
ATTITUDE AND
    RESPONSIBILITY 188
PROFESSIONAL CONDUCT 189

TRANSMISSION AND RECORDING
MULTI-CAMERA
    PRODUCTIONS 192
TRANSMISSION AND
    RECORDING (1) 194
TRANSMISSION AND
    RECORDING (2) 196
OUTSIDE BROADCAST
    PREPARATION 198
AS-DIRECTED 200
AS-DIRECTED REHEARSAL 202
AS-DIRECTED
    TRANSMISSION 204
IT'S A WRAP 206

COMPOSITION
COMPOSITION 208
PERCEPTION 210
VISUAL DESIGN 212
READING AN IMAGE 214
GROUPING AND
    ORGANIZATION 216
THE EDGE OF THE FRAME 218
FRAMES WITHIN FRAMES 220
CLOSED AND OPEN
    FRAMES 222
ASPECT RATIO 224
TRANSITIONAL PERIOD 226
WHY CONVERSION IS
    NEEDED 228
WIDESCREEN
    COMPOSITION 230
RATIO AND PROPORTION 232
LINES AND CURVES 234
BALANCE 236
DISSONANCE 238
DIVIDED INTEREST 240
NATURAL PERSPECTIVE 242
HARMONY AND CONTRAST 244
LIGHT 246
COLOUR 248

MONOCHROME
  VIEWFINDERS   250
WORKING AT SPEED   252

COMPOSITING
COMPOSITING   254
TWO- AND THREE-
  DIMENSIONAL
  BACKGROUNDS   256

CAMERA HEIGHT AND
  CHROMA KEY   258
MATCHING FOREGROUND
  TO BACKGROUND 260
CAMERA MOVEMENT ON
  BLUE SCREEN   262

FURTHER READING   264
GLOSSARY   265

Acknowledgements

My thanks to Alan Bermingham, Bill Curtis, Tony Grant, Andy Hall, Alan Jessop, Robert Kruger and Trevor Wimlett for reading the manuscript of the first edition of this manual and making many helpful and constructive suggestions. Any errors or omissions in the book are mine.

My thanks also to Chris O'Neill, Nick Bonney and Rick Fryer of Vinten Broadcast, Dick Adams, BBC Wales, Claire Owen, BBC TV, Mike Buttolph, Corporate Safety, BBC TV Centre and Margaret Denley, Focal Press. Finally, thanks to my wife Sue and my children, Sally and Edmund, for their help and encouragement in the production of this book.

Photographic Credits

Every effort has been made to find the copyright owners of the photographs used and photographs are reprinted by courtesy BBC TV, BBC Wales, Granada Television, Vinten Broadcast, Bob Ewens, Alan Jessop, Andrew Parr, Trevor Wimlett and 'Zerb', the Guild of Television Cameramen.

Introduction

A large proportion of broadcast, satellite, cable television programmes and corporate conference work is produced using a multi-camera production technique. The programme formats vary from sports coverage, pop concerts, audience discussions, state occasions, game shows to relays of opera and concerts. Multi-camera technique has its own distinct discipline, equipment and operational procedures compared to the single camera, single shot technique practised in film and lightweight video camera operation.

Whereas in the past, broadcast camera operators were trained in the basic skills of multi-camera work and then moved on to single camera operation, many camera operators now start their careers in the single camera mode and have little or no experience of the skills required for multi-camera working. Many students of media courses have no access to professional broadcast multi-camera studios and outside broadcast scanners* and spend the majority of their training using a single camera.

It is not simply a matter of adjusting to additional operational controls on a larger camera; frequently the same model of camera is used on single and multi-camera operations. In any case, an understanding of which 'button' to push does not equip anyone to become a 'camera operator'. The ability to use the operational controls of a TV camera can be mastered relatively quickly. The ability to fluently coordinate a camera and mounting whilst working on a live transmission, getting every shot right first time whilst matching your camerawork to that of others, can take many years.

This style of camerawork grew out of the need to cover a variety of subjects which unfolded in their own time scale. From ninety minute dramas to four hour state events, television multi-camera techniques were invented and adapted to suit virtually any programme format.

When lightweight portable video cameras were developed, it was thought that single camera working would become the norm. In fact a large range of actuality events can never be adequately covered using a single camera. An additional factor in multi-camera coverage is its economy. Studios and outside broadcasts can produce a complete programme in a day and transmit it, if required, without the need for extended post-production. Rather surprisingly to some observers, even mini-soap and drama series are reverting to multi-camera shooting in order to speed up production and cut costs.

Studio and Outside Broadcast Camerawork outlines the basics of multi-camera technique and identifies standard industry practices and procedures that a newcomer to multi-camera working may expect to encounter.

---

*Television terms or jargon words where they are not defined are described in the glossary

At one time they would have been prepared for live and working-as-live TV camerawork by serving time within a camera crew in a broadcast organization and accumulating experience under supervision over a wide range of programme formats. They may now find themselves thrown into a day's rehearsal and transmission without the benefit of this 'apprenticeship' experience. This manual aims to prepare a camera operator new to multi-camera camerawork with the range of techniques they are likely to encounter.

Note: The terms 'cameraman' and 'cameramen' are used in some instances in this manual without wishing to imply that any production craft is restricted to one gender.

Studio and outside broadcast camerawork

Across the wide range of camera techniques employed by film and video camera operators there are certain shared skills that are common to all forms of camerawork. Standard conventions in composition, camera movement and editing requirements (with small variations) are to be seen in the highest budgeted Hollywood blockbuster through to the modest two-minute regional magazine insert. Multi-camera camerawork shares these common characteristics with the addition of a few specialist requirements.

The layout of this manual identifies the following skills needed by a cameraman working on a multi-camera production:

- **Technology:** an understanding of camera technology, lens characteristics and studio/outside broadcast arrangements.
- **Production methods:** an understanding of television production technique and working practices.
- **Rigging and safety:** how to rig safely and operate a camera and a camera mounting.
- **Basic skills:** anticipation, preparation and concentration.
- **Operational skills:** basic camera and pedestal operational skills.
- **Picture making skills:** positioning the camera and lens.
- **Intercutting:** matching shots and edit points.
- **Working in a camera crew:** an understanding of the camera operator's role in programme production and within a camera crew.
- **Recording and transmission:** types of multi-camera production and transmission procedure.
- **Composition:** an understanding of shot composition.
- **Compositing techniques:** blue screen working and virtual studios.

Teamwork

In addition to the above skills is the crucial fact that television programme making is a group activity and good teamwork is an essential ingredient for its success. The ability to work in a team is often overlooked when discussing camerawork as if this is not part of the necessary operational skills required. It is central to the job of a multi-camera television camera operator.

The importance of working both as a team and in a team cannot be overestimated. If you have difficulty working with people you will not enjoy multi-camera camerawork. A television programme is created by a number of technicians exchanging information, modifying and fine-tuning the original concept.

The script or brief is brought to the screen via a number of specialist crafts such as, directing, design, lighting, vision control and camera crew.

There is discussion and consensus between all crafts channelled through the director. The ability to discuss, inform and quite often reach a compromise from what one might consider ideal practice is part of working in a camera crew and being part of a production crew.

Not least of the skills required when working in such a group activity is the ability to communicate. If a large part of TV production involves problem solving then providing and seeking information about the specific project in hand is a key element in multi-camera camerawork.

Invisible technique

The creation of invisible technique

The ability to record an event on film was achieved in the latter part of the nineteenth century. During the next two decades, there was the transition from the practice of running the camera continuously to record an event, to the stop/start technique of separate shots where the camera was repositioned between each shot in order to film new material. The genesis of film narrative was established.

The screen was conceived as an acting area similar to the stage as seen by an audience in a theatre. The action moved within the screen space without either the camera moving or the size of shot changing. All the techniques that we are familiar with now had to be learnt in the first two decades of the twentieth century. The first film makers had to experiment and invent the grammar of editing, shot size and the variety of camera movements that are now standard.

As well as camera movement came the problems involved in stopping the camera, moving to a new position and starting the camera again. The ability to find ways of shooting subjects and then editing the shots together without distracting the audience was learnt by the commercial cinema over a number of years.

The guiding concept that connected all these developing techniques of camera movement and shot change was the need to persuade the audience that they were watching continuous action in real time. This required the mechanics of film making to be hidden from the audience, i.e. to be invisible.

'Invisible' cuts

There was a need for unobtrusive shot transition and camera movement in order to achieve a seamless flow of images in the story-telling. A number of 'invisible' techniques were discovered and became the standard conventions of film making and later television camerawork.

In essence, this convention directs the audience attention to the action rather than to the mechanics of production. Methods are employed to cut between shots, to keep attention on what is contained within the frame rather than beyond its enclosing area and to move the camera smoothly to a new viewpoint without distracting the viewer.

There are alternative conventions of presentation which intentionally draw attention to the means of production. Camera movement in this alternative technique is often restlessly on the move, panning abruptly from subject to subject, making no effort to disguise the transitions and deliberately drawing attention to the means by which the images are brought to the viewer. This breaking down or subverting the Hollywood convention of an 'invisible'

seamless flow of images has a number of different forms or styles. In general, television production adopted the 'Hollywood' model of invisible technique.

Television technique

Standard camerawork conventions

The technique of changing shot without distracting the audience was learnt over a number of years. Reverse angles, point-of-view shots and position matching on cuts were all discovered and became standard technique. The evolution of the grammar of film technique was not instantaneous or self-evident. Each visual technique had to be invented, refined and accepted by other film makers before entering the repertoire of standard camera practice.

The thread that linked most of these developments was the need to provide a variety of ways of presenting visual information coupled with the need for them to be unobtrusive in their transition from shot to shot. Expertly used, they were invisible and yet provided the narrative with pace, excitement and variety. These criteria are still valid and much of the pioneering work from the first decades of the twentieth century remains intact in current camera technique.

Multi-camera live television conventions

Film is a record of an event, edited and assembled after the event occurs. Live television is a presentation of an event as it occurs. The unique quality of an electronic camera is its ability to produce a picture that can be instantly transmitted. Multi-camera coverage entails a production technique which involves a number of people perfecting their individual contribution in a production group simultaneously as the event is transmitted. To coordinate such a group activity, it is essential to plan and have some measure of rehearsal before transmission or to rely on standard production conventions which are understood by everyone involved.

Standard television multi-camera conventions grew out of film technique and the same objectives of disguising technique in order to suspend disbelief in the viewer was adopted. The problem for live television was not to recreate 'real' time as in discontinuous film shooting but to mould multi-camera shooting of an event so that, for example, change of camera angle or cutting between different shot sizes was not obtrusive and distracting to the viewer. The aim once again was towards an 'invisible' technique.

As multi-camera television camerawork deals with uninterrupted action in a timescale created by the nature of the event covered, 'real' time has to be continuously covered in a mixture of shot sizes, camera development and matched shot sizes to allow invisible cuts between cameras.

Multi-camera camera operators have to provide cutting points either pre-rehearsed or by monitoring what the rest of the camera crew are providing. Idiosyncratic personal composition by a camera operator will remain unnoticed only if he/she is responsible for the whole of the visual production. It will immediately become apparent in multi-camera work if his/her work is

intercut with standard camera technique provided by the rest of the crew.

Multi-camera technique remains invisible provided it conforms to certain criteria. These standard conventions are inherited by everyone working within live or multi-camera recordings.

The television signal

The camera as a production tool

Television broadcasting is a high technology industry. Digital manipulation can transform video images and computer graphics can generate scenery, animate characters and create fantasy worlds impossible to build and tape in three-dimensional space.

Despite these visual riches, most television programmes involve people and use cameras as the first stage in acquiring material. The video camera is the most creative production tool available and although a highly sophisticated piece of electronic equipment, its value in programme production depends on the techniques deployed by the camera operator. Its operational characteristics as a production tool are vital but its electronic performance is also crucial in camerawork. A knowledge of how a camera and lens turn light into electricity and the methods of controlling and creatively exploiting that transformation are the foundation on which to build multi-camera operational skills in programme making.

Turning light into electricity

Light passing through the lens is split by a prism into red, green and blue components and filtered on to three or more charge-coupled devices (CCDs). The charge induced in the CCDs by the intensity and colour of the scene brightness is extracted by a series of synchronized lines and combined to make up the standard TV signal (see opposite).

Composite

The PAL colour system is the result of adding a chroma signal to an existing 625 line monochrome system to carry the colour information. The three colour signals obtained from splitting the light in the camera prism are the primary colours for the television additive colour system. Various combinations of these three primaries will produce the remaining colours. The amplitude of the individual colour signals from the three camera sensors is proportional to the mix of colours in shot.

By combining proportions of the red, green and blue signals, a luminance signal (Y) (monochrome picture) is produced which corresponds to picture brightness. The three colour signals generated in the camera are encoded (combined) with the luminance signal to form a single composite signal. This is an analogue signal where the amplitude at any moment is proportional to the picture brightness at that point.

Component

Until recently the composite signal was the normal form of signal passed between all production equipment before being transmitted. With the introduction of digital effects, frame stores and component VTRs it was seen to be

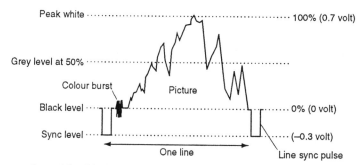

The waveform of the 1V television signal divides into two parts at black level. Above black, the signal varies depending on the tones in the picture from black (0 V) to peak white (0.7 V). Below black, the signal (which is never seen) is used for synchronizing the start of each line and frame. A colour burst provides the receiver with information to allow colour signal processing.

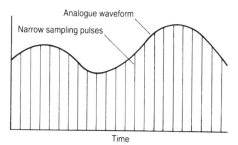

The continuously varying voltage of the TV signal (the analogue signal) is measured (or sampled) at a set number of positions per television line and converted into a stream of numbers (the digital signal) which alters in magnitude in proportion to the original signal.

Storing the signal as binary numbers (ones and zeros) has two advantages. It provides a robust signal that is resistant to noise and distortion and can be restored to its original condition whenever required. Secondly, it enables computer techniques to be applied to the video signal, creating numerous opportunities for picture manipulation and re-ordering the digital samples for standards conversion.

an advantage to keep the signal in a separated form until transmission, sent as luminance (commonly called the 'Y' signal) representing reflected scene light levels, together with two colour components for blue and red (commonly called Cb and Cr). Green information is electronically derived from luminance and the other colour components, at the receiving end of the chain.

Digital
The analogue signal can suffer degradation during processing through the signal chain, particularly in multi-generation editing where impairment to the signal is cumulative. By coding the video signal into a digital form, a stream of numbers is produced which change sufficiently often to mimic the analogue continuous signal.

19

Colour temperature

Additive colour system

Colour television transmission relies on an additive colour system of green, red and blue combining in different ratios to produce all the colours in the spectrum. A combination of 30% of red, 59% of green and 11% of blue will produce one unit of white and it is white that requires the greatest attention in camera line-up.

A white card will change its appearance depending on the colour of the light source that is illuminating it. The eye adjusts to the colour difference between the 'white' of a card lit by daylight and the 'white' of the same card when illuminated by a normal household bulb (tungsten filament) which has more red than mid-day daylight. To the eye, the card under both light conditions simply looks white – an absence of colour.

But the TV camera makes no mental adjustment. It reproduces accurately the predominant colour of the light source illuminating the white card and if the colour of the main source of illumination changes, the camera needs to be adjusted to reproduce the card as white.

Colour temperature range

A convenient way of defining the colour of a light source is to quote its colour temperature in degrees kelvin (K). Typical values of everyday light sources are:

Average summer sunlight	5500 K
Morning/afternoon sunlight	4000–5000 K
Sunrise/sunset	2000–3000 K
Tungsten lamp	3200 K

Colour cameras are designed to operate in a tungsten environment. Processing of the output from the red, green and blue sensors is normalized to signal levels produced by a scene lit with tungsten lighting (3200 K). When the camera is exposed to daylight, it requires significant changes to the red and blue channel gains to achieve a 'white balance'.

In-camera filters

To 'equalize' the daylight to tungsten and so reduce this problem, the cameras are fitted with a filter wheel in front of the light-splitting block. This allows the insertion of a minus blue filter (an orange filter) for scenes when the camera is exposed to daylight (5600 K filter position).

Other filters usually found in a filter wheel (some cameras have two wheels) are various grades of neutral density filter which reduce the amount of light by measured amounts without causing a colour cast. Effects filters are also often fitted such as star bursts which, depending on individual filter design, produce either a four-, six- or eight-point 'star' flare from a highlight.

Additive colour system

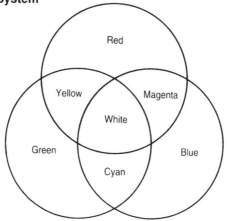

Three colour signals are produced by splitting the light into three channels. Colours that are composed of two or more primary colours produce proportional signals in each channel. The luminance signal is obtained by combining proportions of the red, green and blue signals.

A card placed in front of the lens that produces a signal with the proportions of 30% from the red channel, 59% from the green channel and 11% from the blue channel will be transmitted as white.

Independent of the colour temperature of the light illuminating the card, if the signal can be adjusted in the camera to produce a ratio 30%R + 59%G + 11%B (the process called white balancing) then the card will be transmitted as white.

Colour temperature is measured in degrees kelvin (K)

1 Iron rod at room temperature 18 °C.
2 Iron rod heated to 3473 °C (3200 K) produces light of a colour temperature equivalent to light produced by a tungsten filament.
3 Iron rod heated to 5873 °C (5600 K) produces light of a colour temperature equivalent to North European average summer sunlight.

Operational aspects of the camera

The professional broadcast video camera used in multi-camera production consists of a zoom lens (usually servo-controlled from behind the camera) attached to a camera body containing three or four light sensors (CCDs), electronic circuits to process the signal, an electronic viewfinder mounted on top of the camera and various production facilities such as talkback, filter controls, mixed viewfinder switches, etc.

The three vital facilities that keep the camera operator in touch with programme production are viewfinder, talkback and cue lights. Without a good quality viewfinder he/she is unable to frame up and focus the shot. Without talkback and cue lights, he/she is unaware when the shot will be taken.

Operational controls which have a significant influence on the operation of the camera and transform it from an electronic device into a programme production tool are as follows:

- servo controls of the zoom lens which allow a smooth take-off, precise control of speed of zoom and positive focus.
- a pan/tilt head to enable the fluid control of camera movement. The pan/tilt head should be adjustable to achieve precise balance in order to cater for a wide range of camera/lens combinations and additional attachments such as prompters. It should also have the facility to accommodate the varying centres of gravity (CoG) of different lens/camera/viewfinder combinations.
- a camera mounting which allows the camera operator to position the camera and lens quickly, smoothly and with precision for the desired shot and for the camera to remain at that setting until it is repositioned.

In addition to the operational controls there is obviously a requirement that cameras produce a high quality electronic picture. This will depend on the design characteristics of the camera's performance such as its sensitivity, resolution, contrast range, etc.

The technical quality of the image produced by the camera has an important influence on how the viewer responds to the production. However, the priorities for a camera operator are often centred on the handling ability of the camera, lens and mounting plus the need to work with a reasonable depth of field in an ad-lib situation coupled with the necessity of seeing the focus zone in the viewfinder. In addition, good communications are vital whether in a crowded studio or a remote location. If the operators cannot hear or talk to the control room, then their contribution is severely impaired.

White balance with tungsten

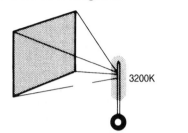
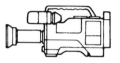

White card illuminated by light source with a colour temperature of 3200 K.
Select filter position on camera – clear glass.
White balance adjusts channel outputs in the proportions of 0.30 red; 0.59 green; 0.11 blue which when combined produce white.

White balance with daylight equivalent

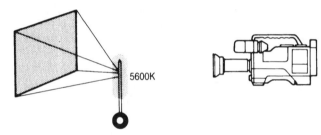

White card illuminated by light source with colour temperature of 5600 K equivalent to daylight.
Select minus blue filter position on camera.
The filter removes a percentage of blue and the white balance returns the output of the 3 channels to the proportions of 0.3 red, 0.59 green and 0.11 blue.

Exposure

A basic requirement in multi-camera productions is that there are no mismatches of exposure or colour rendition when cameras are intercut. This is achieved by remotely controlling the aperture (affecting exposure) and colour adjustment of each camera by vision control where the output of each camera is compared, adjusted and matched. Built-in neutral density (ND) filters and colour correction filters between lens and CCDs can also be switched in when required.

Full facility camera

Lightweight vs main line cameras

Development in technology has allowed cameras used in multi-camera productions to become smaller and smaller. Miniaturization has brought gains and losses for camera operators. The gains have included easier rigs and de-rigs, remote control of cameras on cranes and access to areas previously restricted by the size and weight of larger cameras and mountings. The disadvantages have included tiny switches which are difficult to use at speed, especially when gloves are worn on location, the lack of a full range of production facilities such as controllable cursors in the viewfinder, a range of mixed viewfinder sources, easy access to filter controls, shot box facility and a smaller, limited movement range of the viewfinder.

Lightweight lens servo controls are sometimes not as positive or operationally as sensitive as those found on larger lens packages. A compromise solution is to mount a lightweight camera with large viewfinder and box lens (a large diameter lens encased in a protective cover) in a purpose built harness which has the same approximate 'feel' and zoom range as a standard, full facility camera.

Facilities found on a multi-camera production camera

The operational use of each of the following camera facilities is described in greater detail in a later section of the manual.

- *An electronic viewfinder* which is usually monochrome although some cameras have the choice of colour or mono. Focusing of a broadcast video camera is through the viewfinder. The definition of the electronic picture therefore must allow the camera operator to be the first person in the production chain to see loss of optical focus.
- *Viewfinder controls* – brightness, contrast, peaking (to accentuate edge definition as an aid to focusing); may also have controls for viewfinder image size.
- *Mixed viewfinder controls* enable the viewfinder picture to be switched to other video combinations.
- *Cue lights* in the viewfinder, on the front of camera and on the front of the lens are lit when the camera output is selected at the vision mixing panel. Cue lights outside the viewfinder (on the camera body and lens) can be switched out of circuit if required.
- *Zoom lens* – available in a range of zoom ratios.
- *Lens hood* – helps control flare and degradation and acts as partial protection against rain.
- *Zoom thumb control* on adjustable pan bar.
- *Zoom focus capstan* wheel on pan bar.
- *Range extender* for zoom lens.

- *Shot box* pre-sets a range of zoom angles of views.
- *Headset* and headset jack points for talkback from and to the control room staff.
- *Talkback volume* controls production and engineering talkback and pro-gramme sound level to the headset.
- *Filter wheel* – fitted with a range of colour correction filters, neutral den-sity and effects filters.
- *Crib card holder* and sometimes crib card illumination.

Full facility camera controls

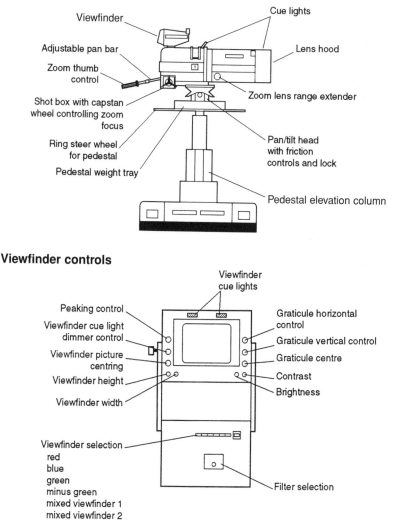

Viewfinder controls

25

The zoom lens (1)

Image size

The image formed by the lens on the face of the pick-up sensors (tube or CCD) is called the image size of the lens. This must match the camera sensor which varies in size although the majority of broadcast cameras are fitted with ⅔ inch CCD. For example, the image formed by a lens designed for a ⅔ inch CCD camera is a circle with a diameter of 11 mm whereas the image size of a lens for a NHK HDTV 1125 CCD camera is 16 mm.

Lenses designed for different sized formats (pick-up sensor dimension) may not be interchangeable. The image size produced by the lens may be much smaller than the pick-up sensor and probably the back focus (flange-back) will not have sufficient adjustment.

Focal length

When parallel rays of light pass through a convex lens, they converge to one point on the optical axis. This point is called the focal point of the lens. The focal length of the lens is indicated by the distance from the centre of the lens or the principal point of a compound lens (e.g. a zoom lens) to the focal point.

The longer the focal length of a lens, the smaller its angle of view and the shorter the focal length of a lens, the wider its angle of view.

Angle of view

The approximate horizontal angle of view of a fixed focal length lens can be calculated by using its focal length and the size of the pick-up sensors of the camera.

For most broadcast cameras (⅔ inch CCDs) the formula would be:

$$\text{angle of view} = 2 \tan^{-1} \frac{8.8 \text{ mm (width of CCD)}}{2 \times \text{focal length (mm)}}$$

Zoom

Although there are prime lenses (fixed focal length) available for some portable ⅔ inch cameras, the majority of cameras are fitted with a zoom lens with an adjustable focal length and therefore an adjustable angle of view over a given range.

This is achieved by moving one part of the lens system (the variator) to change the size of the image and by automatically gearing another part of the lens system (the compensator) to move simultaneously and maintain focus. This alters the image size and therefore the effective focal length of the lens.

Focal length of single lens

Focal length of compound lense

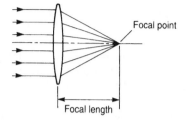

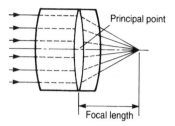

Calculating angle of view

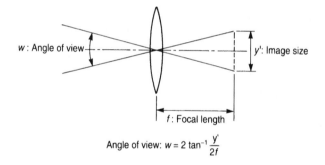

Angle of view: $w = 2 \tan^{-1} \dfrac{y'}{2f}$

Pre-focusing

When the production requirement is for a zoom-in to a subject, the lens must first be fully zoomed in on the subject and focused, then zoomed out to the required starting shot. The zoom will now stay in focus for the whole range of its travel. If possible, always pre-focus before zooming in.

The zoom lens (2)

Zoom ratio

A zoom lens can vary its focal length. The ratio of the longest focal length it can achieve (the telephoto end) with the shortest focal length obtainable (its wide-angle end) is its zoom ratio.

A lens manufacturer will state zoom ratio and the wide-angle focal length in one figure. A '14 × 8.5' zoom lens for a ⅔ inch CCD camera can therefore be decoded as a zoom with a 14:1 ratio starting at 8.5 mm focal length (angle of view = 56°) with the longest focal length of 14 × 8.5 mm = 119 mm (angle of view = 4°). The zoom ratio thus (approximately) equates to '14 ×' i.e. 14 × 4° = 56°.

Lenses with ratios as high as 70:1 can be obtained but the exact choice of ratio and the focal length at the wide end of the zoom will depend very much on what is required from the lens. Large zoom ratio lenses are heavy, often require a great deal of power to operate the servo controls and have a reduced f-number (see below).

Range extender

A zoom lens can be fitted with an internal range-extender lens system which allows the zoom to be used on a different set of focal lengths. A 2× extender on the 14 × 8.5 zoom mentioned above would transform the range from 8.5–119 mm to 17–238 mm but it may also lose 2 stops approaching maximum focal length (238 mm).

f-number

The f-number of a lens is a method of indicating how much light passes through the lens. It is proportional to lens diameter and inversely proportional to focal length. For a given focal length, the larger the aperture of the lens, the smaller its f-number and the brighter the image it produces.

f-numbers are arranged in a scale where each increment is multiplied by $\sqrt{2}$ (1.414). Each time the f-number is increased, the exposure is decreased by half.

1.4   2   2.8   4   5.6   8   11   16   22

Each division on this scale is called a 'stop'. Half a division would be a 'half stop'. The effective aperture of a zoom is not its actual diameter, but the diameter of the image of the diaphragm seen from in front of the lens. This is called the entrance pupil of the lens (see diagram opposite).

When the lens is zoomed (i.e. the focal length is altered) the diameter of the lens which is proportional to focal length alters and also its entrance pupil. The f-number decreases as the focal length of the zoom is altered from its widest angle to its smallest angle. This may cause 'f-drop' or 'ramping' at the telephoto end when the entrance pupil diameter equals the diam-

Typical manufacturer's zoom code

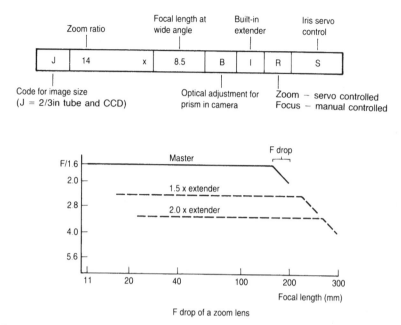

		Focal length at wide angle	Built-in extender	Iris servo control	

Zoom ratio

J	14	x	8.5	B	I	R	S

Code for image size
(J = 2/3in tube and CCD)

Optical adjustment for prism in camera

Zoom — servo controlled
Focus — manual controlled

F drop of a zoom lens

Ramping

When zooming in, entrance pupil becomes larger until it equals diameter of focusing lens group and cannot increase in size. f-drop or ramping may cause underexposure at low light levels.

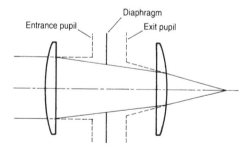

Entrance pupil

In low light conditions (e.g. twilight evening sports events) when the lens aperture may be at its widest at the start of a zoom-in, the picture may be underexposed when the zoom reaches its longest focal length.

eter of the focusing lens group and, due to the lens design, cannot become any larger. Increasing the diameter of the focusing lens group to avoid ramping increases the weight and the cost of the lens.

29

The zoom lens (3)

Depth of field
Changing the f-number alters the depth of field – the portion of the field of view which appears sharply in focus. This zone extends in front of and behind the subject on which the lens is focused and will increase as the f-number increases (see diagram opposite).

The greater the distance of the subject from the camera, the greater the depth of field. The depth of field is greater behind the subject than in front and is dependent on the focal length of the lens.

f-number and therefore depth of field can be adjusted by altering the light level or by the use of neutral density filters.

Minimum object distance
The distance from the front of the lens to the nearest subject that can be kept in focus is called the MOD – minimum object distance. A 14 × 8.5 zoom would have a MOD of between 0.8 m and 0.65 m whereas a larger zoom ratio lens, for example, 33:1, may have a MOD of over 2 m.

Macro
Many zooms are fitted with a macro mechanism which allows objects closer than the lens MOD to be held in focus. The macro shifts several lens groups inside the lens to allow close focus but this prevents the lens being used as a constant focus zoom.

Flange-back (back focus)
Flange-back (commonly called back focus) is the distance from the flange surface of the lens mount to the image plane of the pick-up sensor. Each camera type has a specific flange-back distance (for example, 48 mm in air) and any lens fitted to that camera must be designed with the equivalent flange-back. There is usually a flange-back adjustment mechanism of the lens with which the flange-back can be adjusted by about 0.5 mm. It is important when changing lenses on a camera to check the flange-back position is correctly adjusted (see opposite) and to white balance the new lens.

Glass compensation
A television zoom lens is designed with reference to the beam-splitting prism of the camera it is to be used with. The lens and the prism block glass path needs to be predicted to allow glass compensation to be part of the lens design. Some lens manufacturers indicate the compensation in the lens code number (e.g. Cannon J18 × 9B4 lens – the letter B indicates the lens is glass compensated and the following number 4 indicates the type of compensation).

Depth of field

Depth of field is greater behind subject in focus than in front.

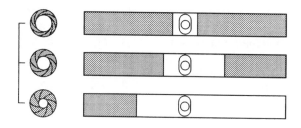

Adjusting flange-back (back focus)

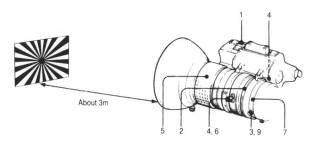

About 3m

1. Set the IRIS selector to Manual.
2. Place star burst lens chart at approx. 3 m or more and open aperture to maximum. Adjust for correct exposure by using either ND filters or adjusting light on the chart.
3. Zoom in on star burst chart.
4. Adjust for sharp focus on chart with front focus ring.
5. Zoom out to widest angle.
6. Loosen the flange-back (fF) adjustment ring lock screw.
7. Adjust fF for optimum definition on chart.

Do not touch zoom focus ring. (NB FLANGE-BACK position should be close to standard marked position on lens)

8. Repeat steps 4 through to 7 until focus is correct at telephoto and wide angle positions.
9. Tighten the fF adjustment ring lock screw.

Switch in RANGE EXTENDER. Zoom in and focus. Zoom out and check that zoom holds focus over complete range.

Camera mountings

Horses for courses

There is a wide range of camera mountings available to cover the diverse requirements of multi-camera programme making in the studio and on location. No one camera mounting will necessarily embrace all styles of camerawork and all weights of equipment.

The first selection criterion is to know if the mounting is to be transported to its operating position (i.e. at a location rather than operated daily in a studio). Equipment that has to be carried up stairs or rigged in difficult locations needs to be lighter and more easily rigged and de-rigged compared to equipment used permanently in a studio.

The second consideration is if the mounting is to be used to reposition the camera 'on shot' or if it is simply needed to reposition 'off shot'. A tripod on wheels (if the ground surface is suitable) can be repositioned to a new camera position but is unsuitable for development shots. A pedestal mounting with steerable wheels and smooth adjustment of height will allow a development on shot if operated on a level floor.

The third consideration is the total weight of camera, lens and, possibly, camera operator, which the mounting will need to support. The simplest way of moving a lightweight camera is to carry it on the shoulder (on or off shot) although this will not give such a smooth movement as using a harness around the torso to steady the camera. There is a range of lightweight tripods, portable pedestals and jib arms that can be used with a lightweight camera. There is also the facility to rig a lightweight camera on the end of a boom arm and move it on a servo driven pan/tilt head and to control the lens using remote controls. At the other end of the scale there are cranes capable of elevating a full facility camera and camera operator to a lens height of over 6 m (20 ft).

Pan/tilt heads

A good pan and tilt head will have adjustment for the centre of gravity (CoG) of the combination of camera/recorder, lens and viewfinder in use. If the CoG is not adjusted the camera will either be difficult to move from the horizontal or it will tilt forwards or backwards. Adjustment of the CoG balance should not be confused with mid-point balance, which involves positioning the camera and lens to find the point of balance on the head.

The setting of the friction or drag control of the head depends on the shot and personal preference. Using a very narrow lens for an extreme close shot (e.g. a bird nesting) may require much more friction than that needed to pan the camera smoothly when following rapid impromptu movement (e.g. skating). Some camera operators prefer a heavy drag or 'feel' on the head so that there is weight to push against while others remove all friction, allowing the head to be panned at the slightest touch.

Full facility camera pan/tilt head

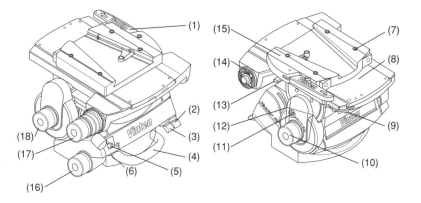

(1) wedge adaptor operating lever, (2) pan friction brake lock, (3) tilt friction brake lock, (4) carrying handle, (5) level bubble, (6) level bubble light switch, (7) wedge adaptor fixing bolts, (8) sliding plate, (9) sliding plate adjustment knob, (10) centre of gravity balance control, (11) tilt axis centre lock, (12) centre lock release, (13) sliding plate clamp, (14) pan bar mounting point, (15) wedge plate adaptor, (16) pan drag adjustment knob, (17) pan bar clamp, (18) tilt drag (friction) adjustment knob.
Warning: Do not rely on the tilt brake (3) when changing cameras. Always engage the centre lock (11).

Lightweight camera pan/tilt head

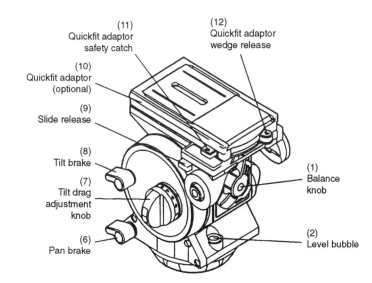

(11) Quickfit adaptor safety catch

(12) Quickfit adaptor wedge release

(10) Quickfit adaptor (optional)

(9) Slide release

(8) Tilt brake

(7) Tilt drag adjustment knob

(6) Pan brake

(1) Balance knob

(2) Level bubble

33

The studio floor

A television studio equipped to mount live and recorded multi-camera productions usually contains three main areas: the studio floor area, the control rooms and a series of production rooms.

The studio floor area

The studio floor surface needs to be absolutely level and free from bumps, cracks or unevenness. One of the basic needs of multi-camera work is to move the camera on shot smoothly and quietly without the use of tracks or boards. If the floor surface cannot accommodate camera movement on shot then it is unsuitable for the production of continuous multi-camera programme making.

Most broadcast studios are equipped with at least three cameras with provision for additional cameras as required. The standard mounting for the camera is usually a pedestal but alternative mountings such as a tripod, dolly, jib arm or crane may be used depending on the requirements of the production. When not in use, the cameras may be stored in a technical storage area which is off the studio floor. Often they are covered and left in an area of the studio floor so as not to obstruct the scenery and lamp de-rigging and the subsequent rig for the following show. Storage area is also required for camera cables, monitors, sound and lighting equipment.

Access for scenery is through large double doors. There must be sufficient grid height overhead to accommodate a cyclorama, a 5 m+ cloth that is stretched taut in an arc around one, two or three sides of the studio to provide a lit backing. Suspended from the grid are lighting hoists that can be lowered for rigging lamps and individually routed to a numbered input into the lighting console. Access to the grid area is often required for rigging lamps, monitors, speakers and suspended scenery. Electrically-driven hoists are used to suspend scenery and for flying in scenery pieces. Other hoists may be available for audience monitors and speakers or simply to liberate more floor space.

The studio walls are usually acoustically treated to improve the sound handling qualities. Installed at strategic positions along the studio walls are the technical facilities commonly called wall boxes. Monitors, microphones, foldback loudspeakers, technical mains and talkback can be plugged into these boxes to provide flexibility in technical rigging depending on the production layout. Positioned on the studio wall may be outlets for water, gas, etc. for production purposes.

Studios require air-conditioning to extract the heat generated by the lamps and a 'house' lighting system (plus emergency lights), when studio lamps are not switched on for rigging and de-rigging. Fire alarms and fire lanes are required to provide an unimpeded route for audiences and production staff to the fire exits.

Close to the studio may be make-up rooms, wardrobe and dressing

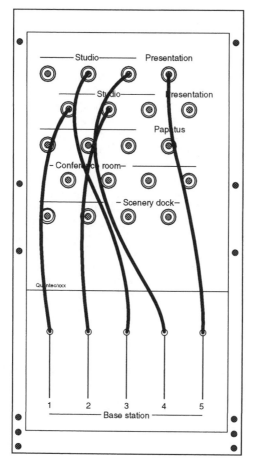

Cable points

Cable points may be part of the wall box or be separate points around the studio alphabetically numbered. This allows Camera 1, for example, to be cabled to camera point D, Camera 2 cabled to camera point G and so forth. The cable point for each camera may be decided at the planning meeting or agreed during the rig. All the cable points terminate in a technical area where, depending on which camera is routed to which point, the appropriate camera channel can be routed to the correct camera.

Warning lights above each entrance to the studio are installed to inform people about to enter the studio of its status – empty (unlit), in REHEARSAL or in TRANSMISSION. A red light indicates that a recording or transmission is in progress and the studio should not be entered.

rooms, property/scenery store all usually equipped with a double door sound lock to prevent noise leaking from these working areas into the studio when recording or 'on transmission'.

Control rooms

The control room

Away from the studio floor area are the production control rooms. If they are sited above the floor level, there is often quick access via stairs straight on to the studio floor. The main studio production control room contains a vision mixing panel, a talkback system and communications to other technical areas, possibly a caption generator for in-vision text and possibly the control system of the prompter device. All the equipment is housed in a long customized desk facing a bank of preview picture monitors displaying each video source used in the production.

Some of the preview monitors may be switchable depending on the number of video sources used in the production. These will include each camera's output, VTR, telecine and frame store outputs, any input from an outside broadcast that may be used or other studio inserts, caption generator and electronic graphics output, electronic VTR clock, a special effects output and a 'studio out' monitor displaying the visual source that is selected at the vision mixing panel. Other monitors may provide feeds of programmes currently being transmitted. Prominent on the monitor bank wall will be a large clock plus an indication of the studio status (e.g. blue light: 'rehearsal', red light: 'transmission')

Sound, lighting and vision control

Adjacent to the production control room (commonly called the 'gallery') is the sound control room where the audio inputs to a programme are mixed. Opposite a bank of preview picture monitors and monitoring loudspeakers is a sound desk used to control the level and quality of all audio outputs. There will also be audio record and replay equipment.

Lighting and vision control usually share the same room and are equipped with preview monitors, a lighting console to control lamp intensity and for grouping lamps for coordinated lighting changes. A diagram of the lamps in use (mimic board) helps the console operator during rehearsal and transmission. Alongside the lighting area is the vision control panel which houses the controls for altering the exposure, black level, colour balance, gain and the gamma of each camera. From this position, the vision control engineer matches each camera's output so that, for example, the skin tones of a face that is in shot on several cameras is the same.

Each studio camera has its associated bay of equipment housed in the vision control room or in a technical area adjacent to the control rooms. Vision control also needs communications to other technical areas.

Other production facilities used in multi-camera programming are a graphics area which feeds electronic graphics, animations and electronic text to the studio, a technical area where telecine, video, slide store machines are centrally available and allocated according to production

Studio control room

requirements. Half inch VTRs are often located in the production control room.

Two other rooms connected with programme making are the production office which is the base for the planning and preparation of a programme, and a green room or hospitality room which is used for the reception of programme guests before and after the programme.

Outside broadcast facilities

Studio and OB equipment

An outside broadcast (OB) is any multi-camera video format programme or programme insert that is transmitted or recorded outside the studio complex. Most of the equipment permanently installed in a studio complex (see Control rooms, page 36) is required for an outside broadcast. Production, sound, engineering and recording facilities are usually housed in customized vehicles (often referred to as 'scanners') or as a travelling kit of lightweight, portable vision mixing panels, video tape recorders and associated engineering equipment, sound mixers, etc. housed in cases and reassembled in a suitable area at the location (e.g. for drama production).

In general terms, studio productions have more control of setting, staging, programme content than an outside broadcast. There is a logistic difficulty in duplicating all these facilities outside the studio but location recording offers the advantage of complex and actual settings plus the ability to cover a huge range of events that are not specifically staged for television. Outside broadcast camerawork tends to be involved in a higher proportion of live or 'recorded-as-live' productions plus a greater number of 'as-directed' programmes (i.e. non-camera scripted).

Covering large-scale events means that cameras are scattered a long way from the scanner and camera operators in general need to be more self-sufficient without the immediate technical back-up often available in broadcast studios.

Outside broadcast vehicles

The main OB vehicle houses the control room which serves the same function as a studio control but the equipment and operating areas are designed and compressed to fit a much smaller space.

Technical support vehicles are used for transporting cable, sound and camera equipment, monitors, lighting gear and other production facilities that may be required. In addition there may be a separate VTR vehicle equipped with recording and slow motion machines, etc.

For a live transmission, there will be a radio links vehicle or portable equipment which may be a terrestrial or a satellite link or alternatively a land line that carries the programme back to a base station or transmitter. The number of vehicles on site will increase with the complexity of the programme and the rig. There may be props, scenery, furniture to be delivered to the site. Dressing rooms, make-up and catering may be required.

Vinten Kestral crane

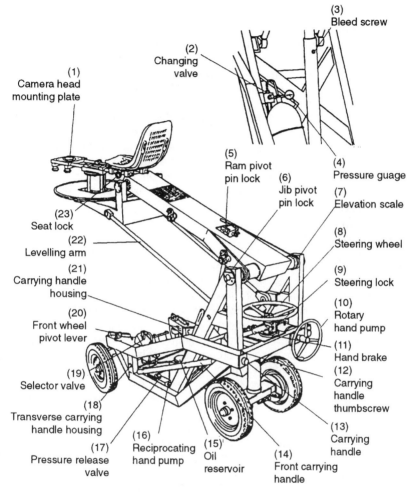

(3) Bleed screw

(2) Changing valve

(1) Camera head mounting plate

(5) Ram pivot pin lock

(6) Jib pivot pin lock

(4) Pressure guage

(7) Elevation scale

(23) Seat lock

(22) Levelling arm

(21) Carrying handle housing

(20) Front wheel pivot lever

(19) Selector valve

(18) Transverse carrying handle housing

(17) Pressure release valve

(16) Reciprocating hand pump

(15) Oil reservoir

(14) Front carrying handle

(13) Carrying handle

(12) Carrying handle thumbscrew

(11) Hand brake

(10) Rotary hand pump

(9) Steering lock

(8) Steering wheel

In many ways an OB convoy is similar to a circus. It travels to a location, rigs and prepares for the show, records or transmits a 'performance', de-rigs and moves on. At all times it must plan to be self-sufficient in facilities and staff and to carry to the location all that is required for the programme.

Control room staff

Production formats

Having looked at the standard facilities provided by a studio and a location facility we can now examine how a multi-camera programme production uses these resources. There are many types of production formats such as, for example, the studio situation comedy which is usually three or four sets facing an audience rostrum, or sports coverage, where six or more cameras will be positioned to cover all aspects of the contest. All of these programme formats require planning, the dissemination of information to the production team before the event and a method of communicating and coordinating everyone's contribution on the transmission or recording.

Multi-camera programme making is a team effort and over the years a production procedure has been evolved which maximizes the efficiency of the production group.

The control room staff

Walk into a control room that is engaged in making a programme and there will usually be a programme director with a script or running order on the desk, talking into a microphone to a number of other production personnel. Talkback – the information from the director and the responses from other members of the crew – is the lifeblood of any multi-camera production.

On one side of the director sits the production assistant who works with the director in the preparation of the programme. She times the show, calls the shot numbers and, in some broadcast organizations, will cue telecine and video machines to replay pre-recorded inserts. On the other side of the director is the vision mixer working from a script and under direction, operating the vision mixing panel switching between cameras and all other vision sources.

Also in the control room there may be a technical coordinator who deals with planning and communications, a producer or editor who, depending on programme formats, will oversee content and running order of items. There may also be a caption generator operator who adds text to the pictures (e.g. name superimpositions abbreviated to 'supers' or referred to as 'Astons').

In the sound control room, the sound supervisor controls the audio and can talk to sound assistants on the studio floor. Possibly there is also a sound assistant playing-in music and effects.

In the lighting and vision control room, the lighting director sits with his/her lighting plot and a console operator at the lighting console and balances the intensity of each lamp in the studio according to the shot and the requirements of the production and groups the lamps for lighting changes and effects if needed. A vision control operator, responsible for the exposure and matching the cameras, sits alongside.

Graphics area

Graphic designers provide electronically generated visual material for the programme as well as two-dimensional graphics.

Control room staff

Caption Generator Operator

Vision Mixer

Director

Production Assistant

Studio floor staff

On the studio floor
The floor manager (FM) relays information from the director during rehearsal and recording/transmission to the front of camera artistes, and liaises and coordinates all other technicians working on the studio floor. The FM may have an assistant floor manager (AFM) and/or a floor assistant (FA) working alongside, depending on the nature and complexity of the programme.

Camera operators wear headsets and can hear the director's instructions and provide shots of the production according to a pre-rehearsed sequence or, in an as-directed production, according to the role allocated to them.

There may be sound technicians on booms positioning a microphone in relation to artiste movement and the lighting design, or they may be rigging and adjusting personal microphones worn by the programme presenters.

A prompter operator may be tucked away in a corner of the studio controlling the text displayed on a television screen attached to the front of the camera. This allows presenters to look straight at the lens while reading scripted links via a mirror reflection of the text monitor. Depending on the studio, a prompter can also be controlled from the control room or another production area. Scene-hands may be needed to reposition furniture and/or scenery during rehearsal and recording/transmission. Electricians working with the lighting director pre-rig and adjust lamps and electrical equipment according to the lighting plot.

Other members of the production team such as the designer, make-up supervisor, costume design and wardrobe may be on the studio floor, in the control rooms or working in their own specific areas (e.g. make-up). Additional crafts will augment the basic production team depending on the demands of the programme (e.g. a special effects designer).

Technical areas
Usually in a central technical area, engineers operate film and video machines to provide pre-recorded and pre-filmed inserts into the programme (although VTRs may be run by control room staff) and also to record the programme if required. Often a studio or maintenance engineer will be responsible for the serviceability and line-up of all studio equipment.

These are the basic crafts involved with everyday programme making. Depending on the type of programme, there may be many other specialist staff on the production team such as property master, special effects, unit managers, painters, carpenters, etc. On outside broadcast units, riggers drive the OB vehicles, rig cables, lay tracks and track cameras.

Studio layout

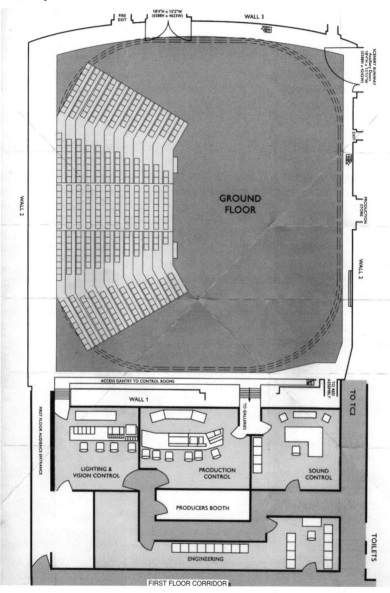

In many smaller productions, there is often an overlap of job functions. Multi-skilled is the name given to staff who have the ability to work in more than one craft skill.

The planning process

Advance planning
Every programme involves some type of advance planning. A two-minute news bulletin, broadcast four or five times a day with a news reader reading straight to camera, will need scheduling of resources and people. It will require the news to be collected and scripted, for the presenter to have access to make-up, the studio facility to be booked and technicians to be scheduled to control the studio facilities. More complex programmes require a longer planning period and a standard procedure to inform and involve all the diverse crafts and skills needed to mount the programme.

Programmes can be roughly divided into those that have a content that has been conceived and devised for television and those with a content that cannot be pre-planned or are events that take place independent of television coverage. Many programmes have a mixture of both types of content. A programme that is planned with the constraints and the facilities that TV can provide (e.g. game shows, soaps, sit-coms, etc.) will have control over every piece of action and the majority of the programme will be pre-rehearsed before transmission or recording.

Planning for the unpredictable
There are many events covered by TV that contain unpredictable action which cannot be rehearsed such as sport, discussion programmes and other ad-lib activities. No one knows when a goal is going to be scored in a football match or how the run of play will develop, but the TV camera coverage must provide for any of the normal eventualities in a match to be covered. Planning for this requires predicting potential incidents and having cameras assigned to cover such eventualities.

From the initial commissioned idea, some form of script or, possibly to begin with, a rough 'running order' of the contents of the programme will be structured. The running order identifies individual sequences in the programme, what the sequences will contain, the vision and sound sources utilised and the duration of each item.

The next stage of the planning involves preparing a script and deciding on design requirements. The flow chart of decisions to be made before recording or transmission depends on the programme format. Scenery needs to be built, scripts written, artistes contracted or programme guests contacted, technical facilities booked and pre-recorded inserts arranged and edited prior to the recording/transmission day. A regular weekly series will have a production planning formula which fits the turnaround time between each programme. It will also have some advanced projects in the planning stage.

Depending on the complexity of the programme, there will be planning meetings and/or recces if it is a location production with engineering man-

Camera operators checking the floor plan

agers, lighting directors, camera supervisors, sound supervisors and all other members of the production team who need advance information in order to plan for the programme.

... .ARY
GUILDFORD COLLEGE
of Further and Higher Education

Camera coverage formats

Shot number system

For many programmes, a camera script will be prepared which breaks down the programme into sections or scenes and then further sub-divides any significant action into separately numbered shots which are assigned to specific cameras. This camera script is usually modified in rehearsal but allows a reference point for all concerned in the production. Each camera operator has his/her own camera cards detailing the shots he/she will be taking.

The production assistant calls each shot number as they are taken during rehearsal and transmission/recording, and the director reminds everyone on talkback of any significant action/event that will occur. The shot number system binds together a whole range of different production activities from lighting changes to equipment repositioning, scenery changes and vision mixing. It is not simply a structure for camera operators.

As-directed coverage

The shot number system provides for the most detailed planning and production precision in, for example, the camera coverage of an orchestral concert where the shots are directly linked to the orchestral score. The score is followed by the director, vision mixer and production assistant and each shot is cut to at a pre-determined point in the score. But multi-camera coverage can use a mixture of other techniques including the following:

- Some sequences of the production are shot numbered but other sequences are 'as-directed' (i.e. they are not pre-rehearsed). In this method of camera coverage, the director will identify what shots are required on each camera during the transmission or recording, combined with appropriate shots being offered by the camera crew.
- Cameras are assigned a role in a structured sequence of shots. For example, a game show where each sequence of the quiz or game will have a defined structure but the order of the shots will depend on the progress of the game, e.g. if 'A' answers, Camera 2 will be used. If 'B' answers, Camera 3 will be used, etc. This is the most common technique in covering group discussions.
- Cameras are assigned a role (e.g. football coverage where one camera holds a wide, one camera is close, one camera picks up 'personality' shots, one camera for slow-motion replay, etc.). With this system, cameras stick to their 'role' and do not attempt to offer additional shots until the event has ended.
- Cameras are assigned a role for part of the event. For example, a state occasion where a camera position allows unique coverage of a location – a section of a street through which the procession will pass – but is subsequently available to pick up other shots to reflect the atmosphere of the event.

- An as-directed shoot such as a pop concert where some cameras concentrate on lead singers, instrumentalists, etc. and other cameras are on wide shots and audience.
- All cameras are individually recorded (isoed) and then edited together in post-production. This technique is more likely to occur using PSCs (portable single cameras).

47

Safety

Individual responsibility

While others working on the programme (e.g. the producer) may have a contractual or insurance obligation for the overall safety of the production, health and safety legislation obliges everyone to take reasonable care of their own health and safety and that of others who may be affected by what they do or fail to do. Everyone also has a responsibility to cooperate, as necessary, to ensure satisfactory safety standards.

If you comply with the requirements for safety and something goes wrong, then your employer will be held to account. If you fail to comply, you may lose any claim for compensation for injury and could even be prosecuted individually.

What you must do

- Follow the safety requirements and any instructions that are given, especially in relation to emergencies (e.g. know the location of fire exits).
- Ask for further information if you need it.
- Report accidents (or a 'near miss'), dangerous situations or defects in safety arrangements.
- Do not interfere with or misuse safety systems or equipment, or engage in horseplay that could be dangerous.
- Work within the limits of competence which means a knowledge of best practice and an awareness of the limitations of one's own experience and knowledge.

Assessing risk

The key to good, safe working practices is to assess any significant risk and to take action to eliminate or minimize such risks. The procedure is as follows:

- Identify precisely what is required in the production.
- Identify any potential hazards in that activity.
- Identify the means by which those risks can be controlled.

The key terms in risk assessment are:

- **hazard** – the inherent ability to cause harm;
- **risk** – the likelihood that harm will occur in particular circumstances;
- **reasonably practicable** – the potential improvement in safety is balanced against the cost and inconvenience of the measures that would be required; if the costs and inconvenience do not heavily outweigh the benefits, then the thing is reasonably practicable and should be done;
- **residual risk** – the risk remaining after precautions have been taken.

An example of the above four terms in action might be when it is proposed

to rig a camera hoist near overhead power lines because it is claimed that this is the best position for the required shot. The power lines are a *hazard*. Touching them could result in death. What is the likelihood (*risk*) that harm will occur in particular circumstances? There may be the risk of a high wind blowing the hoist onto the power lines. Is the weather changeable? Could a high wind arise? What is *reasonable and practical* to improve safety? The obvious action is to reposition the hoist to provide a usable shot but eliminate all risk of it touching the power lines. As weather is often unpredictable, the hoist should be repositioned as the costs and inconvenience do not heavily outweigh the benefits. There remains the *residual risk* of operating a camera on a hoist which can only be partially reduced by wearing a safety harness.

Rigging a studio

The importance of safety

Nearly all television production environments are temporary rigs and therefore potentially hazardous. One of the most dangerous times is during rigging and de-rigging. Apart from the risks of lifting heavy equipment, hoisting, climbing and cabling, there is, when de-rigging, the universal tendency to want to get the job done as quickly as possible, coupled, on location, with a de-rig that is often carried out at night. It is in such situations that a couple of minutes of thought could prevent a lifetime of backache.

Fire

Make yourself aware of the fire procedure and alarms in studios and on location. A staff member of an organization is usually familiar with every corridor, exit and shortcut in a studio complex. A freelance may need to read signs when finding their way around. Make certain that you could find your way through smoke-filled corridors to the nearest exit.

Location work means continuously operating in new or unfamiliar buildings or stadiums filled with spectators. When rigging, walk the quickest route you can find to an outside exit in the case of fire.

Studio rigging

Allocated rigging time may be shared by many different craft groups. The simultaneous activities of rigging lights, setting, set dressing and sound and camera rigging can lead to a potentially dangerous situation. Ensure that all precautions are taken to ensure the safety of yourself and others. In particular observe the following:

- Check when pulling cables that they will not trip or unsettle other colleagues carrying weights.
- Do not continue to pull a cable that is out of sight and snagged. Apart from the possible damage to the cable end, it may be snagged on a ladder in use, etc.
- Get help when lifting heavy weights and use the advised procedure of bending at the knees and keeping the back straight when lifting. Lift in two stages – chair height, then up to required height.
- Do not go into the grid area without observing the proper procedure (see Slung monitors, page 54).

Cable routing

Camera cable routing should ensure that access routes are not obstructed. Where necessary (e.g. crossing fire lanes, audience or performer entrances and exits), cables must be flown or ramped. Take special precautions in unlit areas of the studio (behind sets, etc.) which may be used by performers and crew in a hurry during a production. Ask for working lights to be rigged.

A cable 'eight'

Where possible, camera cable runs should take the safest and shortest route to the cable point avoiding floor areas that are access points on to the set or to production rooms (e.g. make-up, wardrobe etc.). If a safety rail is fitted around the base of the studio wall, the camera cable should pass under the rail before being plugged into the cable point.

A cable eight (see above) is a convenient way of storing camera cable that is not immediately needed.

Floor monitors

Monitors

Monitors play an important part on the studio floor and are used by different members of the production crew. Their positions are often very carefully sited to provide an unobstructed eyeline for the presenters, floor manager or boom operators (if the booms are not fitted with mini-monitors) and camera crew. Never stand in front of a monitor when watching the show. Stand to one side of the monitor and check that you are not obstructing anyone who is using the monitor. The same discipline applies to standing in front of an audience and obstructing their view of the show.

On location, monitors are crucial for keeping reporters, commentators, etc., in touch with the transmitted or recorded output.

In-vision monitors are used to conduct interviews with participants who are not in the studio or to display visual material. Large screen displays and video walls (numerous monitors stacked close to each other displaying a segment of a video image) are also used for a variety of purposes in-vision.

Switched feeds

A monitor can be fed with a single video source such as the output of the studio or location or it can be fed with two or more sources which are switchable on the monitor and therefore serve a dual purpose during a production.

It can also be remotely switched and fed a number of video sources from a technical area or vision mixing panel. It is therefore important when rigging a monitor that the video cable is plugged to the correct monitor video point on the wall box. These monitor points can be cross-plugged in the studio technical area to provide whatever video feed is required.

Studio monitors require a mains cable which is usually bound with the video cable or may be an integral dual video/mains cable. Location monitors may be battery fed if a mains power supply is inaccessible. Check the condition of the power cable before plugging into the technical mains socket. This is a separate power supply to isolate broadcast equipment from any induced interference on the standard mains supply of the studio complex.

Secure the combined power/video cable to the wall box by passing it under the safety bar (if installed) and then tie off the cable using a clove hitch (see opposite).

All monitor cables crossing fire lanes should be ramped or covered with appropriate rubber mats, flown (above head height) or stuck down with special gaffer tape that has printed hazard stripes. If the cables are flown, remember to use quick-release knots to avoid wasting time at the de-rig untying tight and complicated 'granny' knots.

Prompters

Prompters attached to cameras are in effect specialist monitors and may require a feed from the prompter controller and a power supply.

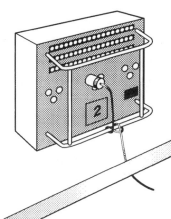
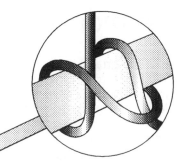

Run all cables under the bar (if fitted) beneath the wall box. When possible tie off the cable using a clove hitch to prevent any accidental pulling on the cable disconnecting the cable or damaging the wall box connection.

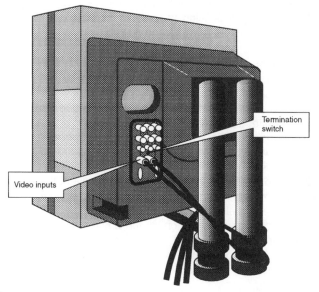

Termination switch

Video inputs

Monitors

Monitors in general production use are generally mounted on a wheeled trolley. Check that the monitor is securely attached to the trolley by safety straps or is a permanent fixture. Tie the combined cable to the monitor stand in the same way as at the wall box giving sufficient slack between the tied point and the inputs on the back of the monitor so that if inadvertently the monitor cable is pulled, it will not pull out the cable or damage the input connectors. If the feed for the monitor is the only video input, check that the monitor is terminated (i.e. switched to 75 ohms).

Never pull a monitor along by its cable and get assistance if it needs to be repositioned across cables or ramps. It is better to pull a monitor and lift it over obstructions rather than to push and risk the front end suddenly tipping when it hits an obstacle resulting in the monitor sliding off its stand.

Slung monitors

Working in the grid

Sometimes it is necessary to enter the grid area in order to sling a monitor above the studio floor. Extreme care should be taken that nothing taken on to the grid falls through on to the studio floor below. Access to the grid must be strictly controlled while people are working on the studio floor and the following procedures enforced:

- remove any loose item either worn or pocketed when entering the grid e.g. coins, keys, screwdrivers, spanners and especially video barrels;
- if tools are essential for the rig, then they must be kept secure when working overhead;
- do not allow video or mains cable ends to fall though the grid but lower them to the floor;
- if possible, clear the floor but if this is not practical, have an 'exclusion zone' with someone 'policing' it;
- only suspend monitors from agreed suspension points (hoists etc.).

Slung monitors

- Check that the safe working load (SWL) of the hoist or support is suitable for the slung monitor and cradle.
- Check the monitor cradle is safe and all adjustable struts are tight and hold the monitor securely.
- Use two people to lift and present the monitor/cradle to the suspension arm and have another to attach the monitor to the spigot or whatever method is used to attach the monitor cradle to the hoist.
- Attach a steel safety bond (see opposite) to prevent the monitor falling if the primary means of attachment to the hoist should fail.
- Video cable and mains cables should be tied off at the grid and also tied to the monitor cradle. Always check there is a sufficient amount of slack cable before lowering a hoist.
- When the mains/video cable is plugged to the monitor, switch on and check the monitor is functioning with the correct feed and termination, before hoisting.
- Do not manually assist the hoist.
- The hoist must be under surveillance when being raised or lowered.
- There must be nobody under the load.
- Check that the hoist movement does not foul adjacent suspended items and sufficient slack cable is available when lowering.

Electricity

Rigging camera cables, monitors, and dolly power supplies is a daily occurrence but, however familiar, an electrical supply is a potential hazard unless

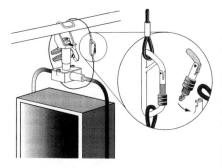

Safety bonds

A safety bond is used to protect every overhead rigged linkage in case of failure of the means of attachment to the suspension component. A safety bond is a flexible steel wire rope fitted with a quick release fastener. It is looped between a suspended item and a firm support and is a safeguard against the accidental release of a rigged connection. It is entirely separate from the primary means of support and normally carries no load.

Scenery: Remember that scenery is often a three dimensional 'fiction' – a flimsy and temporary framework. Structures that appear weight bearing may be of very slight construction. Do not attempt to use part of the scenery as a camera platform unless the specific area has been pre-planned for the intended load capacity.

Smoke effects: Although most effects smoke machines produce a smoke of low toxicity it can irritate the nose, throat and lungs. An asthmatic may suffer a severe attack. There is a balance to be struck between generating the required density of smoke and the ventilation needed to clear it. Do not attempt to operate close to the smoke source for long periods.

safe handling procedures are observed. The electrical safety of plugs and connectors should be inspected before plugging into a supply and a periodic check should be made on earthing and the condition of cables for signs of cuts or worn insulation. Electrical equipment should be periodically tested by a competent person and date stamped.

On location, water (rain, sea, rivers, swimming pools, etc.) in contact with electricity poses a special hazard. When more than one power source is used at a location dangerous voltage differences can occur. There should be segregation between different power supplies.

Only open the side of the camera and alter controls if you can see what you are touching and are competent to carry out the adjustment. Never feel around for a control while looking in the viewfinder.

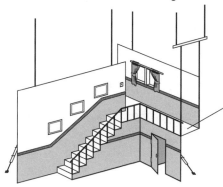

Some parts of studio sets are designed simply as 'dressing' and are not intended to be practical.

This 'floor' surface is only supported by ropes slung from the studio grid. It is non-load bearing and cannot be walked on.

Never sit, stand or walk on any scenery unless you know it is designed for that purpose.

Rigging cameras

Basic checks need to be carried out before rigging or de-rigging a full facility television camera on to a wedge plate pan/tilt head attached to a mounting:

- Check the stability of the mounting and the head is secured to the mounting (e.g. on a four-bolt fixing, all bolts are in place and tight).
- **Tripod** – is level and the base and legs are secure and locked.
- **Pedestal** – the column is locked down with safety locks and the head is locked off with safety chains in place.
- **Crane or jib arm** – the arm is locked or restrained with a security strap or someone is securing the boom. NB: do not stand on the crane platform when rigging or de-rigging a camera. The crane arm will require weights to be added at the rear of the boom arm to balance out the combined weight of camera operator, camera and lens.
- Know the route you are carrying the camera and check that the route is clear and free from obstructions (e.g. closed doors can be pushed open in the direction of movement).
- Check the safety locking pin on the wedge plate on the pan/tilt head is removed and the retaining spigot is clear of the shoe of the wedge plate and is in a condition to accept the wedge on the base of the camera (see opposite).
- Check the back of the pan/tilt head (i.e. the widest part of the wedge plate) is facing the direction in which camera will be slid on to the head.
- Check that the camera is seated in the wedge plate before sliding in the securing spigot and replacing the locking pin.
- When rigging a lens, protect the back element and keep the pedestal/crane or arm locked off at minimum height to facilitate hanging the lens on the camera. Remove the back element lens cap (if fitted) and the cap/protection for camera prism block. When rigging most box lenses, present the top of the lens to the hinge at the top of the camera and then lower the lens down to engage securing spigots. Slide the retaining clamp and tighten.
- Connect lens cables and zoom controls checking that they are routed correctly and that there are no excessive loops of cable that could snag the pan/tilt head in operation.
- When connecting a multi-core camera cable, check the position of the key ring configuration inside the cable connector and match this to the cable connector on the camera.
- Remove the security bar or locking pins on the pedestal column, unlock any column brake and check the pedestal is balanced (see opposite).

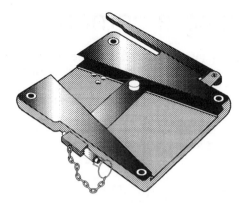

Wedge plate shoe showing the spigot that slides into the channel in the base of the camera wedge plate.

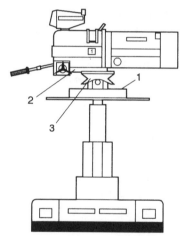

Raise the column and check the pedestal is correctly pressurized for the rigged camera/lens combination. Many camera mountings use compressed gas to balance the camera/lens on the column. The pressure of this gas must be adjusted by a competent, trained person.

Move the column of the pedestal through its complete range of operating heights and check that it remains at any height it is set to without rising or sinking. Use the trim weights (1) on the pedestal to adjust. Gas pressure varies with temperature and the pedestal may need further trim weight adjustment during operations.

When pan bars, viewfinder and zoom controls are adjusted for operation and the camera cable is connected, check the balance of the head with all friction removed and if required, unlock the wedge plate (2) and move the camera to reach a point of balance (i.e. the camera will stay at any angle of tilt). If after balancing, the camera either returns to a level position or it falls forward or backwards to the maximum tilt, it is likely that the wrong size of cams (3) are fitted for the camera/lens combination that has been rigged.

When the camera is balanced, apply the degree of friction that is operationally required for the production.

De-rigging a camera

- **Pedestal** – check that the column is locked down and the safety chains are secured on the pan/tilt head and that, ideally, the pedestal wheels are oriented 90° to the wedge plate sliding section.
- **Crane or jib arm** – check that the arm is locked or restrained with a security strap or someone is securing the boom.
- Fit front lens cap and switch the camera off before disconnecting the camera cable and all lens cables.
- Recheck that no cables remain connected before removing lens and refitting back element lens cap.
- Pan the camera so that both people sliding the camera out of the wedge plate are comfortably positioned and are able to move the camera away from the mounting without obstruction.
- Remove the locking pin on the head and slide the restraining spigot out of the wedge plate channel.
- Slide the camera back on the head and lift clear.
- Leave the pedestal/crane/jib arm in a secure and balanced condition.

Rigging a lightweight camera

- Check the fitting on the base of the camera matches the tripod adaptor plate on the pan/tilt head fitting.
- Check the cam size of the pan/tilt head if fitting a lightweight camera and box lens combination.
- When fitting a lightweight camera into a harness equipped with a box lens, take care to protect the back element of the lens as the camera is presented to the lens.
- Make sure the height adjustment of the camera plate is correct so that no weight or pressure is applied to the lens to camera flange.
- When fitting a lightweight camera/lens on to a lightweight head, check that the holding pin is not in the centre of the wedge. Move lever to reseat the holding pin in its inoperative position. Slide camera into the tripod adaptor plate until a click is heard. Check that the camera is locked by testing if it can be slid out of the adaptor plate. The method of securing the base of a lightweight camera to the tripod adaptor varies with make of camera. Adjust balance, CoG and required friction.
- Cable up zoom, viewfinder, cue lights, mixed viewfinder and check if lens can be powered from camera cable or if it is to be battery driven.
- Check that the connecting cable between lens and camera will supply the correct voltage on the correct pins.

Rigging a crane/jib arm

■ Route the camera cable and any other cable required to provide sufficient loop at any point on the mounting which moves. Check there is sufficient cable slack by positioning the arm throughout its complete operational range.

■ If the dolly is motorized, check that the correct power supply is available before connecting. Secure the power cable to the camera cable with gaffer tape along the length of cable in use.

■ Always leave an unattended crane in a secure and locked condition.

Balancing a lightweight head

The head is correctly balanced when the minimum amount of even effort is required to move the head and the camera can be set in any tilt position and the head will remain in that position when the hand is removed from the pan bar. Pan/tilt head balance procedure will vary depending on design. The following instructions apply to the Vinten Vision range. Prior to balancing any head, ensure that the pan bars and any ancillary equipment have been fitted in the operating position in order to prevent upsetting the balance once it has been achieved.

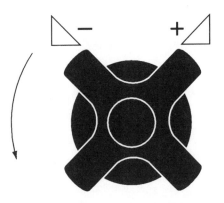

1. Release tilt brake. Turn balance knob counter-clockwise until head falls away from horizontal under weight of camera.

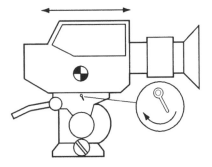

2. Release slide lock and slide camera backwards and forward until it balances horizontally. Apply slide lock.

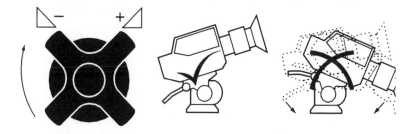

3. Turn balance knob clockwise until camera does not fall away when head is tilted and released.

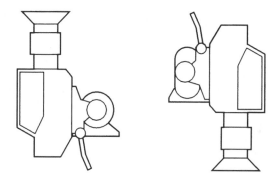

4. Repeat steps 2 and 3 until perfect balance is achieved, when the camera will remain set at any angle from +90° to −90° without falling away or springing back. Re-apply the tilt brake.

Outside broadcast rigging

Lightweight design

An outside broadcast is a programme that is recorded or transmitted away from normal studio facilities and therefore every item of equipment required by the production needs to be transported to the location.

Although in the past outside broadcast units were usually equipped with full facility cameras, it is now possible to use portable cameras for every type of production. Smaller cameras provide the obvious advantages of ease of rigging and greater flexibility in choice of camera position and smaller cables. Their disadvantages include lack of full production facilities found on larger cameras, sometimes a lack of positive zoom controls and smaller zoom lens ratios. Large box lenses are often used with a rigging harness on to a lightweight camera to allow greater zoom ratios.

At a location, camera mountings often have to be positioned on scaffolding, in stadiums or inside buildings inaccessible to wheeled transport. Every item has to be manhandled, for example, up stairs or to a remote part of the stadium before being rigged. Mountings need to be broken down into manageable sections that can be carried. In general, OB mountings are smaller and lighter than their studio equivalent although sharing the same operational range of height and manoeuvrability.

Once the camera and mounting have been carried to their operating position, a cable or a radio link is required to allow for the return signal, picture control and communications. Power may be supplied to the camera via cable, battery or from a local mains supply via an adaptor.

If possible, avoid rigging in isolation on location as this increases the risk of being hurt while lifting heavy weights without assistance or the risk of electrocution without immediate help.

OB rigging hazards

As well as the general details of rigging previously discussed, rigging cameras and mountings at a location involves solving problems caused by:

■ lifting and carrying heavy weights when rigging;
■ working among the public;
■ working at heights (see opposite);
■ personal and equipment protection against adverse weather.

Hoisting and lifting equipment

Although instruction is available on lifting heavy weights to avoid back injury, the nature of access to some stadiums, public buildings, etc., makes recommended procedure impossible. Always attempt to maintain the advised body posture of chin in, straight arms and back when lifting heavy weights.

Rigging a camera onto a freestanding scaffold rostrum.

- Visually check that the structure is safe and competently assembled.
- Check that a gallows arm is fitted at the corner of the rostrum with at least a 2:1 block and tackle fitted for hauling up the equipment.
- The gallows arm should be high enough to allow the equipment to be swung over the hand rail. Great care should be taken if the height of the arm only allows equipment to be swung on board between the hand rail and the kicking board.
- Hauling equipment up by a single pulley attached to the hand rail or by hand over the hand rail is dangerous and places everyone involved at risk.
- Check the rope to be used to haul the equipment is of sufficient strength and is well stretched. New ropes tend to twist under strain and make hauling the equipment dangerous and difficult.
- Check that a guard is fitted to the pulley to prevent the rope slipping out of the guide.
- A lifting bag marked with the maximum carrying weight should be used but if this not available, make a 'parcel' of the equipment box by attaching the rope to the carrying handles.
- Attach a second rope to the lifting hook to allow the load to be controlled from the ground when lifting and pulled clear from the rostrum on the way up. This also allows the lifting hook and bag to be pulled down for the second load.
- At least three people should help with the rig, and with a full facility camera and mounting ideally four people – two at the top and two at the bottom of the scaffold.
- If possible, send the equipment up in the order of rig, i.e. mounting, pan/tilt head, camera, lens, etc.

When hoisting equipment up to a height, use block and tackle if available and double check anchor points and securing arrangements on the equipment. Have someone policing the area below the hoisting position and whenever possible use an approved and tested lifting bag.

Make certain tripods and bases are secure, stable and level before rigging camera and lens. In an exposed position or on uneven ground, use additional ropes to anchor the mounting to prevent damage by high winds. Always leave the camera weather protected and with the smallest area of camera/lens facing the prevailing wind.

The appropriate route for a cable is where it is not constantly being stepped on or likely to trip up people and will not be damaged by vehicles. Camera cables need to be ramped, flown or buried where they are exposed to vehicles or the public and their presence identified with hazard striped tape.

Working among the public

Public interest
Most people watch television and therefore most people have an interest in how programmes are made. On location there will often be an interchange between the production crew and the public. Try to accommodate their genuine interest whilst safeguarding their safety.

Never rig or de-rig camera equipment above an audience unless a 'safe area' has been cleared and is being continuously 'policed'. If a camera is positioned among the public (e.g. in an audience), make certain that there is someone, in addition to the camera operator, who can assist with organizing and controlling an operational area. Check that the condition of the camera, lens and mounting cannot cause harm if there is accidental contact in a crowd

Organize additional help if the camera is cabled and requires repositioning among the public. The rigger should ensure that sufficient slack cable is available at all times and be ready to pay it out as and when the camera moves. To a large extent, roving cameras are now equipped with radio links and therefore cable bashing for a mobile camera is redundant (e.g. running the touch line at a rugby or football match).

Cameras mounted above an audience must be rigged before the audience is seated and checked for any loose or movable items that could be displaced when operating. Cranes manoeuvring above an audience should be no lower than the height of a person suddenly standing up and with no trailing loops of cable. There should always be an observer of the camera's physical position when manoeuvring a remotely controlled camera. On location, clearance to work a crane above an audience may be required from the local authority.

Camera crews working in front of audiences or spectators at public events or performances should wear the appropriate clothing to integrate with the event (e.g. avoid very casual clothes at a church service).

Security
Precautions must always be taken against loss or damage to equipment. When working in public places, avoid leaving equipment unattended. Overnight security of equipment is necessary unless the camera position is secure and inaccessible. If there is a risk of someone scaling a scaffold tower then blockboard can be used to clad the base and the access ladder removed.

Hostile crowds
No story is worth a life. During public disorder or a civil disturbance, stay together as a crew and avoid conspicuous display of cameras etc. Withdraw immediately if the presence of TV cameras intensifies a dangerous situation.

Portable microwave link

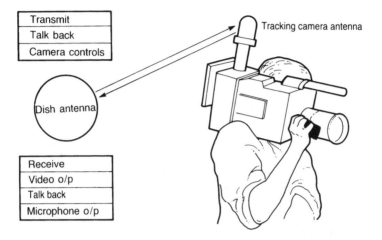

The microwave transmitter/antenna module is attached to the camera. Typical portable microwave link frequencies are between 2.5 GHz and 13 GHz.

The camera antenna transmits to the location control truck, video and audio output plus camera operator talkback.

The tracking base antenna transmits production talkback, camera controls (iris, lift, gain etc.) and a return video feed to allow the camera operator in the field to monitor on the camera viewfinder (if required) the 'on air' picture or any other video source that is needed.

Working at height

Working at height

There is always the risk of a person or object falling from a height. The operating height at which a camera is a risk is any distance likely to cause injury, and certainly any drop in excess of 2 m. Either safety barriers must be erected (at least 1.1 m high) plus toe boards and intermediate rails or equivalent protection.

If the edge cannot be protected, then people must be kept at least 3 m from the edge or wear a harness attached to a securely anchored safety line. Any object that could fall or be blown off the structure (e.g. lens cap) should be removed or anchored. Equipment in exposed positions must be adequately secured to withstand the foreseeable wind force. Check when a camera cable is connected to an elevated camera that it is tied off so that the weight of the cable does not stretch the cable or pull on the camera.

Scaffolding

Scaffolding should be erected by an approved contractor and certified for its intended use before being rigged with camera/lens/mounting. There should be the normal 'edge protection' of a 1.1 m barrier and a 'kick' or toe board to indicate to the camera operator while operating the camera that he/she is approaching the edge of the platform.

Sometimes the base of the scaffolding is sheeted with blockboard for cosmetic or safety reasons (e.g. it prevents unauthorized personnel clambering up the scaffolding). Sheeted scaffold structures may suffer considerable strain at high wind speeds.

Be especially vigilant in the use of zip-up towers built from 'snap-together' components. The height to least-base ratio must not be more the 3:1 in light winds and a 3.5:1 ratio when used inside. Guy ropes and ground anchor/ballasting may be used to improve stability.

Ladders

Check that access ladders are securely attached to the scaffolding, and that rungs are free from mud, grease, etc. If a free-standing ladder is used for rigging, check that the foot of the ladder is on a firm and level surface and someone is using his/her weight to stabilize the ladder when in use.

Hydraulic platforms

- Check that a competent person is operating the hoist and will be in continuous attendance while the hoist is in use.
- Check safety inspection cards and date of last inspection.
- Check the arrangements to communicate between the cage and the ground.

A scaffold clamp in operation at a rugby match

A quick and convenient method of mounting a camera on a scaffold structure is by the use of a scaffold clamp. This consists of a metal pod attached to two scaffold poles rigged on the scaffolding onto which the pan/tilt head is fixed. Usually this restricts the amount the camera can be panned left or right before the operator begins to lean out over the scaffold bar in order to see into the viewfinder.

- Check the emergency procedure if the camera operator is trapped aloft (e.g. bleeding down the system, rescue by another hoist, etc.).
- Check the operation of any self-lowering system.
- Check that the base of the hoist will be continuously supervised to prevent unauthorized operation.
- Check the condition of the hoist and look for hydraulic oil leaks, cracks in the welding of the cage, etc.
- Check that the legs are positioned for adequate load spreading of the rig and are not positioned on or near drain covers.
- Have a system for measuring wind speed and know the maximum wind speed for safe working on the specific rig and height to be worked.
- Use a harness and properly attached lifeline.

Height and overhead power cables

Be careful when using mast scaffold poles, mic booms, etc., when close to overhead power lines. Operating positions should be no closer than 15 m from wire suspended on a metal structure and no closer than 11 m from a wire suspended from a wooden structure.

Adverse weather

Planning the weather?

Often the most unpredictable factor in an outside broadcast is the weather. The positions of the cameras are usually controlled by the nature of the event but they are often sited to avoid looking into the sun. Extreme weather changes may be experienced during the period of rig, rehearsal and transmission, and therefore adequate precautions must be made to protect:

- equipment against adverse weather;
- personnel against adverse weather.

Adverse weather conditions

The standard advice in weather protection for equipment or people is to prepare for the worst.

This means checking weather forecasts and assessing, if in exposed positions, that scaffold towers or hoists can withstand any anticipated high winds and if equipment requires additional anchorage. Often, long before the structure is at risk, the winds may be too high to hold a camera steady on anything other than a fairly wide angle.

A weather cover should always be fitted to a camera before use as it offers protection from rain and heat. Water and electricity do not mix and there should be precautions taken to protect all electrical connections such as headsets, zoom controls, cable plugs, etc. Often the simplest but most satisfactory method is covering hand controls with small plastic bags. In driving rain, keep the camera panned away from the wind whenever possible and use the front lens cap during any extended break in coverage. Check there is adequate ventilation if the camera is covered and left switched on overnight.

Rain building up on the front element of the lens will be more obvious on a wide angle shot and lens cloths will be needed to periodically clean the lens. In rainy conditions, the lens shade, if adjustable, should be positioned to provide the greatest protection with gaffer tape stuck along the top and bottom of the hood to reduce rain penetration or flare. Check that it does not vignette (i.e. appear in shot) when the widest angle of the lens is selected.

Extremes of cold or heat can have an adverse affect on the performance of cameras. Use additional thermal linings inside camera covers and/or shade from direct sun if feasible.

Personal weather protection

Large-scale events (e.g. golf) involve cameras being scattered a long way

Specialist clothing can be purchased designed for outdoor pursuits such as mountaineering, sailing, etc. which are waterproof but allow a measure of physical activity without a build up of perspiration within the garment. Lightweight thermal gloves are available which allow the sensitive control of zoom and camera switches in very cold weather. One of the problems with camera miniaturization is that switches (talkback, mixed, viewfinder, etc.) have got smaller while gloved hands have remained the same size.

Condensation within wet weather clothing is a shared problem with a camera when it is moved from a cold environment to a warm moist interior (e.g. touch line to interview room).

from the scanner. They also involve long transmissions. A camera operator setting out for the day therefore needs to equip him/herself with a choice of clothing to match any changing weather conditions.

Those who work regularly out of doors must make themselves aware of the risks involved and how to protect themselves against sunburn, skin cancer, heat stress and heat stroke, hypothermia, white finger and frost bite.

Risk assessment during a thunderstorm
A check on the effects of any extreme weather forecast must be made each day on exposed camera positions. Individual safety requires a personal assessment and only the individual on a scaffold tower or hoist can judge when it is time to call it a day and retreat from the threat of lightning.

Outside broadcast hazards

A checklist of potential OB safety hazards includes the following:

- Boats – it is essential to wear life lines and life jackets when operating on a boat or near water such as on a harbour wall.
- Confined spaces – check the quality of air and ventilation when working in confined spaces such as trench, pipes, sewer, ducts, mines, caves, etc.
- Children are a hazard to themselves. When working in schools or on a children's programme, check that someone is available and responsible to prevent them touching or tripping over cables, floor lamps, camera mountings, etc.
- Explosive effects and fire effects must be regulated by a properly trained effects operator and special care should be taken with those effects that cannot be rehearsed.
- Excessive fatigue is a safety problem when operating equipment that could cause damage to yourself or others and when driving a vehicle on a long journey home after a production has finished.
- Fork-lift trucks must have a properly constructed cage if they are to carry a camera operator and camera.
- Lamps – all lamps should have a safety glass/safety mesh as protection against exploding bulbs. Compact source discharge lamps must always be used with a UV radiation protective lens. Lamps rigged overhead must be fitted with a safety bond. Check that lamp stands are secured and cabled to avoid being tripped over and that they are securely weighted at the base to prevent them being blown over.
- Location safety – in old buildings, check for weak floors, unsafe overhead windows, derelict water systems and that the electrical supply is suitable for the use it is put to. Check the means of escape in case of fire and the local methods of dealing with a fire. Check for the impact of adverse weather and, in remote locations, the time and access to emergency services.
- Level floor – every OB vehicle should be earthed and vehicles that require people to work inside should be parked and levelled with adequate ventilation. If operating a camera on the roof of a vehicle, it should either have a fully guarded edge or a safety harness and safety line should be worn by the camera operator. Check the risk from radio frequency radiation if there are aerials mounted on the same roof.
- Noise – high levels of location noise (machinery etc.), effects (gunshots, explosions) as well as close working to foldback speakers can damage hearing. Stress will be experienced attempting to listen to talkback with a very high ambient noise. Wear noise-cancelling headsets. If wearing single sided cans, use an ear plug in the unprotected ear.
- Stunt vehicles – motor vehicles travelling at speed involved in a stunt are

Camera operator working with a heavy duty tripod anchored against high winds

likely to go out of control. Leave the camera locked-off on the shot and stand well away from the action area in a safe position agreed with the stunt coordinator.

■ Filming from a moving vehicle – the camera must be either securely mounted or independently secured on safety lanyards. Operators should be fitted with seat belts or safety harnesses attached to safety lines securely anchored.

■ Roadside working – wear high-visibility clothing and have the police direct traffic if required. Police may give permission for a member of the crew to direct traffic but motorists are not obliged to obey such instructions.

Cables and monitors (1)

Reporting

If you are working on a multi-camera studio production for the first time you will be involved in a number of standard daily routines. After reporting to the camera supervisor you will be delegated to assist someone with rigging. As discussed in the previous section this involves rigging cameras, cables and monitors plus any special mountings or camera positions required for the production. Then make yourself acquainted with the production schedule for the day. For example, check the start of rehearsal time, recording times and meal breaks.

Never leave the studio or location unless you know what time working will recommence especially if you are not on talkback. If you are new to multi-camera working, try to keep in touch with the camera crew during production breaks – in television there are frequently last minute changes to the daily schedule.

Cabling

The first job a trainee will often be given on a studio multi-camera crew will be to look after cables and monitors. The time honoured role of 'cable bashing' may appear to be a long way from camerawork but it is a vital job on a fast moving show and if it is done well, will make just as big a contribution as any other production activity. It should also teach you six basic principles of multi-camera camerawork:

■ preparation;
■ anticipation;
■ concentration;
■ invisible technique;
■ silent operation;
■ teamwork.

Preparation

Look at the script to find out how the show is broken down into sections, recording periods, etc. Try to get an overall picture of the working day. Check that all camera cables are eighted with no obstruction (e.g. a ladder has not been parked on top of a cable since it was rigged). Check the floor plan and see where each camera is working and if there are repositions during recording or transmission. If there are rapid moves between shots or on shot you will need to assist with the cable. Make a note at what point in the production this happens.

Anticipation

During rehearsal, watch for cameras that work into other camera cable

A harness for a portable camera and large lens

loops and make certain there is sufficient cable laid out in front of a camera tracking into the set so that it does not push another camera's cable.
Make certain a camera moving on shot is not pulling a length of cable
stretching across the studio. Give sufficient slack cable close to the camera
on the move so that the camera operator is pulling the minimum length of
cable. Be aware at all times of how much cable is available to each camera
and that the cable is free of obstruction (e.g. not snagged around a boom
wheel, caught on a stage weight, etc.).

Cables and monitors (2)

Cable clearing
Be particularly vigilant when clearing cables behind large cranes. Often the cable will be bound with a power cable and possibly a camera headlamp cable. These additional cables require very careful lashing with gaffer tape to prevent small loops of cable developing which can easily catch under the cable guards. Do not allow the back or front of the crane to push large loops of cable when moving. Keep all cable away from the guards to prevent the speed and weight of the crane overriding the cable.

Concentration
Do not let your attention drift towards the content of the show unless it is linked with cues for camera movement you are involved with. You have probably done a good job if, on leaving the studio at the end of the day, you can only supply details of the production which were linked with camera moves and cables.

Invisible technique
Being invisible when cable clearing is an asset to the production. Your activity will not disturb the front of camera people or audience and it is good preparation for practising 'invisible' technique when you progress to camerawork. Be aware at all times which camera is on shot and keep out of shot. Constantly check left, right and behind you to avoid appearing in vision.

Silent operation
One of the reasons that someone is needed on cables, especially in quiet shows such as discussion or orchestral music, is that cables being dragged across the floor can be noisy. Your job in cable clearing is to lift the cable off the floor if it is generating noise. Also remember that you may be ultra-efficient dashing here, there and everywhere throwing cables out of the way as you go but if you create noise in the process you will have failed. Wear soft-soled shoes.

Tracking a pedestal
Often a camera operator will want complete control of the move on the pedestal but if this is impossible then he/she will indicate when to move and leave it to you to judge the speed of the move to match the action. One of the most awkward moves to make is to crab parallel with the action. Pedestal tracking requires the same basic technique for all movement on shot. Start with the action and end the move with the action. If it is a precisely rehearsed move, then the start and the end position should be marked on the floor.

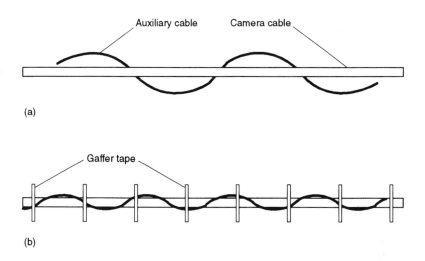

The quickest way to lash one cable to another is to lay both cables side by side (a) and to bind loops of the smaller cable to the camera cable with gaffer tape (b). Bind the cables tightly together leaving no stray loop of cable that could be caught under a cable guard. This method is quick to de-rig and presents the smallest area of cable in contact with the floor reducing friction (and therefore weight when dragging the cable) and noise. Do not wind one cable around and around the camera cable as this is difficult to remove and will develop loops which can catch under guards.

Monitors

Frequently, a monitor may need to be repositioned during a recording or transmission. If it is your job to move it, mark up the positions and make a note when it is to be moved. A basic rule in any simple activity such as repositioning a monitor is applicable all the way through multi-camera production practice – if possible, never do something on recording or transmission that was not done on rehearsal. There are many exceptions to this injunction but until you have sufficient production experience – stick to the rule.

Camera rehearsal

Working as a team

The individual skills of many crafts combine to work together under the guidance of the director to transmit or record a programme. Sometimes the programme format requires a planned and precise camera script which is followed from opening titles to closing credits (e.g. a concert). Other programmes require the ad-lib technique of jazz where each camera is allocated a role but may shift and modify the shots they offer according to circumstances (e.g. sports coverage, public events, pop concerts).

Once a transmission (and sometimes a recording) has started, there is no opportunity to stop and sort out production problems or make substantial alterations to the camera coverage of the programme. The basic requirement of live multi-camera camerawork is to get it right first time – there are no retakes.

Preparation and anticipation

The rehearsal period is the time to discover what the contribution from each craft group will be. Each member of the camera crew has to establish what his/her role in the production is via a two-way exchange of information with the director and by talking to the other camera operators. In many rehearsals, all the information may be supplied on pre-planned camera cards and a floor plan marked with camera positions. The feasibility of the planning is then tested by a rehearsal of every shot.

With other programme formats, the barest information on a running order is supplied and the camera operator has to seek details of the camera coverage that may affect him/her. Experience enables the right questions to be asked as this is the only opportunity to discover what is required before a cameraman is faced with a 'live' performance.

Each member of the crew has to work in the real time of the programme and all decisions are governed by the timescale of the event. While the planning may have taken months or weeks and the rehearsal days or hours, transmission is governed by the timescale of the event covered. Shot decisions have to be made in seconds with no time-out to consider the best way of tackling a particular situation. Preparation and anticipation are essential in order to create the time for fast camerawork.

Customary technique

The nature of many programmes (e.g. sport, discussion programmes) does not allow precise information about shots either to be rehearsed or confirmed. What should be clear in the mind of each camera operator is the range of shots he/she will be involved with.

Multi-camera production technique relies on the assumption that every member of the production crew is equipped with a knowledge of the con-

The language of camera movement

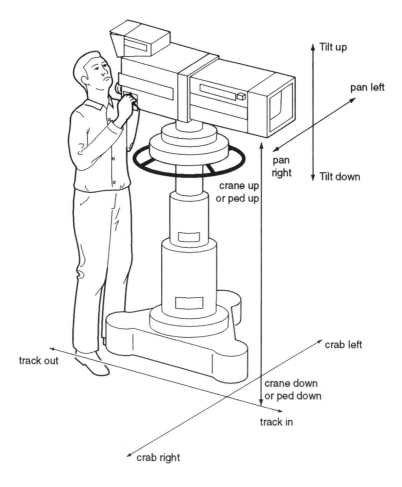

ventions of the specific programme format and has a thorough mastery of the basic skills in his/her particular craft. Information about shots will be supplied during rehearsal and/or during transmission/recording but it will be assumed by the director that the camera crew will respond with customary technique to the specific programme requirements (example – matched shots for interviews, see Interviews/discussion, page 160).

Rehearse/record

There are two main methods for recording a programme using multi-cameras:

- Rehearse a section of the programme and record that section.
- Rehearse the whole of the programme and then record or transmit the programme 'live'.

To some extent, the first method of rehearse/record is efficient in that only small sections are rehearsed and remembered but it does require a high level of concentration throughout the shooting day because the production is periodically in 'transmission' conditions and sometimes allows insufficient time for all disciplines to get it right.

The second method requires extended rehearsal unless production content is so flexible that coverage is arranged by assigning a role for each camera during the programme (e.g. Camera 1 on a wide shot, Camera 2 on close-ups, etc.). If content is precisely known (e.g. drama serials/soaps, sitcoms, etc.) then the camera rehearsal will involve working through the programme shot by shot so that everyone associated with the production is aware of what is required.

Camera rehearsal

The rehearsal period is structured in a variety of ways depending on the programme.

Blocking or looking at shots allows the whole production team to make the necessary adjustments section by section. The programme is rehearsed shot by shot, stopping each time there is a problem (e.g. unsatisfactory framing, unacceptable sound, unflattering lighting etc.). During this phase of the rehearsal, shots are established, lighting and sound adjusted. A solution is found or will be found before continuing with the rehearsal.

This may be followed by a run-through of a particular sequence adding pre-recorded inserts and this gives an indication of the time needed for camera moves, pace of movement and change of shot.

Finally, depending on the programme, there may be a full dress run-through from opening titles to end credits. This final rehearsal is an attempt to run the programme exactly as it will be transmitted or recorded with no stoppages. The dress run may reveal logistical problems of moving cameras, presenters, scenery, etc., between sequences and all the other craft adjustments that need to be made in continuous camera coverage. Any significant alterations to the production as the result of this rehearsal may be rehearsed again (time permitting) or the production crew will be made aware of any unrehearsed material or shots before the recording or transmission.

The rehearsal period should be used to check the production require-

Essential points

- Use the rehearsal period to establish what your specific contribution will be. Ask questions if you are unsure.
- Make notes on your camera card or running order and mark up camera position (see Camera card notes, page 174).
- Make yourself aware of the role of other cameras.
- Plan for the unexpected and have contingency plans for any eventuality.
- Do not over-commit yourself with numerous camera repositions if you are unsure of the time available to implement them.
- Check the cable routing of the camera and any potential object on which it could get snagged (e.g. rostrum corners, stage weights, boom wheels).

ments for the whole programme. There is no point in having a perfectly rehearsed third of a programme if the remaining two thirds could not be rehearsed because of lack of time.

Always check the time available to reposition the camera if no rehearsal is available. Do not offer shots from a number of positions during the slow blocking of the show unless you are convinced that when the sequence is run at speed you can make the necessary moves and that you are not preventing other camera movement.

Tracking

Assisting with pedestal work

As we will see in the section on operational skills, a camera mounted on a pedestal is a very flexible method of repositioning the camera on and off shot. Most camera operators operating on such a mounting usually like to control all camera movement themselves. The pedestal can be controlled in a very precise manner by the camera operator but sometimes a shot requires the assistance of a tracker.

Assisting with a pedestal development shot may be the first involvement a trainee will experience with camera movement on shot. There are a number of reasons why a camera operator operating a pedestal may need assistance but crabbing the camera at speed parallel to the action is one reason for a request for a tracker.

It is easier to push the pedestal at speed than to pull it running backwards. Make certain during rehearsal that the start and end positions of the camera are marked and that the end position mark can be seen during the move to avoid an overshoot. Decide on the best method of dealing with the camera cable keeping it clear of the feet of the camera operator and of the pedestal. Mark up a running order or make a rough camera card for all movements that need your assistance with a description of the action rather than shot number if you are not wearing a radio headset.

Agree with the camera operator how he/she will signal when the movement is to begin. He/she may ask you to take your own cue from the artiste movement or may want to cue you him/herself. Always be ready to adapt and adjust to the artist movement rather than simply going to a pre-rehearsed mark. In general, camera movement will start with artiste movement and end with artiste movement (see Camera movement, page 126).

Help with pedestal work may also occur because of the precision needed in focusing while moving. The camera operator may need an extra hand to ring-steer the pedestal while he/she reframes and shifts focus. Very fast moves on shot and fast reposition between shots are additional reasons why pedestal work requires assistance.

Tracking a dolly

The technique required to track a dolly is one step up from assisting on a pedestal because of the important additional responsibility that the camera operator, seated on the front of the dolly, places on the tracker to get him/her and the camera to the rehearsed position. If the rehearsed tracking line is missed or the speed of the track is mismatched with the action, there is nothing the camera operator can do to salvage the shot. The same criteria applies for accurate marking up the floor and camera card plus the need to watch the camera operator for signals to adjust the dolly if required.

The tracker will now be wearing a headset and this will be his/her first

Essential points

- Before rehearsal, equip yourself with marker/pen and marking up material – tape/timber crayon, etc.
- Check cable guard clearance and ensure there are no loops of ancillary cables attached to the camera cable (e.g. lighting cables, prompt, etc.) which could catch under the cable guards.
- Mark the floor according to position and movement.
- Note all positions and movements by marking the card for quick reference.
- Pace the movement to the action.
- Watch your cable and get assistance with cable clearing if necessary.
- All movement must be silent and safe.
- Never endanger yourself, other members of staff, the public or equipment.
- Check that all your marks are still legible before transmission/recording.
- On transmission/recording watch for camera operator's hand signals.
- Anticipate fast repositions before they occur.
- Work to the cue light and the shot number.

opportunity of experiencing the flow of shot numbers, director's instructions synchronized with programme sound which underpins all continuous multi-camera camerawork.

If there are a number of positions on the same tracking line, mark a ladder (i.e. a large 'ruler' on the floor with equal spaced units) and number them alphabetically so that each shot or movement can have a start and a finish letter assigned. Make certain that all shots have an assigned position marked on the camera card and any additional information such as a fast move, etc., is easily read quickly from the page. There is frequently no time to read long elaborate instructions.

Any movement with a dolly must not endanger yourself or the cameraman, other members of the production crew and cast or any audience or members of the public present. Finally, movement must not endanger the equipment you are using.

Operating a camera for the first time

Basic skills

The basic operational skills learnt by cabling and tracking apply equally to camerawork. When the day arrives for a trainee to operate his/her first camera on transmission or recording, he/she will have already acquired the habits of preparation, anticipation and concentration.

The basic skills required for multi-camera camerawork are as follows:

■ The skills needed to control smoothly the camera and mounting.
■ The skills needed to prepare for a recording/transmission and to repeat what was rehearsed or agreed at a specific time in the programme.
■ The skills needed to match the tempo of the camerawork to the timescale of the programme. In practice this means that every shot has to be delivered precisely when it is required with no opportunity for the cameraman to hold the action while last-minute preparations are made.
■ The ability to work as part of a camera crew.

It is obviously not possible to acquire all the techniques associated with multi-camera camerawork on day one. These will be mastered after exposure to a wide range of programme making. What can be practised by the trainee when not involved in rehearsal is the control of camera movement, focusing and pedestal technique.

In rehearsal

At the start of rehearsal remember that you are part of a camera crew and your work must match their shots. Despite the concentration required to master the steep learning curve before transmission/recording, keep in touch with what other members of the production team are doing. You need to display individual initiative plus the ability to be aware of what is happening around you. Do not bury your head in the viewfinder all the time. On many shows a camera operator will often be looking around the camera more than in the viewfinder.

Listen to talkback and mark up any information that concerns your shots and watch the cue lights in the viewfinder to check when you are off and on shot. If you are asked a question on recording or transmission 'nod' the camera in the tilt mode to communicate 'yes' and move the camera in the pan mode to communicate 'no' provided you are not on shot.

Coping with change

If there is a major change during the programme, anticipate how it will affect your shots and be prepared to adjust to a new and unrehearsed situation.

Pre-rehearsal checklist
All of these topics will be discussed in turn but the following basic preparations should be followed when operating a camera for the first time.

■ Check over camera, mount, remove chains if fitted and unlock pan/tilt head.
■ Check that the cable is 'eighted' and free to follow any camera movement.
■ Look through the camera cards if supplied and check opening position on floor plan.
■ Check that you can clearly hear production/engineering talkback and programme sound on your headset.
■ Check the viewfinder controls and mixed viewfinder facilities.
■ Get the feel of the camera movement and adjust friction.
■ Adjust pan bar and position of the zoom demand unit according to personal preference. Position of pan bar may need to be altered to accommodate very high or low shots during rehearsal.
■ Check focus and the varying zone of focus depending on zoom angle.
■ Reduce the headset cable loop to the minimum operational requirements and tie off to the camera. A long loop can easily get snagged.

Never underestimate the importance of anticipation in making time for yourself. Do not allow the excitement and confusion of a situation to get in the way of thinking clearly in order to act decisively.

Hold rather than grip the pan bar. White knuckles and a sweaty palm will not improve your ability to control the camera. Nerves are natural and often a stimulus to concentration but ignore how many hundreds of thousands of viewers may be watching your work and put your attention on the next shot. If you do make a mistake forget about it until after the show and then consider how you can avoid making the same mistake again. Look for comment about your work after the programme has finished and mentally make a note of any advice after your first day as a camera operator has ended.

Pedestal design

Continuous adjustment

Live or 'recorded-as-live' television production requires a camera mounting that can be quickly and silently repositioned off shot and have the flexibility to be smoothly positioned on shot to accomplish pre-rehearsed camera movements. It must also be capable of instant small adjustments in track or crab mode to compensate for masking by artistes or wrong positioning. A usable shot must always be provided in a continuous programme even though the position of the artistes is not as rehearsed.

In a studio these requirements are best served by a pedestal camera mounting controlled by the camera operator who can instantly compensate without misunderstanding or delay between tracker and camera operator.

The camera operator, while operating the camera, can also move the camera forwards, backwards or sideways by means of the ring steering wheel which alters the direction of the double wheel positioned at each corner of the base and he/she can alter the camera height. This must be accomplished silently, smoothly and with minimum effort. Continuous adjustment of the pedestal requires a smooth floor and complete mastery in the use of a pedestal.

The pedestal design

The most common camera mounting in a multi-camera production studio is the pedestal. The majority of studios are equipped with Vinten pedestals which are designed for a range of different weights and models of camera. These mountings have a triangular base with a pair of wheels at each corner controlled from a large ring steering wheel attached to the top of a hydraulically balanced column which can be smoothly raised or lowered (see opposite).

The larger pedestals (e.g. the Fulmar) with pan/tilt head, mainline camera, lens and lens controls can have a total weight of over 300 kg while a smaller lightweight pedestal and camera can be less than 140 kg. Moving 300 kg from a standing start, paced to the speed of the action covered while maintaining good composition and focus requires a specialist technique that is developed with experience. If you are new to multi-camera camerawork, do not underestimate the skills needed to move and stop the pedestal fluently, on cue and with precision.

Smoothly positioning the camera on and off shot requires learning skills in the use of the mounting. Practise as much as possible when not engaged in rehearsal but remember to defocus or cap up the camera to avoid distracting control room staff (who may be involved in rehearsing another sequence) by the moving images on your camera's preview monitor.

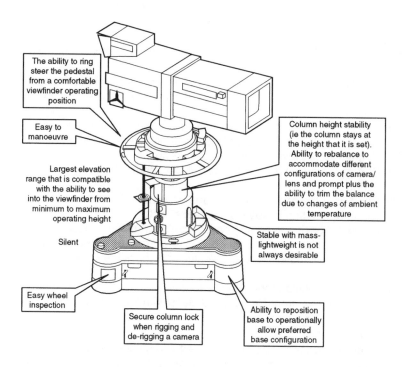

The ability to ring steer the pedestal from a comfortable viewfinder operating position

Easy to manoeuvre

Largest elevation range that is compatible with the ability to see into the viewfinder from minimum to maximum operating height

Silent

Easy wheel inspection

Column height stability (ie the column stays at the height that it is set). Ability to rebalance to accommodate different configurations of camera/lens and prompt plus the ability to trim the balance due to changes of ambient temperature

Stable with mass-lightweight is not always desirable

Secure column lock when rigging and de-rigging a camera

Ability to reposition base to operationally allow preferred base configuration

Essential operational points are as follows:

■ The camera and the mounting must be balanced and the head fitted with correct cams to ensure smooth operation.

■ The wheels must be free from any debris picked up from the studio.

■ Always try to operate with the flat side of the pedestal base behind the camera.

■ Whenever possible, position wheels 90° to action so that instant adjustment to avoid masking can be achieved.

Pre-rehearsal checklist

Before rehearsal commences, check that all the operational controls of the camera, pedestal and pan/tilt head are functioning and set correctly and that they are adjusted to suit your operational technique.

Camera

- Check that zoom drive cables are clamped and will not snag when the camera is in use.
- Check that the pan bar and zoom control/shot box are positioned to your operational requirements and that the crib card-holder is conveniently positioned.
- Check the range of viewfinder movement and adjust if necessary.
- Set up viewfinder – contrast/brightness/peaking/edge of frame and that all cue lights are switched on and working.
- Check and adjust the back focus of the zoom if the lens has just been rigged.
- Check that the camera channel and viewfinder definition is adequate for you to be the first to see loss of optical focus.
- Check talkback and tie off headset cable for minimum loop.
- Set up shot box angles if this is your preferred method of working.
- Check zoom and focus control setting and check the smoothness of their operation.
- Check the setting of the zoom extender.
- Check the lens front element and clean with lens tissue if necessary.

Pan/tilt head

- Remove locking chains or bar if fitted and unlock the pan/tilt head.
- Adjust balance of camera and check correct size cams are fitted for lens/camera/viewfinder configuration.
- Adjust the degree of pan and tilt friction required for the programme format.

Pedestal

- Remove safety locking pin or bar if fitted.
- Check the balance of the column is correct by raising the column to its highest point and check if the camera stays in this position. Reverse the procedure by depressing to the lowest point and check if camera rises. Add or subtract trim weights to balance the pedestal.
- Check that there are sufficient trim weights in the storage tray to accommodate any change of temperature during rehearsal/recording.
- Check that the camera cable is clamped and there is sufficient loop of cable to allow nearly 360° movement on the head.

A universal camera 'operating' position. Sitting on the corner of the ped waiting for the start of rehearsal, the next shot or the next meal break!

- Check that cable guards are correctly set to avoid riding over the camera cable.
- Check the camera cable is eighted and will provide an unimpeded flow of cable when the camera moves.

Noise
Check that movement of the camera, mounting and pan/tilt head is silent and that you have the means to mark up camera position and to mark up camera cards if supplied.

Pedestal technique (1)

The main elements affecting smooth pedestal movement on shot are:

- the condition of the floor;
- lens angle;
- movement and composition;
- mechanical condition of the pedestal;
- camera cable;
- viewfinder;
- space for the development;
- focus;
- eye, hand and body coordination.

The condition of the floor

Check over the floor for dropped nails or other small debris left from the scenery set and lights. Check over painted or 'martacked' floor areas for over-painted marking tapes, bubbles or general wear and tear of the floor surface. Have the floor swept and if possible plan the camera movement to avoid the worst conditions. The effects of an uneven floor will be exacerbated by working at the top of the pedestal column or by tracking on a narrow lens angle.

Lens angle

Select the correct lens angle from the zoom range for the camera development required. A long track on a narrow angle will not only be difficult to hold steady and in focus but will provide little or no change in the perspective of mass in the shot (see Perspective of line, page 122). There is no motivation for a camera move if there is no significant change in the composition of the shot.

In general, the wider the lens angle in use (e.g. > 30°) the steadier the movement and the greater control of framing and focus. Often a small amount of camera movement on a wide angle provides a substantial change in the shot (see The development shot, page 136).

Movement and composition

Good composition must be maintained throughout the pedestal movement. This can be achieved by starting and ending with good compositions and ensuring a smooth transition between these frames by the use of pivot points (see Zooming, page 108), by motivating the movement with action within the frame and at a speed that matches the content of the shot. A good pedestal development shot should provide a smooth, unobtrusive, continuous change in visual interest with no 'dead' area between the initial and final image.

Pedestal technique

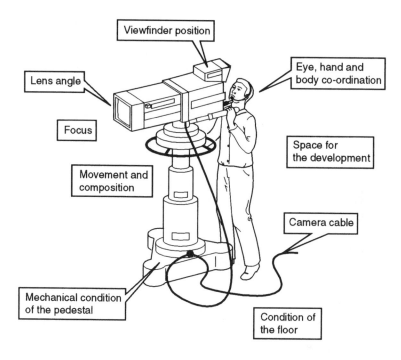

Viewfinder position

Eye, hand and
body co-ordination

Lens angle

Focus

Space for
the development

Movement and
composition

Camera cable

Mechanical condition
of the pedestal

Condition of
the floor

Mechanical condition of the pedestal
Check for pieces of gaffer tape, nails or small debris embedded or stuck to
the pedestal wheels. Check that the column of the pedestal is balanced.
Changes in temperature affect the hydraulic system of the pedestal. If necessary transfer the trim weights stored at the base of the pedestal to the
weight tray above the ring steering wheel. The balance of the camera
should have been adjusted in the 'start-of-day checks' and a check made
at the same time that the correct cams are fitted in the pan and tilt head for
the camera/lens and prompter (if fitted) in use. Other mechanical checks
such as cable guard clearance, slackness in the ring steer assembly will
also affect the smoothness of the pedestal movement.

Pedestal technique (2)

Camera cable

More pedestal movements on shot have suffered from cables being fouled, snagged or stood on than possibly for any other reason. If there is no one on the crew cable clearing, make certain that there is a sufficient length of unimpeded cable available for the intended movement. If possible, reduce the amount and distance the cable has to be pulled during the move. A long length of cable dragged across the studio floor adds to the weight of the pedestal/camera and the amount of effort required to move the pedestal.

Check that the camera cable is clamped to the base of the pedestal and that the loop of cable between clamp and camera will not become snagged on any part of the pedestal as the camera is panned and moved and that there is sufficient loop of cable when panning the camera at maximum elevation. Check that no ancillary cable wrapped around the camera cable has loose or exposed loops that could be trapped under the cable guards and stop the pedestal movement.

Viewfinder

If there is a change of height of the camera or, during a crabbing movement, it is necessary to position the body away from the centre of the viewfinder, provision must be made to alter the viewfinder hood in order to see the whole of the viewfinder image. If this cannot be achieved with a quick adjustment by the right hand released from the ring steer while the camera is moving, then the best compromise is to start in a difficult viewfinder viewing and body position and, as the shot develops, to arrive at a comfortable operating position at the end of the move.

Sometimes the camera has been positioned so far back on the pan and tilt head to balance out a heavy lens and prompt that the viewfinder ends up a long distance away from the ring steering wheel. In order to reach the ring steer even at full arm stretch, the face of the operator is almost pressed up against the viewfinder. This is a near impossible operating position for any kind of pedestal development camera work and either a larger ring steering wheel must be fitted to the pedestal or additional weights added to the back of the camera in order that balance can be achieved with the viewfinder positioned in a normal operating position.

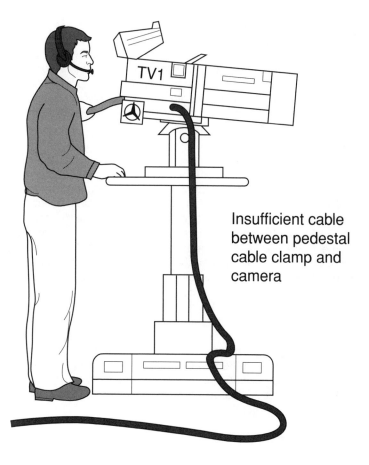

Insufficient cable between pedestal cable clamp and camera

There should be a sufficient loop of camera cable between pedestal base clamp and camera cable entry point to allow almost a 360° pan of the camera.

Pedestal technique (3)

Space for the development

It seems self-evident that a camera move can only be attempted if there is sufficient floor space unimpeded by other equipment, set or artistes, that there is sufficient set to cover the whole of the move (including 'shooting off' the top of the set) and that the camera will not end up 'in vision' in the following shot. Although the above criteria may be obvious, it is not unknown for camera operators to set out on a complex development shot to find that they have fallen foul of one of the above pitfalls.

Focus

Needless to say, however fluent the camera development may be the significant subject in the frame must stay in focus during the whole of the move. There is no short-cut technique to focus pulling on the move. You need one hand on the pan bar to continuously reframe the shot, one hand on the ring steer to control the direction and to provide the impetus for the movement and one hand on the focus wheel to adjust focus. Three-handed camera operators are in great demand on multi-camera pedestal work.

Some development shots involve staying the same distance from the principal subject and therefore focus is not a problem. A wide angle lens development with a large depth of field may also allow control of the pedestal with both hands but with most tracks and crabs some stage is reached when the right hand must be freed to give a quick tweak to the focus. The right direction of wheel travel and a 'kick off' with the foot often allows the left hand on the pan bar to keep the camera moving while the right hand can be positioned on the focus wheel. Try to arrange the direction of the pedestal so that this type of movement control is achieved if a large focus pull is required.

Eye, hand and body coordination

Moving the pedestal on shot should become as familiar and easy as driving a car. Practice and experience, anticipation of the unexpected and the avoidance of impossible moves are all part of good pedestal control.

One of the most difficult moves on a pedestal is to crab right and around an artiste in a semi-circle. To push the pedestal, the body needs to be behind the direction of the move but this involves the panning handle, which is normally on the left of the camera, pushing into the body and preventing the operator from panning left to compensate for the crab right. If you can achieve this with fluency and precision you can remove your L plates from the pedestal.

Repositioning the ped

Control of pedestal
At each corner of the base of the pedestal are a pair of wheels. Their direction is controlled by the large steering ring positioned under the trim weight storage tray. The direction of the alignment of the wheels is communicated to the hand by a raised red indicator attached to the steering ring so that without looking away from the viewfinder, information is always available as to the direction the pedestal will move when pushed (see opposite).

This centre ring control allows the camera operator to crab, steer and adjust height on shot with one hand (usually the right hand) while controlling framing via the pan bar with the other hand.

The alignment of the base of the pedestal can be adjusted to avoid constantly working with a corner of the base directly behind the camera.

Moving between shots
Practice is required to move the pedestal efficiently and quickly via the ring steering wheel. Multi-camera camerawork often involves a number of repositions of the camera during a sequence or scene and so movement off shot has to be fast and precise. Move the pedestal to the new position first before adjusting height.

If the framing of the shot relies on an exact position of the lens (e.g. a reflection in a mirror, an over the shoulder two shot, etc.) then the base of the pedestal requires a precise mark on the studio floor. Mark an arc following the base of the pedestal and add a number or letter which corresponds to the shot number (see opposite) and note this on the camera card.

The marks made with a floor crayon are quickly erased by pedestal and cable movement across them. They will need re-marking as there is a great deal of activity across the floor between rehearsal and transmission/recording. 'Lo-tack' tape (designed to be easily removed on de-rig) is more permanent but there is a risk, if there are too many marks on the studio floor, of bumping over the tape when moving on shot and causing a jump in the framing.

Repositioning the camera at speed
When repositioning the camera at speed across the studio floor, turn the camera in the direction of travel as it is easier to push a camera than to run backwards. Make certain that you walk around the pedestal in a direction that provides sufficient slack cable between camera and cable clamp on the pedestal base rather than winding the cable loop around the column.

Pushing the camera onto a new set also allows you to start composing the shot before you come to rest and speeds up the move.

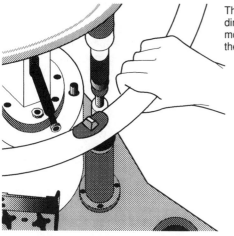

The raised red pointer indicates the direction in which the pedestal will move and is a constant reminder of the position of the pedestal wheels.

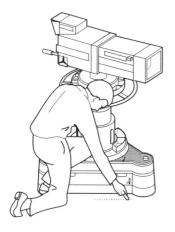

Mark up any critical camera position and number or letter the position and make a note on the camera card. The position marked 'STEER' on the base of the pedestal allows one set of wheels to be unlocked and the pedestal base swivelled to the optimum operating position. Return the wheels to 'CRAB' for normal movement.

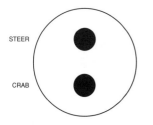

STEER

CRAB

Tracking on a pedestal

Tracking is moving the camera towards or away from the principal subject in the frame. The three operational adjustments required in tracking are control of camera mounting and camera, framing and focusing. In addition, there is the need for the track to have a reason or some type of motivation (see Camera movement, page 126).

Before tracking
If possible, arrange the pedestal base so that you are working within an arc of the base. Position the angle of the viewfinder so that you can see the whole of the image from the start to the end of the track. Have sufficient slack cable for the whole of the track to avoid pulling a large length of cable across the studio floor. Check that nothing will impede your movement throughout the range of the track such as floor coverings, furniture, other cameras, cables or people! Check that your end position will not finish in the succeeding shot. Check that the lens angle selected is suitable for tracking (see the topic Lens angle, page 88).

To track in
Position the ring steering wheel to point the wheels in the direction of the track (preferably off shot) and holding the ring steer with the right hand at the position of the indicator and holding (not gripping) the pan bar with the left hand, push with the right foot to get the pedestal moving and continue the movement with the hand on the ring steer.

Adjust the framing of the shot as you track in (see Pivot points, Zooming, page 112) and while keeping the momentum of the movement with the left hand on the pan bar, the right hand can be released from the ring steer to the focus capstan in order to adjust focus if necessary as you approach the principal subject in the frame. If the design of the focus capstan is sufficiently robust, the right hand can also be used to push the pedestal.

Reduce the push on the pedestal towards the end of the track to allow the track to glide imperceptibly to a halt. Avoid abrupt changes of movement unless this is required by the motivation for the move. Most camera movement follows a non-linear rate of change. The move or zoom is started imperceptibly before accelerating to the maximum speed required and then falling off as the move reaches its end point. Audio fades often use the same technique with the sound gradually receding until it unobtrusively disappears so that the listener is unaware of the exact point of the completed fade. This is another aspect of invisible technique – visual or audio changes are softened to ease the transition.

To track out
Tracking out is operationally more demanding than a push-in as moving

Essential operational points when tracking

■ Select a lens angle wider than 25°.
■ Adjust the pedestal to allow you to work within an arc of the base.
■ Adjust the viewfinder to fit the movement.
■ Have sufficient slack cable.
■ Check the floor space is clear for the move.
■ Position ring steer in the direction of track.
■ Use hand on ring steer and foot to 'kick' off movement.
■ Concentrate on steering and shot development before adjusting focus (if needed) when approaching the principal subject in frame.
■ Glide to a halt following a non-linear speed of movement.
■ When tracking out, focus change is critical at the start of the move and movement has to be maintained without the use of the ring steer.
■ Avoid sweeping cable under your feet with the base of the camera when tracking out.

backwards is more awkward than a track-in. Overcoming the inertia required to get the 300 kg pedestal/camera moving has to be provided by the right hand on the ring steer without the benefit of a push off with the foot. Also, the biggest correction of focus will occur in the first part of the movement which requires the right hand to be controlling the capstan focus.

The technique is to pull on the ring steer with the right hand to get the pedestal moving and then quickly transfer this hand to the capstan and refocus while keeping the pedestal on the move with the left hand on the pan bar. A fast move will cover an unsynchronized focus pull provided the shot is sharp when the movement ends. Focusing is much more critical during a slow move and the camera movement must be activated through the pan bar and focus capstan as the right hand cannot be released to the ring steer or loss of focus will not be corrected in time.

All the conditions connected to a track-in apply to tracking out with the additional requirement to make certain that as you track out, the base of the pedestal does not pile up the camera cable around your feet creating the risk of loosing your footing.

Crabbing

Combined move

A pure crabbing movement is a camera move where the distance between the principal subject and the lens remains unchanged during the move. Frequently, however, a crab is combined with a track to provide a more visually interesting and dynamic camera development.

The name was probably coined from the ability of the crab to move sideways but it is almost impossible for a camera operator working with a full facility camera on a heavy duty pedestal, unaided, to move a pedestal sideways (parallel to the principal subject) from a standing start. This is because it is not practical to look into the viewfinder and reach around the camera to a point on the ring steer close to 90° from the lens in order to pull the pedestal parallel to the action. Most camera operators are unable to crab the pedestal by gripping the ring steer below the viewfinder. The same move, however, is relatively simple when operating with a lightweight camera and pedestal.

Pan bar conventions

Many countries have adopted the convention of pan bar on the left of camera and focus control on the right-hand side of the camera. The pan bar prevents the ring steer to the left of the camera being used by the cameraman to crab the pedestal.

The usual crabbing technique with a full facility camera and heavy duty pedestal is therefore to turn the wheels slightly into the subject so that the crabbing movement starts as a mixture of crab and track. The movement can be kicked off with the foot and then the shot development controlled with the steering ring. The position of the hand on the steering ring will depend on the degree of rotation of the wheel required by the shot development. The further the hand is positioned away from the wheel below the viewfinder, the less power there is in the arm to keep the pedestal moving. Once the pedestal is on the move, it is usually possible to steer into a crabbing line that is parallel to the principal subject's movement.

A common technique to provide more physical power to move the pedestal is to offset the body on the right side (or opposite side to the pan bar) of the viewfinder in order to reach further around the ring steer and either pull (for a crab right) or push (for a crab left).

From bad to better

A good rule of thumb for any camera movement which involves at some point a bad body posture for operating or a bad sightline to the viewfinder, is to start from the worst operating condition and, during the camera development, unwind to a good operating position. This allows framing and focus at the end of the shot to be adjusted when working in the best operating position.

Keeping the whole of the viewfinder image in view is frequently difficult with a crabbing move. A side opening viewfinder hood or a viewfinder that

Crabbing operating requirements are similar to tracking viz:

- Select a lens angle wider than 35°.
- If possible adjust the pedestal to allow most of the movement with-in one arc of the base.
- Adjust the viewfinder to fit the movement.
- Have sufficient slack cable.
- Check the floor space is clear for the move.
- Position ring steer in the direction of track.
- Use hand on ring steer and foot to 'kick' off movement except a crab right.
- Concentrate on steering and shot development before adjusting focus as necessary when approaching the principal subject in frame.
- Glide to a halt following a non-linear speed of movement.

To maximize the effect of a crab see The development shot, page 136.

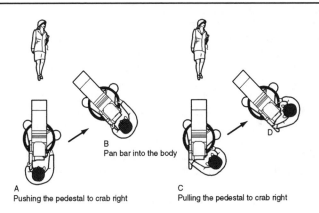

A
Pushing the pedestal to crab right

B
Pan bar into the body

C
Pulling the pedestal to crab right

D

swivels helps if the final operating position is not jeopardized. A common problem during such a move is that the cue light becomes obscured.

Crabbing right in an arc

Because of the conventional position in the UK of the pan bar to the left of the camera, care should be taken when positioned in line with the viewfind-er that a crab right does not develop with an operating position increasing-ly to the left of the viewfinder. This can easily happen if the crab right is started with a kick off with the foot (A) and as the movement develops the camera is increasingly panned left which pushes the pan bar further and further into the body trailing behind the camera (B). For a crab right, start with the body to the right of the viewfinder (C) and use the ring steer to develop the shot (D). This also places you in a more comfortable position to adjust focus if required.

Craning

Straight back

An average pedestal has an elevation range of approximately 95 cm (37.5 inches). Visually, the effect of a 95cm change in lens height can be significantly enhanced if the wider angle of the zoom lens is selected and there is suitable content in the frame. It is usually a shot using the wider lens angle where camera height becomes the most critical. Frequently the camera height is adjusted off shot to improve the composition of the shot by altering perspective of line.

The pedestal counterbalances the combined weight of camera and lens by pressurized gas and small trim weights. These trim weights can be added to the column to compensate for changes in gas pressure due to ambient temperature change. Even though the counterbalance system provides for very little effort to effect a change in height once the column is moving, there is an initial inertia to overcome and care should be taken in craning the camera up or down.

To avoid back strain or injury when lifting a heavy weight, it is recommended to keep the back straight and bend the knees. Unfortunately it is often not possible to follow this advice when operating a television camera. Viewfinder height is controlled by lens height which is frequently below normal standing eye height. Even with tilting viewfinders, the camera operator spends a great deal of operating time crouching in order to look into the viewfinder. With a bent back in this position he/she then has to crane the camera, for example, to follow an artiste standing up.

The safest body posture and the technique with the greatest control of movement is to position the shoulder over the ring steer and use the torso to force the pedestal down. To crane the camera up, use the reverse of this technique and with the shoulder over the pedestal pull the ring steering wheel up.

The most difficult manoeuvre, and potentially the most physically dangerous, is to attempt to crane up and down gripping the ring steer with the arm outstretched. A small adjustment of the pedestal height in this way can be made off shot but if the crane up is matched to artiste movement, then it is probably prudent to position the shoulder as close to the ring steer as possible before 'lifting' the ring steer.

Viewfinder

Craning the pedestal on shot through its full elevation range will cause problems with viewfinder position. At the lowest operating position of the pedestal, the viewfinder will need to be tilted up. As the camera is craned up (if not adjusted) the tilted viewfinder will eventually be pointing up at the studio lights and be inaccessible. It is sometimes possible to correct the angle of the viewfinder during the movement with the forehead or to give it a quick 'knock' at the end of the movement but the more usual solution is as illustrated.

Viewfinder position when craning

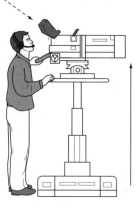

(a)   (b)

When craning the camera up, if the viewfinder is tilted up to provide a comfortable operating position at the start of the move, unless it is repositioned during the move, its position at the top of the column will be inoperable.

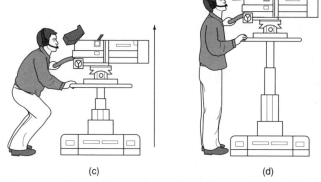

(c)   (d)

Start at the lowest camera position with the viewfinder tilted down at an angle that can just be usable in its highest position (c). Most viewfinders have the bottom part of the visor either open or able to be opened and therefore the face of the viewfinder can be seen at most heights. Again the rule of thumb can be applied of starting with a difficult operating position and during the crane up to move to an easier situation (d). Craning down simply reverses this technique.

Check that there is sufficient cable loop between camera and pedestal base cable clamp for any craning movement.

Terminology

The camera movement description to 'crane up' originally came from the camera crane movement. Some directors use 'ped up' or 'ped down' to describe changing the lens height of a camera mounted on a pedestal. Also 'tilt up' or 'tilt down' may be described as 'pan up' or 'pan down'.

Focus

Depth of field
Focusing is the act of adjusting the lens elements to achieve a sharp image at the focal plane. Objects either side of this focus zone may still look reasonably sharp depending on their distance from the lens, the lens aperture and lens angle. The area covering the objects that are in acceptable focus is called the depth of field.

The depth of field can be considerable if the widest angle of the zoom is selected and, while working with a small aperture, a subject is selected for focus at some distance from the lens. When zooming into this subject, the depth of field or zone of acceptable sharpness will decrease (see opposite).

Capstan servo control
If the television camera is being operated from behind the camera using a large viewfinder, focusing is usually achieved by a capstan servo control mounted on the right of the camera. The position of the focus control and its operation will vary depending on country but the standard convention in the UK is to turn the capstan clockwise to focus forward (i.e. objects closer to the lens) and to turn it anti-clockwise for objects further from the lens (see opposite). If a portable camera is being used with a monocular viewfinder then focus is usually controlled by the focus ring on the lens.

Follow focus
Television is often a 'talking head' medium and the eyes need to be in sharp focus. Sharpest focus can be checked off shot by rocking the focus zone behind and then in front of the eyes. Detecting on shot which plane of the picture is in focus is more difficult. You, as the camera operator, must be the first to detect loss of focus but this can only be achieved if the viewfinder definition is better than that of the viewer and the plane of sharpest focus can be seen without rocking focus.

As camera or subject moves there will be a loss of focus which needs to be corrected. The art of focusing is to know which way to focus and not to overshoot. Practise following focus as someone walks towards the lens (UK convention – turn the capstan clockwise). Turn capstan anti-clockwise as the subject moves away from camera. Practise throwing focus from one subject to another.

Pre-focusing
Sometimes it is not possible to focus on a subject before the shot is required. Typically, as a presenter appears in the frame, the camera is cut to. Without some method of pre-focusing, the chances are that the shot will be soft and

Focus capstan wheel

The three variables that affect depth of field are :
- distance from camera of principal subject in focus
- aperture of the lens
- lens angle selected

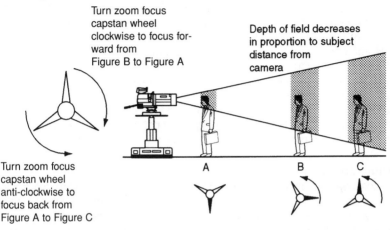

Turn zoom focus
capstan wheel
clockwise to focus for-
ward from
Figure B to Figure A

Depth of field decreases
in proportion to subject
distance from
camera

Turn zoom focus
capstan wheel
anti-clockwise to
focus back from
Figure A to Figure C

A   B   C

Focus problems

It is sometimes advantageous when a patterned subject is causing strobing – a patterning on the screen (e.g. a check coat which cannot be replaced or a monitor) – to slightly pull the focus forward of the surface of the material.

Aperture adjustment in multi-camera productions is centralized in vision control. A common technique is for the apertures of cameras in use to be set to an agreed value and left until all lighting adjustments are made during rehearsal. If correct exposure is not obtained by the lighting balance the aperture may require adjustment. This adjustment to the depth of field may occur late in the rehearsal period. If a critical camera move is contemplated where both hands are in use to develop a shot and focus is maintained by working within the prevailing depth of field beware that with a decrease in depth of field on transmission/recording the same move may now not be possible without adjusting focus.

---

focus will have to be tweaked on shot. The solution is to focus up on the subject during rehearsal and then swing the camera (without altering focus) to find another part of the set which is sharp. On transmission/recording pre-focus on that object and then reposition for the subject to enter frame. Make certain that both camera position and subject position are marked.

Zoom focus

Zoom lens and focus
A zoom lens is designed to keep the same focal plane throughout the whole of its range (provided the back focus has been correctly adjusted). Even if a zoom has not been rehearsed, always pre-focus whenever possible on the tightest shot of the subject. This is the best way of checking focus and it also prepares for a zoom-in if required.

Some focus demand units have small indentations which can be adjusted (off shot or during rehearsal) to indicate a specific focus point on the zoom. This allows a pre-rehearsed second focus point to be arrived at (after the first pre-focused point) by turning the capstan focus and feeling with the hand when the pre-set indentations are aligned.

Blind zooming
When zooming into a subject on which the focus has not been pre-determined (blind zooming) it is best to be focused slightly back behind the subject so that you know where your zone of focus is. As focusing becomes more critical at the end of the zoom range, focus can be pulled forward. This helps to correct focus the right way. Correcting the wrong way, for example, focusing back when you should have focused forward because you did not know where the zone of focus was positioned, is more obvious than a slight out of focus shot for part of the zoom. Practise focusing by fast zooming into a subject and then hitting the correct focus in one movement. Keep varying the distance of the objects zoomed into so that fast accurate focusing becomes instinctive.

Pulling focus
Within a composition, visual attention is directed to the subject in sharpest focus. Attention can be transferred to another part of the frame by throwing focus on to that subject. Use the principle of invisible technique and match the speed of the focus pull to the motivating action.

If the focus is on a foreground person facing camera with a defocused background figure and the foreground subject turns away from camera, focus can be instantly thrown back to the background. A slower focus pull would be more appropriate in music coverage, for example, moving off the hands of a foreground musician to a background instrumentalist. Avoid long focus pulls that provide nothing but an extended defocused picture before another subject comes into sharp focus unless this is motivated by the action (e.g. the subjective experience of someone recovering consciousness).

Differential focus
Differential focus is deliberately using a narrow depth of field to emphasize the principal subject in the frame in sharp focus which is contrasted with a heavily out of focus background.

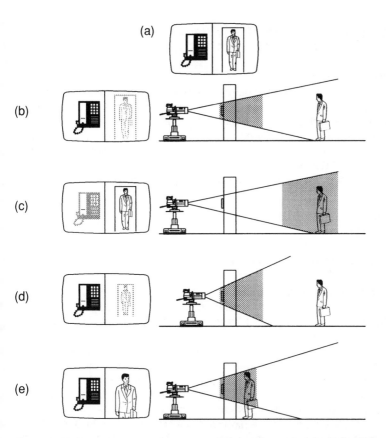

Figure (a) illustrates the required framing of the shot with a telephone mounted on a wall and a person entering a doorway in the background both in focus. Camera position and lens angle can achieve this framing but focused forward on the telephone (b) puts the background figure out of focus. Focusing back on the figure (c) puts the telephone out of focus. A wider angle lens (d) will not provide a greater depth of field if the camera is tracked-in to return to the original framing (a). Altering the light level may allow a smaller aperture and a larger depth of field but usually the best solution is to restage the action (e) to provide for both telephone and person to be covered by the existing depth of field.

A narrow depth of field can be achieved by either reducing lighting levels and opening up the lens aperture to achieve correct exposure or by using a neutral density filter to reduce light entering the lens requiring the aperture to be opened and reducing depth of field or by increasing the shutter speed.

Split focus
Because of aperture or lens angle it is sometimes not possible, in an unrehearsed situation, to hold two subjects at different distances from the lens in sharp focus. The focus therefore has to be split between them with either one or the other slightly soft.

105

Panning and tilting

Control of camera
Invisible camera technique requires camera movement to be unobtrusive and matched to content. Panning and tilting the camera is a basic skill that requires considerable practice until there is complete coordination between the eye and the hand on the pan bar. A requirement of good camerawork is the ability to move the camera smoothly and to be able to accelerate movement and decelerate movement.

The control of the camera during panning and tilting requires a combination of:

- correct friction (and cams);
- anticipation;
- correct body posture;
- correct choice of lens angle.

Condition of the pan/tilt head
Controlled smooth camera movement cannot be achieved unless the correct friction has been selected for the programme format. The amount of friction constraining vertical and horizontal movement is often a personal choice. Each camera operator needs to balance out the need for easy flexible movement against the operational difficulties of holding the camera steady when tracking, crabbing and panning the camera without friction.

A compromise amount of friction is therefore selected which suits the programme requirements and weather conditions. Using a long lens continuously at its narrow end in a high wind may require more friction than the same operation in a flat calm. It has been observed that when using the extreme narrow end of a 70-1 zoom lens (2x range extender lens angle approximately 0.28°) the pulse in the operator's hand on the pan bar can be detected by a rhythmic movement in the frame.

Anticipation
Panning along a line of objects of unequal height will quickly demonstrate the need to anticipate change in framing. Good camerawork requires fast reflexes in reframing during a continuous move combined with smooth and unobtrusive transitions. Anticipating the direction of a compensating diagonal move at an early stage will avoid jerky and erratic camerawork. Practise smooth controlled camera movement by panning, in a tight shot (close-up), across a camera cable which is snaking across the floor. This also provides focus practice.

Non-linear movement
A pan often requires a non-linear rate of movement (see opposite).

Non-linear movement

When motion begins, camera pans faster than subject to create space in front.

Constant speed of subject is matched by constant speed of pan.

Rapid change of direction requires an instant reframing to maintain space in front of the skater

A pan often requires a non-linear rate of movement. Following a moving person requires a quick acceleration of the pan to create space in front of them to move into (a), a constant speed of pan as they move (b) and settling to a static frame as they stop. If the movement is continuous and constantly changing direction such as a skate board, then unobtrusive camerawork will require a constantly varying pan and tilt rate (c) combined with diagonal movement. If the viewer is unaware of this activity then the camera operator has exactly paced the movement correctly.

Body position

Anticipating the end of a pan or tilt allows the camera operator to position him/herself so that a comfortable operating stance can be adopted. The more body stress there is in following action, the more likely that changes in camera movement will be erratic and noticeable.

Choice of lens angle

Even the most experienced camera operators will experience difficulties in accomplishing very small detailed pans and tilts when using a very narrow lens angle. The difficulty of controlled movement will be exacerbated if camera and lens are fitted with ancillary equipment such as prompters, lamps or microphones. Panning with a lens angle of less than 1° requires a very small movement on the pan bar for a very big movement in the frame.

107

Zooming

Variable lens angle

A zoom lens has a continuously variable lens angle and is therefore useful in multi-camera TV production for adjusting the image size without moving the camera position. When operating from behind the camera, the adjustment is controlled on most television cameras via the thumb on a two-way rocker switch which alters the direction and speed of the zoom. A good servo zoom should allow a smooth imperceptible take-up of the movement of the zoom which can then be accelerated by the thumb control to match the requirements of the shot. There is usually provision to alter the response of the thumb control so that a very slow zoom rate can be selected or a very fast zoom speed for the same movement of the thumb control.

When operating with a monocular viewfinder on a portable camera, the zoom lens can be controlled from a rocker switch mounted on the lens as well as a thumb control remoted to the pan bar or on a pistol grip.

Shot box

As the zoom lens has a continuous range of lens angles, individual settings can be pre-selected on a shot box. This is clamped to the pan bar sometimes as an integral part of the focus capstan and has a number of buttons which can be individually set to a required lens angle. When a shot box button is pushed, the zoom automatically moves to the pre-selected lens angle associated with that button.

Most shot boxes also have the provision to vary the rate at which the zoom lens moves to a selected lens angle. This allows the lens angle at the start of a shot to be programmed on one button and the lens angle at the end of the shot to be assigned to another button. The speed that the lens angle alters between the two buttons can then be adjusted to provide a precisely timed zoom in or out.

Use of the zoom

In general, the zoom is used in three ways in multi-camera TV production:

- to compose the shot;
- to readjust the composition on shot;
- to change the shot size in vision.

Pan bar zoom demand control

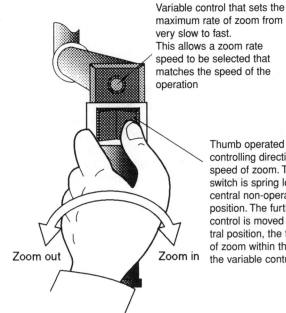

Variable control that sets the maximum rate of zoom from very slow to fast.
This allows a zoom rate speed to be selected that matches the speed of the operation

Thumb operated rocker switch controlling direction and rate of speed of zoom. The rocker switch is spring loaded to a central non-operating 'neutral' position. The further the thumb control is moved from this central position, the faster the rate of zoom within the limit set by the variable control.

Zoom out   Zoom in

Thumb operated rocker switch controlling direction and rate of speed of zoom

Composition

The zoom lens allows the desired framing of a shot to be quickly achieved. Shot size can be quickly altered out of vision to provide a range of shots. Each shot can have the required size and framing to match other cameras (see Intercutting, page 156). Extended zoom ranges (30:1, 40:1, 70:1) allow a wide range of shots to be obtained from a fixed position (e.g. on an OB scaffold tower/hoist) and provide visual movement across terrain where tracking would not be possible.

The speed of response of the thumb control can be adjusted to allow a compromise between the need for a fast reposition out of vision balanced against a slower speed of movement on shot. If the very fastest speed is selected, there is a tendency to overshoot on the framing making small changes in lens angle difficult. At the other extreme, a slow rate of zoom to allow good control of an 'in vision' zoom may be too slow for fast repositioning out of vision.

Readjustment on shot

The zoom is often used to trim or adjust the shot to improve the composition when the content of the shot changes. Someone joining a person in shot is provided with space in the frame by zooming out. The reverse may happen when they leave shot – the camera zooms in to re-compose the original shot. Trimming the shot 'in vision' may be unavoidable in the coverage of spontaneous or unknown content but it quickly becomes an irritant if repeatedly used. Fidgeting with the framing by altering the zoom angle should be avoided.

Shot box

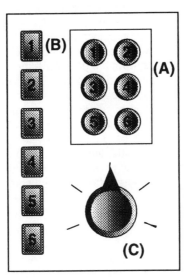

Each button on the shot box can be pre-set to a specific lens angle by variable controls (A).

When a button is pushed (B), the lens will be set to the pre-set lens angle at a speed controlled by (C).

The speed of zoom between two pre-set positions can therefore be precisely controlled. The speed between the pre-sets is normally set at the maximum setting for rapid change between pre-selected lens angles.

The shot box lens angle setting is instantly overridden when the thumb zoom demand is moved away from the neutral central position.

Pivot points

Zooming

Zooming into or away from the subject occurs in many programmes. There is a significant distinction between the perspective changes provided by tracking and zooming (see Tracking and zooming, page 138) but zooming is often the only choice to alter the image size because of the inability to move the camera. Zooming can be smoother, quicker and provide a greater change in image size than would be practical in tracking. It allows multi-camera coverage at a distance from the principal subjects and avoids cameras moving close to the subject and appearing in adjacent shots. Working at a distance also helps to keep clear the audience's view of the performers and to reduce the distraction of camera movement.

Like all changes in shot, the application of invisible technique requires this type of visual transition to be unobtrusive (except that type of programme content which draws attention to its method of presentation). Because a zoom involves no change of perspective, its harsh abrupt magnification or diminution of an image often requires some means of softening or disguising the transition. This can be achieved by combining the zoom with a camera movement and by the use of a pivot point.

Pivot points

A common mistake with users of domestic camcorders is to centre the subject of interest in the frame and then to zoom towards them keeping the subject the same distance from all four sides of the frame. The visual effect is as if the frame implodes in on them from all sides.

A more pleasing visual movement is to keep two sides of the frame at the same distance from the subject for the whole of the movement. This is achieved in a track or a zoom by pre-selecting a pivot point in the composition which is usually the main subject of interest and, while maintaining their position at a set distance from two adjacent sides of the frame, allow the other two sides of the frame to change their relative position to the subject (see opposite). This allows the subject image to grow progressively larger (or smaller) within the frame while avoiding the impression of the frame contracting in towards them.

It may be necessary on a combined track and crabbing movement to change this pivot point during the move but again, as in all camera technique, the changeover to a different pivot point must be subtle, unobtrusive and controlled by the main subject of interest.

Pivot point

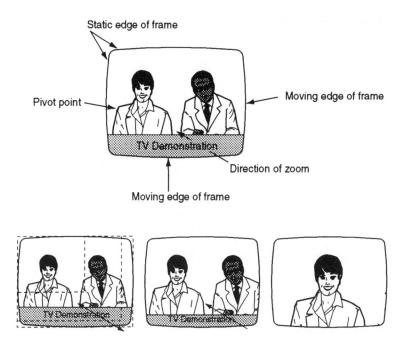

Pre-select one or two adjacent sides of the frame to the main subject of the zoom and whilst maintaining their position at a set distance from the main subject of the zoom allow the other two sides of the frame to change their relative position to the subject.

Keep the same relationship of the adjacent frame edge to the selected subject during the whole of the zoom movement.

The point that is chosen to be held stationary in the frame is called the pivot point. Using a pivot point allows the subject image to grow progressively larger (or smaller) within the frame whilst avoiding the impression of the frame contracting in towards them.

Picture making

Picture-making skills
Central to the craft of camerawork are the skills required to create arresting and informative images. Having discussed how to smoothly move the camera on and off shot, where should the lens be positioned to provide the most effective shot? What rules govern the craft of picture making?

'I see what you mean!'
There is usually a reason why a shot is recorded on tape or film. The purpose may be simply to record an event or the image may play an important part in expressing a complex idea. Whatever the reasons that initiate the shot, the camera operator should have a clear understanding of the purpose behind the shot.

After establishing why the shot is required, and usually this will be deduced purely from experience of the shot structure of the programme format, the camera operator will position the camera, adjust the lens angle, framing and focus. All four activities (including knowledge of programme formats) rely on an understanding of the visual design elements available to compose a shot within the standard television framing conventions. Effective picture making is the ability to manipulate the lens position and the lens angle within a particular programme context.

Primary decisions
The basics of visual communication are discussed in the section on composition (pages 208–53). This section of the manual deals with the seven primary decisions to be made when setting up a shot and their effect on the image viz:

- camera angle;
- lens angle;
- camera distance;
- camera height;
- frame;
- subject in focus;
- depth of field.

Positioning the lens
Whether in a complex studio production where each shot has a pre-planned position and shot size (e.g. drama) or at an outside broadcast location where the siting of fixed camera positions will be crucial in achieving comprehensive coverage (e.g. the camera coverage of an 18-hole golf course), positioning the camera lens in space is central to multi-camera production technique.

Physically changing the lens position and altering the lens angle controls

114

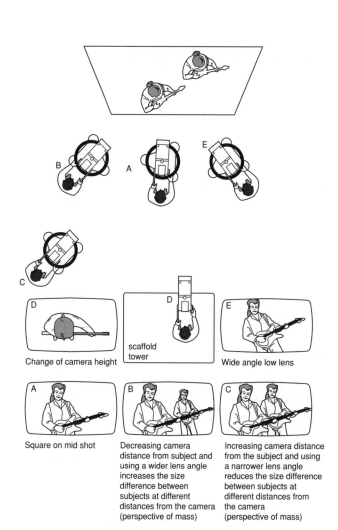

Change of camera height   scaffold tower

Wide angle low lens

Square on mid shot

Decreasing camera distance from subject and using a wider lens angle increases the size difference between subjects at different distances from the camera (perspective of mass)

Increasing camera distance from the subject and using a narrower lens angle reduces the size difference between subjects at different distances from the camera (perspective of mass)

In addition, there are many variations provided by the lighting treatment, framing, canting the camera and selective focusing

the appearance and the information contained in a shot. One essential skill required by a camera operator is the ability to visualize a shot from a lens angle in any position in space without the need to move the camera to that position in order to discover its visual potential.

If a shot on a camera is unsatisfactory, the camera operator should be able to assess how much movement and/or change of lens angle is required to improve its composition. This is doubly important when a camera has to be rigged and from a static position provide a variety of shots. Anticipating the visual potential between different camera positions is part of the craft of television camerawork.

Positioning the lens

Content
The subject of the shot is the predominantly influential element when arranging a given subject for maximum visual effect. The camera operator's role usually centres on deciding between a choice of techniques on how best to handle the given material. In everyday programme production, there may be opportunities for the camera operator to select material that provides good visual potential but frequently the subject is prescribed by script, brief or design and the camera operator has to devise the best shot that can be achieved with the available material.

Design
When the action is staged in a set that has been specially constructed for the programme, the director, designer and lighting director will have pre-planned the visual appearance of the basic shots. This is especially true of game and entertainment shows where the design element of the setting will often have an overriding influence on shot structure and camera position.

Camera angle
Camera angle describes the camera's position relative to the subject. A three-dimensional subject will display different facets of its design according to the viewpoint of its observer. Moving the camera's position left or right, up or down will substantially change the appearance of the image.

Lens angle
Varying the angle of view of the lens includes or excludes additional information. It can magnify subject size and emphasize the principal subject.

Camera distance
The distance of the lens from the principal subject controls the linear perspective of the shot and this can have a significant influence on composition through the variation in converging lines. Often the camera distance and the lens angle are adjusted simultaneously to produce changes to size relationships in shot.

Camera height
Changing the height of the camera alters the relationship between foreground and background. A low camera height emphasizes foreground and condenses or eliminates receding horizontal planes. A high camera position allows a 'plan view' and shows position relationships over a wide area. There is also a subjective aspect of lens height which influences how the image is perceived.

The purpose of the shot

The position of the lens and which lens angle is selected are dependent on the purpose of the shot which may be one or a number of the following:

- To emphasize the principal subject.
- To provide variation in shot size.
- To give added prominence to the selected subject.
- To provide more information about the subject.
- To provide for change of angle/size of shot to allow unobtrusive intercutting.
- To allow variety of shot and shot emphasis.
- To create good shot composition.
- To favour the appearance of the performer.
- To alter the internal space in the shot.
- To alter size relationships in shot.
- To improve the eyeline.
- To comply with the lighting rig or natural light.

Camera tilt

Camera tilt is often used in combination with lens height and shifts the horizon (real or unseen) in the frame and adds emphasis to ground or sky.

Structural skeleton of a shot

Form and content

One of the skills required in picture making is the ability to interest and hold the attention of the audience. Although the content of the shot such as a house, animal or personality may be the initial reason why a viewer's interest is captured by an image, the method of presentation is also a vital factor in sustaining that interest.

A television image is a two-dimensional picture but most shots will contain depth indicators that allow the audience to understand the two-dimensional representation of three dimensions depicted. Text on a blank background has no depth indicators but the text is still perceptually seen as 'in front' of the page.

There are therefore two aspects of the composition. The content – house, animal or face – and the front surface arrangements of lines, shapes, contrasts, etc., which form the recognizable images. The majority of the audience may only remember the content of the shot – the specific house, animal or face – but they will also be affected by the series of lines, shapes, brightness points and contrasts, colour, etc., which constructs the front surface plane of the image. This 'abstract' element of the shot may be crucial to the way the viewer responds to the image.

Each visual element in a shot can therefore serve two functions:

- As *content* – that part of the composition that provides depth indicators and information about the physical subject of the shot.
- As *form* – part of the design that lies on the surface plane of the screen and forms an overall abstract design which can produce a reaction in the viewer independent of any response to the content of the shot.

The reduction of this aspect of the shot, its form, to a simplified diagram of line and shape has been termed the structural skeleton of the image. It reveals the perceptual elements that potentially can hold the viewer's attention over and above the interest in the content of the shot.

The structural skeleton of the shot is only partially formed by content. For example, every camera operator knows that a shot of an object can be made more interesting if the camera is moved from a square-on, symmetrical viewpoint to an angle of view favouring more than one side or surface and/or if the height of the lens is varied. Repositioning the camera is altering the structural skeleton for, while the content of the shot remains and is recognizable as 'a car' or 'a building', converging lines of rooftop, windows, doors, etc., have been altered and restructured to provide a more pleasing 'front surface' design (see opposite).

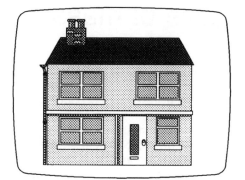

(a) A 'square on' shot

(b) An angled shot

Diagonal arrangements of lines in a composition produce a greater impression of vitality than either vertical or horizontal lines. The square-on shot of a house (top) is visually static because it maximizes the number of horizontal lines in the frame. Angling the camera position to show two sides of a building (bottom) converts the horizontal lines into diagonals. A line at an angle is perceptually seen as a line that is in motion. Compositions with a strong diagonal element imply movement or vitality.

Although the subject of the shot remains the same – a house — the structural skeleton of the shot has been rearranged to increase the viewer's perceptual attention independent of their interest in the specific content of the shot.

The degree to which these convergences can be controlled by lens height, lens position and lens angle requires an understanding of perspective.

Perspective of mass

Three dimensions

One of the perceptual methods we use to determine depth is to assess the rate by which objects appear to diminish/increase in size as they recede/approach us and the appearance of parallel lines that converge and vanish at the horizon.

Other depth indicators are atmospheric or aerial perspective. This is the optical effect of light being absorbed by mist, dust or moisture causing colours to become de-saturated and bluer, and a reduction of contrast between tones with increasing distance from the observer. Binocular vision allows depth to be assessed by contrasting the two viewpoints of our eyes. This form of depth calculation is obviously not available in a two-dimensional image but overlapping of objects is and gives clues to relative distance.

Two dimensions

When a camera converts a three-dimensional scene into a two-dimensional TV picture, it leaves an imprint of lens-height, camera tilt, distance from subject and lens angle.

We can detect these decisions in any image by examining the position of the horizon line (or determine where it would be) and where it cuts similar sized figures. This will reveal camera height and tilt. Lens-height and tilt will be revealed by any parallel converging lines in the image such as the edges of buildings or roads. The size relationship between foreground and background objects, particularly the human figure, will give clues to camera distance from objects and lens angle. Camera distance from subject will be revealed by the change in object size when moving towards or away from the lens.

For any specific lens angle and camera position there will be a unique set of the above parameters. Each one can be adjusted when setting up the shot.

Perspective of mass

The composition of a shot is affected by the distance of the camera from the subject and the lens angle that is used. This will make a difference to the size relationships within the frame.

The size relationship of objects in a field of view is known as the perspective of mass. Put simply, the closer an object is to us the larger it will appear and vice versa. The image of an object doubles in size whenever its distance is halved. This is a simple fact of geometric optics and it applies to a camera as it does to the eye. Adjusting the camera distance and the lens angle can provide the size relationships required for a composition.

Basic influences on a shot

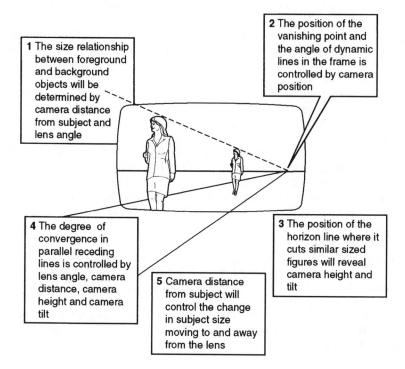

2 The position of the vanishing point and the angle of dynamic lines in the frame is controlled by camera position

1 The size relationship between foreground and background objects will be determined by camera distance from subject and lens angle

4 The degree of convergence in parallel receding lines is controlled by lens angle, camera distance, camera height and camera tilt

5 Camera distance from subject will control the change in subject size moving to and away from the lens

3 The position of the horizon line where it cuts similar sized figures will reveal camera height and tilt

Perspective of line

Horizon line and vanishing point

Our normal perceptual experience of someone of our own size moving on flat ground towards us is that the horizon line will always intersect them at eye level.

It was a fifteenth-century writer/architect, Leon Alberti, who realized that the controlling factor when creating a three-dimensional effect on a two-dimensional plane was the distance of the 'recording' eye from the scene and its height from the ground.

The crucial element in his construction was the horizon line. This illusionary line where the ground plane meets the sky is also the point where all orthogonals, that is, parallel lines running at right angles to the horizon line, meet. This point is called the vanishing point.

Of course Alberti's explanation of our normal perception of linear perspective does involve two visual illusions. The first illusion is that the sky meets the ground plane (land or sea) when it obviously does not. Secondly, that a visual sight line parallel to the ground plane would eventually meet this illusionary line at what is termed the vanishing point.

Camera height

Looking from behind the camera, we will see that the horizon line will intersect the camera at lens height. If the lens height is 1.5 metres, then all 1.5 metre objects in front of the lens will be cut at the same point by the horizon line in the frame.

If we tilt the camera down, the horizon line moves up the frame. If we tilt up, the line moves down. But if we crane the camera up, keeping it level, the horizon line follows and continues to bisect the frame.

If the camera is level, any object between the lens and the illusionary vanishing point on the horizon will be intersected by the horizon line at the same height as the lens.

Line convergence

Understanding how the perspective of line is created by viewpoint provides the means to control placement within the picture. Converging lines in a composition are often an important part of the visual design of an image. The camera operator, by careful selection of lens angle, camera height and camera tilt can position them in frame to emphasize the principal subject or use them as a strong compositional element (see opposite).

122

Horizon line

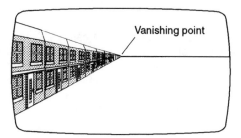

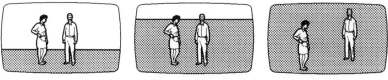

Low angle   Lens at eye height   High angle

On a flat surface, the horizon line cuts similar size figures at the same point. The height of that point is the height of the lens.

Emphasizing the principal subject using converging lines

123

Camera distance

When setting up a shot, the decision on camera distance to the principal subject and the choice of lens angle is the controlling factor in the way that depth is depicted in the image. Lens height and camera tilt will control line perspective. Shooting low with a level camera will produce one type of line perspective. Shooting from a high vantage point tilted down will produce another set of line relationships in the frame.

The important point to remember is that the relative subject size relationship is a product of camera distance. How the subject fills the frame is a product of lens angle.

Camera distance from subject

In practice, camera distance from subject is often decided first and then the final framing is adjusted on the zoom. This can result in an awkward composition which could be avoided if the effect of camera distance was taken into consideration.

The way distance and lens angle can influence composition can be illustrated by a shot seen daily on television – a presenter seated at a desk talking to camera. Frequently news or other factual information is being delivered to camera and therefore the shot composition usually attempts to avoid dramatic, eccentric framing.

If the camera is positioned too close to the desk, the lens will need to be zoomed out to its widest angle to accommodate desk and presenter. This combination of short camera distance from subject and wide angle will result in distortion of the desk and exaggerated hand movements, possible camera shadows on the foreground and, if a prompter is being used, a 'shifty' eye movement when reading the text. When the prompter reading distance is too close to presenters it is possible to see their eyes moving as they scan the lines of text. This not only destroys the concept of eye contact with the viewer but due to the constant eye movement it can also create an impression that the presenter is uncertain and uneasy. Also, the closer the lens is to the presenter the greater the effect of camera height. Small movements of the body towards and away from the lens will significantly alter the headroom. Small variations in height will require a greater tilt of the head by the presenter in order to look at the lens compared to the camera positioned further away on a longer lens (see opposite).

If the camera is positioned too far from the presenter, the resultant perspective of mass will flatten the depth of the set, make reading the prompter difficult and increase the risk of someone inadvertently walking between lens and presenter.

The correct distance for this type of subject is to position the camera for easy reading of the prompter with a lens height slightly above eye height.

Camera too high and too close to presenter

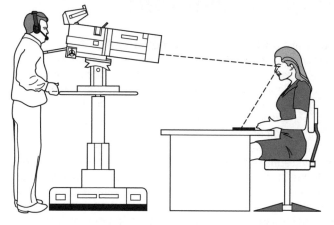

This camera position can cause shadows, produce 'shifty eyes' if the presenter is reading from a prompt or a large head movement from script on desk to lens.

Camera height and its affect on headroom

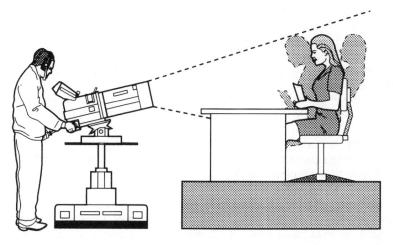

With a low camera height, if the presenter leans forward, their head will touch the top of the frame. If they lean back, the headroom will increase.

Camera movement

Single camera and multi-camera movement
Film is a record of an event edited and assembled after the event occurred. Live television is a presentation of an event as it occurs. Although camera movement in single and multi-camera shooting share many similarities, they are to some extent conditioned by the differences imposed by the practice of recording a single shot and the practicalities of recording or transmitting a number of shots continuously.

Live, or recorded-as-live, multi-camera coverage presents an event in real time and requires flexible camera mountings able to provide a variety of shots. In the studio, camera movement can be maximized on or off shot by tracking over a level floor. Film and single camera coverage can break the action into single shots and lay tracks and devise movement without the need to compromise or be inhibited by other camera movement.

Staging action for continuous coverage by multi-cameras frequently requires a great deal more visual compromise than action which is conceived for a single shot. There are limitations on set design and lighting for multi-camera shooting which may be easily overcome or simply not a consideration in single shot/single camera recording.

Continuous adjustment
In general, because of the constraints of time and/or budget, multi-camera operation often requires constant minor adjustments to the frame in order to accommodate actor position or staging that could have been re-plotted if time/budget (and the ever present need for multi-camera compromise) was available.

Multi-camera actuality coverage requires a great deal of reframing to keep the subject in shot. As subject movement is frequently unplanned, the composition of the shot will need continuous adjustment. This requires a pan and tilt head that can be instantly adjusted in discrete movements. Multi-camera coverage requires maximum flexibility with camera movement to follow often unrehearsed action.

Two types of movement
Camera movement can be conveniently grouped as functional movement and decorative movement. This over-simplified division will often overlap but functional movement is reframing to accommodate subject movement whereas decorative movement can be defined as a planned, deliberate change of camera position or zoom to provide visual variety, narrative emphasis or new information, motivated by action or dialogue.

Objects on edge of frame

Be positive about including or excluding items on the edge of frame such as a glass of water on the desk, etc. If possible get them removed because they are simply a distraction. Make certain the edge of the desk is parallel to the bottom of the frame or, if an angled shot is required, that the desk edge is a distinct angle to the bottom of the frame.

Frequently, the importance or emotional intensity of a line of dialogue will naturally draw the camera closer but the move has to be handled with sensitivity and feeling and timed to match the emotions expressed. Just as camera movement will be synchronized with the start/stop points of action, movement motivated by dialogue or emotional expression will be controlled by the timing and nuances of the performance.

Expert camerawork, whether single or multi-camera, provides invisible camera movement by matching movement to action.

Invisible movement

Camera movement and invisible technique

There is the paradox of creating camera movement to provide visual excitement or visual change while attempting to make the movement 'invisible' in the sense that the aim is to avoid the audience's attention switching from the programme content to the camerawork. This is achieved when camera movement matches the movement of the action and good composition is maintained throughout the move. The intention is to emphasize subject or picture content, rather than technique.

Intrusive and conspicuous camera movements are often used for specific dramatic or stylistic reasons (e.g. pop promotions) but the majority of programme formats work on the premise that the methods of programme production should remain hidden or invisible.

Motivation

A camera move is usually prompted either:

- to add visual interest;
- to express excitement, increase tension or curiosity;
- to provide a new main subject of interest;
- to provide a change of viewpoint.

A camera move is therefore a visual development that provides new information or creates atmosphere or mood. If the opening and closing frames of a move, such as a zoom in, are the only images that are considered important, then it is probably better to use a cut to change shot rather than a camera move.

Match the movement to the mood or action

Two basic conventions controlling camera movement are firstly, match the movement to the action so that the camera move is motivated by the action and is controlled in speed, timing and degree by action.

Secondly, there is a need to maintain good composition throughout the move. A camera move should provide new visual interest and there should be no 'dead' area between the first and end image of the movement.

Movement that is not motivated by action will be obtrusive and focus attention on the method of recording the image, making the camera technique visible. It is sometimes the objective of obtrusive camera movement to invigorate content that is considered stale and lacking interest. If there is a lack of confidence in the content of a shot, then possibly it is better to rethink the subject rather than attempting to disguise this weakness by moving attention on to the camera technique.

Frame adjustment during panning

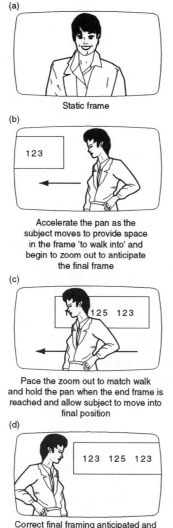

(a)

Static frame

(b)

123

Accelerate the pan as the
subject moves to provide space
in the frame 'to walk into' and
begin to zoom out to anticipate
the final frame

(c)

125   123

Pace the zoom out to match walk
and hold the pan when the end frame is
reached and allow subject to move into
final position

(d)

123   125   123

Correct final framing anticipated and
made invisible by the walk

Accelerate and decelerate in the correct ratio: the rate of movement may alter during a camera move. If the composition is such that the subject is close to the edge of the frame when they begin their move, it will be necessary to make a swift adjustment of the frame to give them 'walking' room before settling down to the movement framing. Likewise, at the end of the move, the final frame may have to be arrived at by a similar speedier reframing of the subject to achieve a balanced final frame. If possible, the action should be staged to avoid sudden changes of pace and to provide a fluid, smooth movement.

Camera movement – panning

The pan
The simplest camera movement is the pan. It is often used to give visual variety among a number of static shots but usually the main use of a pan, apart from keeping a moving subject in frame, is to show relationships.

There is obviously the need to begin a pan with a well-balanced shot that has intrinsic interest in its own right. The second requirement is to find visual elements that allow the pan to flow smoothly and inevitably to the end framing.

The end frame must be well balanced and again of intrinsic interest. The pan alerts the viewer that the camera is moving to reveal some image of importance or interest. If this anticipation is denied and the end framing is quickly cut away from because it contains no visual interest, then the movement is an anticlimax.

Speed of movement matched to mood and content
The speed of a panning shot must be matched to content. Panning fast over complex detail produces irritation – it is impossible to take in the information. Panning slowly over large, unbroken, plain areas may provoke boredom.

The speed of a pan across a symphony orchestra playing a slow majestic piece will be at a different speed to a pan across the orchestra when it is playing at full gallop. Speed of movement must match mood and content. If it is required to be discrete and invisible then movement must begin when the action begins and end when the action ends. A crane or tilt up with a person rising must not anticipate the move, neither must it be late in catching up with the move. Any movement that is bursting to get out of the frame must either be allowed camera movement to accommodate it or there is a need for a cut to a wider shot.

Using dominant lines and movement
It is almost always necessary to help with the visual change caused by a pan by finding some visual connection between the first and the last composition. One of the ways of achieving 'invisible' movement is to use dominant horizontal, vertical or angled lines to pan along in order to move to a new viewpoint. Panning on lines in the frame allows for visual continuity between two images and appears to provide a satisfactory visual link.

Using movement to motivate a pan
The same visual link can be achieved by using movement within the frame to allow a pan or a camera movement from one composition to another. The most common convention in establishing a shot is to follow a person across the set or location to allow new information about the geography of the set-

ting as the shot develops. The person the camera follows may be unimportant but is used to take the camera visually from a starting composition to possibly the main subject.

Lens angle and apparent speed of movement

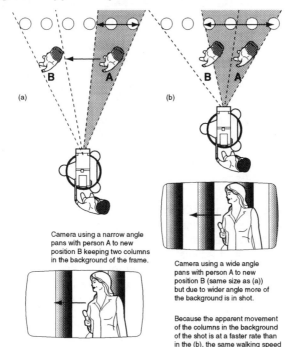

Camera using a narrow angle pans with person A to new position B keeping two columns in the background of the frame.

Camera using a wide angle pans with person A to new position B (same size as (a)) but due to wider angle more of the background is in shot.

Because the apparent movement of the columns in the background of the shot is at a faster rate than in the (b), the same walking speed will appear faster in (a)

The choice of lens angle will affect the apparent panning speed. Using a very narrow angle will show less background which will flash past in a close-up. The opposite effect will be seen with a wider lens closer to the movement. The background will appear to have less movement but unless the artistes walk in an arc, their size will alter during the shot.

Essential operational points when panning:

- Motivate the pan by action, to show relationships or to reveal new information.
- Ensure that the end frame has significance.
- Match speed of movement to mood and content.
- Synchronize all reframing with the action.
- Use dominant lines or movement to bridge first and end frames.
- Use the appropriate lens angle.
- Accelerate and decelerate the pan in the correct ratio.

Static and moving objects

Static camera, moving subject

Lens angle, camera distance and camera height dictate the characteristics of a moving subject composition. On a long lens with the subject at a distance from the camera, space is compressed and movement appears to be disproportionate to the change in image size. For example, a subject can walk ten paces towards the camera on a long lens in mid-shot and hardly register a change in size. This contradicts our normal perception of perspective change and sets up a surreal 'running on the spot' feel to the image.

A close position with a wide angle lens accentuates movement and any movement towards the camera makes the subject size change disproportionate to the actual movement taken. Action that crosses from corner to corner of the frame will be more dynamic than action which sweeps horizontally across the frame.

Moving camera, moving subject

One of the most common forms of moving camera/moving subject shot is to follow, in the same size shot, someone walking or driving. This provides a static principal subject against a continuously changing background. A popular version of this effect is the parallel tracking shot where two people in conversation walk with the camera crabbing with them, often slightly ahead so that both faces are seen. For this technique to be 'invisible' the frame must be steady, horizontal and the same size shot maintained over most of the move. The effect is as if the audience is a third person walking with them and listening in to their conversation.

Other variations of this visual convention are people in cars, trains and even the interiors of glass-walled lifts which are used to frame a static principal subject against a moving background.

Moving the camera while the subject moves towards or away from the lens can be more difficult to handle. Unless there are other visual elements moving in and out of the frame, the change in size of the subject can appear as if the camera is unable to keep up or is gaining on the subject. When the movement is across the frame, as in a crabbing shot, then change of size may not be so apparent and is visually acceptable.

Understanding the image

It is important to understand the content of a moving shot. If the camera movement, pan or zoom is too fast, then the information will be unreadable. If the shot development is too fast for content then there will be a mismatch of a mood.

Containing movement

Movement within the static frame

In setting up a shot where, for example, a background figure walks to join a foreground figure, try to find a camera position that avoids constant reframing. Try to contain the action by appropriate lens position and lens angle without the need to reframe for small movements.

One of the weaknesses of television camerawork is that there is a tendency to cover action by small zoom movements or camera movement. Single-camera film or video usually settles on either staging the action so that it can be contained in a static frame or having tracks laid down and devising a positive camera movement to contain the action. In television productions, continual small minor adjustments of framing detract from content and become an irritant, although with unrehearsed action there is no way of avoiding constant frame adjustment.

Often a common dilemma is when to pan with a subject who is swaying in and out of reasonable framing. The shot may be too tight for someone who can only talk when they move or they may make big hand movements to emphasize a point. The solution is to loosen the shot. It is seldom a good idea to constantly pan to keep someone in frame as inevitably you will be wrong-footed and compensate for an anticipated movement that does not happen. If the shot cannot be contained without continuously reframing, then the incessant moving background eventually becomes a distraction from the main subject of the shot.

Frame adjustment while tracking

One of the compositional conventions of camerawork with profile shots, where people are looking out of frame, is to give additional space in the direction of their gaze for 'looking room'. Similarly when someone is walking across frame, give more space in front of them than behind.

This space in the frame to 'walk into' needs to be maintained throughout a development. This can be difficult if the subject, for example, is standing to the left of frame and moves to camera left (i.e. towards the left-hand side of the frame). This requires an accelerated rapid pan left in order to provide space on the left (the direction of movement) before settling down to match the speed of the pan with the walk. The appropriate framing for the end composition must be achieved before the subject stops to avoid the camera reframing after the action has ended. If the subject is walking to take up a similar position left of frame with another 'results board', then the camera must stop the pan when the board is correctly framed making certain there is sufficient space on left of frame for the subject to walk into. In general, anticipate any change in frame size whilst on the move and do not leave the reframing until the subject has settled. Come to rest with the subject.

(a)

(b)

Person in doorway walks downstage to end at position B beside foreground figure. The camera pans left to accomodate the two shot

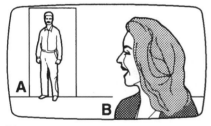

(c)

(d)

The pan left to accommodate the two shot can be eliminated if the camera crabs left and positions the door to the left of the foreground, Figure (c). This allows the background figure a walk to foreground without any need for camera movement to compensate.
NB. On rehearsal, memorize key points about the final framing if any significant elements are required to be in the frame (e.g. a background door for an entrance). It is better to jot down on the camera card some detail of the end frame after a move rather than to rely completely on visual memory.

135

The development shot

Panning, tracking or crabbing the camera to emphasize another visual element in the frame is a standard convention that has been used for many years. A development shot, as the name implies, is a shot which smoothly and unobtrusively moves towards a new viewpoint and is an alternative to a cut. It can start with a composition that emphasizes one set of visual elements and then moves, motivated by action or driven by the audience's curiosity, to an image that emphasizes another set of visual elements. In dramatic terms, it has no real equivalent in theatre or literature and when staging, pace and execution are fully integrated it can provide the most visually exciting images.

To achieve its greatest impact, a development often requires either foreground elements to wipe across the frame to emphasize movement or a significant change in the background of the shot. It requires a progressive change of viewpoint from its starting position and it needs a main subject of interest that can be followed through various dynamic compositions. The movement must be fluid and changing through a series of compelling images. A crab around a performer, for example, will have little visual impact if it is staged against a plain cyclorama. There will be no background markers to indicate movement other than moving from a frontal viewpoint to profile.

Combining tracking and zooming

Many development shots require either a wide opening to the move or they end wide. As we have discussed, camera movement is accentuated when using the wide angle end of the zoom (plus appropriate set design) but if part of the development involves a medium close-up or close-up of a face, then at some stage, on a wide angle ($< 40°$) there will be unacceptable distortion and probably camera shadow.

This can be avoided by starting the move on the wide angle and then, at some point in the development, continuing the move on the zoom. The transition between track and zoom needs careful selection but usually the movement can be carried over by continuing with a slight crab while ending in a tight shot on the zoom. This obviously involves 'blind zooming' with no opportunity to pre-check focus. Critical focus will occur in close-up just at the point when subtle control of framing is required. On a crane or a dolly, the camera lens can be tracked to a pre-determined position while the cameraman controls framing, pivot and focus. The same type of development shot on a pedestal may require the assistance of a tracker to 'sweeten' the move. The reverse development shot of zoom first, track later, requires even more precise focus and attentive camera control.

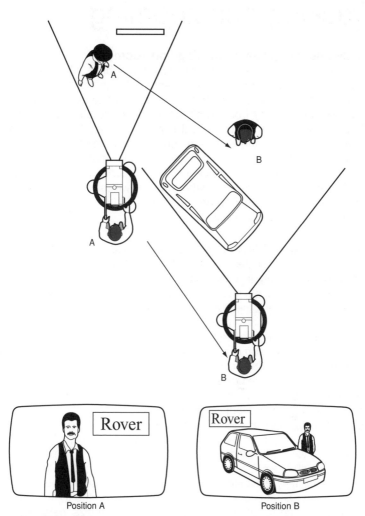

Position A   Position B

A simple development
Camera at position A crabs/tracks and zooms out as presenter walks behind car to end on a wideshot at B of car and presenter. The movement is emphasized by the car roof crossing the frame and the presenter crossing the 'Rover' logo.

Visual anticipation
A development shot moves from one set of visual elements on to another viewpoint. This visual transition requires reframing, using pivot points, tracking, crabbing and zooming and therefore it is essential that the camera operator anticipates what the final frame will be in order to smoothly progress the move to achieve that objective. Visual anticipation is organizing all the necessary adjustments before the end frame is reached. 'Tidying up' the composition cannot be left until the move has ended.

137

Tracking and zooming

The distinction between tracking and zooming

Moving the camera towards or away from the subject alters the size relationships between foreground and background objects. The perspective of mass changes in a similar way to our own perceptual experience when we move towards or away from an object. Tracking the camera therefore not only conforms to our normal visual expectations but sets up interesting rearrangements of all the visual elements in the camera's field of view.

Changing the camera distance alters all the image size relationships apart from very distant objects near or on the horizon. The size of a range of hills remains unaffected no matter how far we travel towards them until we reach a critical distance where we have a part of the hills as foreground with which to compare a background.

The compositional distinction between zoom and track

Tracking into a scene extends the involvement of the viewer in that they are being allowed visually to move into the two-dimensional screen space. In normal perception, depth indicators can be appraised or checked by moving the head or the body to seek a new viewpoint of the field of view. Viewing a series of static images on a two-dimensional screen does not allow this visual 'interrogation'. If depth is to be indicated it must be self-evident and contained in the composition of the image. A tracking shot provides a change in viewpoint and allows the viewer greater opportunity to experience the depth of the space pictured compared to either a zoom or a static shot.

A zoom in or out contains no change in size relationships, it simply allows either a greater magnification of a portion of the shot or wider view of the same size relationships. The arguments for zooming (apart from convenience and budget) is that as a television production is a highly artificial process, the viewer is already experiencing a radically different visual sensation watching a two-dimensional image of an object (which is either magnified or extremely diminished) compared to their visual experience when observing the actual event. If so much is changed in the translation by the film and television medium using techniques of shot size, perspective, two dimensions, small image, etc., why quibble about zooming which fails to reproduce some small physical aspect of human perception?

A television production is an approximation of an event which often includes attempts to induce an experience of the event in the viewer. Zooming creates a visual experience and therefore, it is argued, is as valid a technique as any other artifice employed.

Accentuating the effect of camera movement

The greatest impression of movement can be observed by using a wide angle lens and tracking between similar size objects such as a row of trees

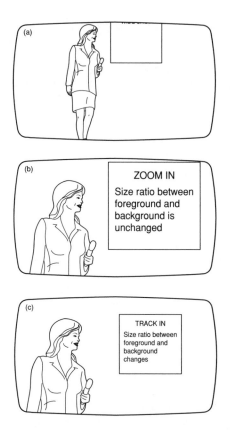

(a)

(b) ZOOM IN

Size ratio between foreground and background is unchanged

(c) TRACK IN

Size ratio between foreground and background changes

each side of a road. The apparent size of each tree to its neighbour changes dramatically as it approaches the lens. There is a constant visual flow of size ratio expansion as we track down the road.

Zooming along the road between rows of trees does not have anything like the same visual dynamics. The camera does not move and therefore there is no change in size relationships. The zoom simply magnifies the central portion of the field of view preserving the existing size relationships. They remain unaltered as in a still photograph when a portion of it is enlarged. The perspective of mass is decided by the camera distance and zooming simply expands or contracts a portion of the field of view.

The feeling of flatness or deadness produced by zooming arises because there is no anticipated change to the perspective of mass which in normal perception accompanies changes in magnification or diminution of subject. This compositional inertia can be disguised by building in a camera move such as a pan with action or even a crabbing movement to accompany a zoom. The camera movement provides some relational changes to the visual elements that the zoom is magnifying.

139

Wide angle/narrow angle

The wide angle/narrow angle effect

Size relationships or the perspective of mass can be confused with the wide angle effect and the narrow angle effect. To increase the size of a background figure to a foreground figure it is common practice to reposition the camera back and zoom in to return to the original framing. The size relationships have now altered. It is not the narrower angle that produced this effect but the increased distance from the camera.

By tracking away from the two figures we have altered the ratio between lens and first figure and lens and second figure. It is a much smaller ratio and therefore the difference in size between the two of them is now not so great. When we zoom in and revert to the original full frame for foreground figure we keep the new size relationships that have been formed by camera distance. The two figures appear to be closer in size.

As part of our perception of depth depends on judging size relationships – the further away the smaller they are – our perception of this new size relationship produced by tracking out and zooming in leads us to believe that the distance between equal height figures is not so great as the first framing.

Possibly, the narrow angle and the wide angle effect should be renamed the distant viewing effect. The important point to remember is that subject size relationship is a product of camera distance. How the subject fills the frame is a product of lens angle. This, of course, is the crucial distinction between tracking and zooming. Tracking the camera towards or away from the subject alters size relationships – the perspective of mass. Zooming the lens preserves the existing relative size relationships and magnifies or diminishes a portion of the shot.

Movement within the shot and lens angle

A two-dimensional television image of three-dimensional space can involve a compromise between action and the requirements of the camera. A common adjustment is the speed of the actor movement to the size of the shot or the lens angle in use.

A small movement in a close-up can be the equivalent of a big movement in long shot. A full figure, three-pace walk towards a wide angle lens will create a much bigger change in size than the equivalent full figure walk towards a 25° lens. The 'internal space' of the lens in use becomes a critical consideration when staging action for the camera (see opposite).

One of the most common adjustments is the speed of a rise from a chair which may need to be covered in close-up. A normal rise will often appear frantic contained in a tight shot (head and shoulders) and is often slowed down. This also helps with the problem of achieving good framing when covering a fast-moving subject on a narrow angle lens.

Crabbing arcs

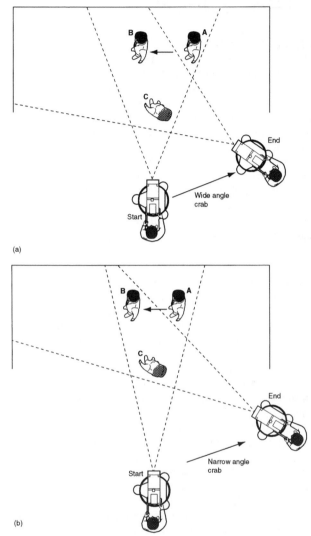

(a)

(b)

A common development shot is keeping a foreground artiste or object in shot (person C) while crabbing to follow the background movement of another actor (from A to B).

This is fairly straightforward using a wide angle lens if the camera position is tight to the foreground subject as this allows the arc of the crab to be relatively short (a). A metre or so of camera movement will accommodate a 3 m change of position of a background artiste. If a longer lens is used (b), for the same size foreground image, the camera is much further back and the arc of the crabbing line now becomes considerably extended in order to keep the same background actor movement in shot. Using a narrower lens also alters the apparent movement of the camera as less background scenery is covered by the sweep of the lens.

THE LIBRARY
GUILDFORD COLLEGE
of Further and Higher Education

Internal space

The internal space of a shot

The internal space of the shot is a subtle but important part of the look, mood and atmosphere of the shot. As we have seen, when three-dimensional objects are converted into a flat two-dimensional image, size relationships are controlled by camera distance to subject and lens angle. A small room can appear large using a wide angle lens and a large room can appear cramped and condensed using a narrow angle lens.

A medium shot of an actor can be achieved using a lens angle that varies between more than 75° down to less than 5°. The wider angles produce possible distortion of features or exaggerated body movement but the crucial distinction between using these ranges of lens angles is that to keep the same size medium shot the camera moves further and further back from the main subject as the lens angle is decreased. This alters the size relationship between foreground and background – the internal space of the shot is altered.

Production style and lens angle

So what lens angle should be selected? Assuming that lighting, sound, set design or location constraints can accommodate the resultant framing, the lens angle depends on the mood or feel of the shot and the action that it is to contain. For visual continuity during a scene or even for the whole production, it would seem to be necessary to keep within a limited range of lens angles. One style of production may consistently use a wide-angle lens, producing a series of shots which emphasizes movement towards or away from the lens and therefore creates an apparent increase in the internal space of the shots. This is often accompanied by a low lens height emphasizing ceilings and dynamic converging lines of walls, buildings, etc.

Another 'internal space' style is to use narrow angle lenses producing compressed space, extended movement towards and away from camera and a general mood of claustrophobia. Frequently this style is accompanied by a lack of 'geography' shots – shots which provide information about setting or locale. Shot in tight close-up, the action is followed without revealing the location resulting in a series of images with swirling backgrounds which generates pace without information. The viewer is sucked into the mystery and teased with a lack of precise visual clues to the surroundings.

The choice of the lens angle is therefore dependent on how the action is to be staged and the visual style that is required.

The narrower the lens angle, the more difficult it becomes to achieve smooth and fluid camera development and movement. The camera has to travel further to achieve size change or movement on a narrow angle lens

Changing the 'space' of a shot with lens angle and camera distance

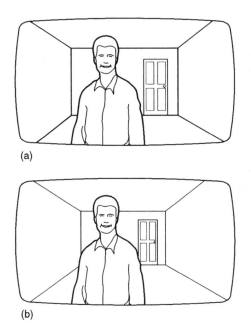

(a)

(b)

The same size of foreground subject achieved with a narrow angle lens (a) and a wide angle lens (b) and repositioning the camera.

than on a wide angle lens, is more prone to movement vibration or unsteadiness on very narrow lens angles and requires larger and more precise focus pulls.

143

Space and atmosphere

Visual qualities

Camera movement must have visual elements that change their relationship depending on camera position. A crab around a subject set against a featureless background will provide slight indication of change of viewpoint. The same movement with the subject set against a varied and broken background now has markers to indicate the change of viewpoint. If foreground features sweep across the frame there are even more indicators that the viewpoint is changing and the movement (if that is what is required) becomes more dominant and visual.

Camera movement using a narrow lens angle has a distinct visual quality but requires greater operational precision than with a wide angle lens movement which is easier to achieve and where there is greater apparent movement in the frame for the distance covered.

The internal space of a shot often underlines the emotional quality of the scene. 'Normal' perspective for establishing shots is often used where the intention is to describe the locale plainly and straightforwardly. A condensed or an expanded space on the other hand may help to suggest the mood or atmosphere of the action.

The choice of lens angle and resulting composition should not be accidental unless, as is too often the case, camera position and angle is a *fait accompli* created by a multi-camera compromise.

Control of background

A small area of background can be controlled by lighting or by limiting the depth of field by neutral density filter or shutter but the greatest control is by choice of camera position, lens angle, camera distance and foreground subject position. Consideration must also be given to how the shot will be intercut and often a matching background of similar tonal range, colour and contrast has to be chosen to avoid a mismatch when intercutting.

Too large a tonal difference between intercut backgrounds results in obtrusive and very visible cuts. Visual continuity of elements such as direction of light, similar zones of focus and the continuity of background movement (e.g. crowds, traffic, etc.) in intercut shots have also to be checked.

Lens angle

The choice of lens angle and camera distance from the subject is the controlling factor in the way that depth is depicted in the image but the 'internal' space of a shot often plays a crucial part in setting up the atmosphere of a shot.

A long lens positioned at a distance from a cramped interior will heighten the claustrophobia of the setting. Subject size ratios will be evened out from foreground to background and movement to and away from camera

Changing a pivot during a movement

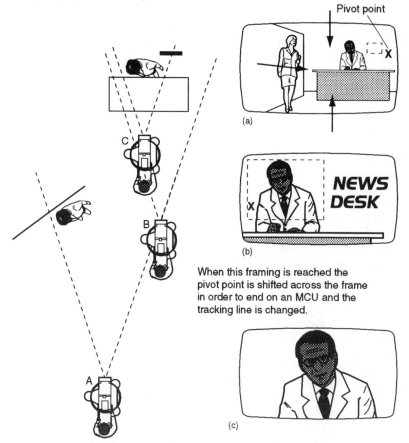

Pivot point

(a)

NEWS DESK

(b)

When this framing is reached the pivot point is shifted across the frame in order to end on an MCU and the tracking line is changed.

(c)

Sometimes it is not possible to maintain the same pivot point during the whole of a camera move. (a) is the opening frame and (c) illustrates the end frame of a camera move. At the start of the move up to camera position B, the pivot point is to the right of the presenter at the desk. This side of the frame is held static in relation to seated presenter in order to keep the programme logo 'NEWS DESK' in shot. As the development requires the end frame to be an MCU, when frame (b) is reached, the point is transferred across to the left of the presenter and the right hand side of the frame now closes in losing the logo. If the programme logo had been positioned to the left of the seated presenter this pivot point switch would not have been necessary.

will show no significant change in size and therefore give a subjective impression that no distance has been traversed.

A wide angle lens close to the subject will increase space, emphasize movement and, depending on shot content, emphasize convergence of line and accentuate the relative size of same size figures at different distances from the lens.

145

Tracking lines

Maintaining good composition when moving

When tracking, it is often necessary to adjust the height of the camera particularly when moving into the human figure. In shots closer than full figure, lens height is often eye height but when the camera is further away, depending on the shot, the lens height is usually lower to reduce the amount of floor/ground in shot. A low lens height places emphasis on the subject by avoiding distracting foreground level surfaces such as roads, grass or floor. Like all 'rules of thumb', this convention is probably ignored more than it is employed but changes in lens height often accompany tracking movements in order to bring emphasis onto the main subject.

Another reason for altering the lens height when tracking into the subject is to enhance the appearance of actors by shooting slightly down on faces, rather than shooting up and emphasizing jaw lines and double chins, etc.

Finding the right tracking line

We saw in the description of zooming that keeping two sides or even one side at a constant distance from the principle subject throughout a zoom or track creates a more pleasing visual result than simply allowing all four sides of the frame to implode in on the subject.

In zooming, the control of the pivot point is achieved by panning and/or tilting to adjust the frame during the zoom. Control of the framing during tracking (to keep a constant distance between one side of the frame and the subject) can also be achieved by panning/tilting but it is more effective if it can be controlled by the line of the track.

The figure opposite illustrates a tracking line to produce an end frame of presenter plus scoreboard. The tracking line chosen requires no constant reframing during the move and no change in the direction of the pedestal wheels to maintain the pre-selected pivot point. It is the tracking line angle that maintains the pivot point. Operationally it is simpler, smoother and visually unobtrusive – the motivation for selecting a pivot point.

Finding the right camera height when tracking

The same technique can be used to maintain a pivot point at the top of the frame when tracking in or out, for example, on a singer. When tracking in, the camera is craned up at a rate which holds the pivot point at the top of the frame without the need to reframe the camera. The lens height automatically arrives at the more flattering position, slightly above eye height, for the closer shot while avoiding crossing the key light and shadowing the artist! Tracking out, the camera is craned down at a rate which maintains the top-of-the-frame pivot point arriving at a lower angle wide shot which compresses the amount of floor area in shot.

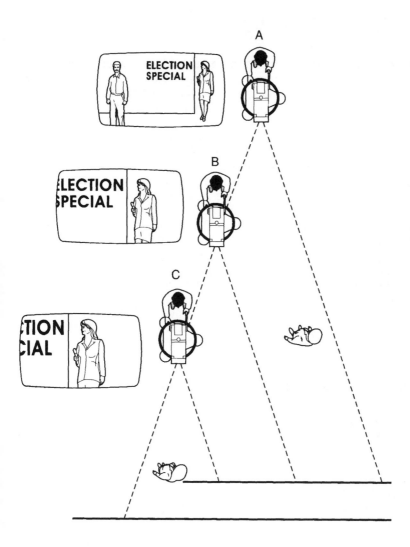

Finding a tracking line

Moving from the wide shot at A the camera tracks in on a straight line to close the shot at C. This movement produces a more pleasing effect with a consistent pivot point position than a track-in which involves steering the pedestal into the final framing.

The same technique can be used on a track-in and crane-up. A line can be found where it is not necessary to reframe to change the headroom by maintaining a constant increase in height during the track.

Camera height

Horizon line and camera height as a compositional device

American silent film production at the turn of the twentieth century used a convention of a 50 mm lens at eye level and actor movement was restricted to being no closer to the lens than 12 feet. With an actor standing 12 feet from the lens, the bottom of the frame cuts him/her at knee height. By 1910, the Vitagraph company allowed the actors to play up to 9 feet from the lens and the camera was lowered to chest height.

From these static camera positions developed a Hollywood convention of frequently placing the camera at eye level which in turn allowed the horizon line to cut the foreground actors at eye level. Whether the artistes are standing or sitting, the camera is often positioned at eye height which places the horizon behind the eyes. This emphasizes the main subject of the frame, the face, and the main area of interest of the face, the eyes.

A more prosaic factor controlling lens height is the need to avoid shooting off the top of studio sets. Keeping the camera at eye level speeds up production as actor movement to camera can be accommodated without panning up and shooting off the top of the set or the need to relight.

A lens height of slightly above presenter eye height (whether standing or sitting) is usually kinder to the face, provides a more alert and positive body posture and often improves the lighting on an artiste with deep set eyes, etc.

The subjective influence of camera height

Lens height will also control the way the audience identifies with the subject. Moving the horizon down below a person makes them more dominant because the viewer is forced to adopt a lower eyeline viewpoint. We are in the size relationship of children looking up to adults. A low lens height may also de-emphasize floor or ground level detail because we are looking along at ground level and reducing or eliminating indications of ground space between objects. This concentrates the viewer's interest on the vertical subjects. A high position lens height has the reverse effect. The many planes of the scene are emphasized like a scale model.

Usually it is better to divide the frame into unequal parts by positioning the horizon line above or below the mid-point of the frame. Many cameramen intuitively use the 'rule of thirds' (see Ratio and proportion, page 232) to position the horizon. A composition can evoke space by panning up and placing the line low in frame. Placing a high horizon in the frame can balance a darker foreground land mass or subject with the more attention-grabbing detail of a high key sky. It also helps with contrast range and exposure.

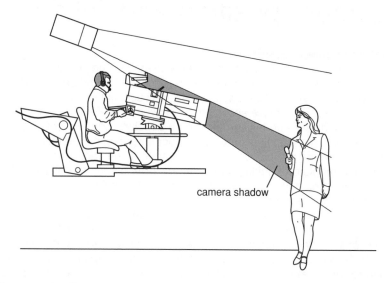

camera shadow

Camera shadows

Camera shadows are always a risk once the camera begins to work close and high to the subject. Adjustment of the camera height, camera position and/or light source may resolve the problem. Frequently, pulling back on a tighter shot also helps. With the situation pictured above, if the shot is tightening above the shadow line, the camera can track in along the key throwing the shadow outside the frame. Alternatively, the arm swinger will position the camera either side of the key to avoid the camera shadow falling on the artiste.

Camera position and lighting

Planned camera positions

Most multi-camera productions require pre-planning. The planning includes decisions on design and set, presenter positions, a lighting rig and camera positions. There may not be a camera plan as such, but frequently the lighting director will have made assumptions on where the cameras will be and what shots they will be taking based on a director's brief. He/she requires this essential information in order to produce a lighting plot. Lamps have to be rigged in specific places before rehearsal commences. There is the additional problem of lighting each set for several camera positions. The lighting effect on any subject is determined by the angle between the camera and the light source.

A camera operator has to be aware of the lighting rig and the placing of key, fill and back light when positioning the camera. Lamps can be re-rigged to accommodate a 'new' camera position during rehearsal but there is a limit to the amount of relighting that can be carried out before the time taken up to re-light uses up all the available camera rehearsal to the detriment of the whole production.

Camera position and key light

Key lights are positioned to produce the desired modelling on the presenter and are typically set to between 10–40° either side of the eyeline position to the planned lens position. If the camera is crabbed beyond this point and the presenter turns to face the lens then the modelling on the face becomes either non-existent (camera under key light) or 'over modelled' which results in an ugly nose shadow that spreads across the face.

If the camera continues to crab away from the key light then possibly the back light will start to illuminate the face with a key light acting as back light and there is no fill (see figure opposite).

Camera height: Camera height has an influence on the lighting treatment. A high camera position with the presenter looking to lens may tilt their head so far back that the backlight may hit the front of the forehead. A low camera angle always risks shooting into lights.

Flares: Although not always seen in a monochrome viewfinder, coloured flares can have a disturbing and unwanted effect on the composition. Sometimes they can be lost by a slight change in height or position. If this is not possible due to shot content, then either an additional 'impromptu' ray shade is added (a piece of black gaffer tape fastened across the top of the lens hood) or it may be possible to raise the offending lamp to lose the flare, or use a flag on the light source. Another quick and easy way to overcome 'flare' problems is to have a small flag attached to the camera via a flexible arm.

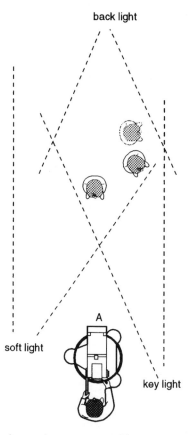

back light

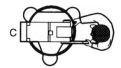

soft light

A

key light

Unplanned camera positions

The presenter has been lit for a camera position at A. If the camera repositions to B, it may be possible to add a soft light between positions B and C. If the camera repositions to C the key and back light are now lighting both sides of the presenter's face and there needs to be a major re-light to accommodate this position.

Shadows on backgrounds: These can occur accidentally when a camera is repositioning or if a camera is forced to take up an unrehearsed position due to artiste being off their marks or when following impromptu action. Shooting off the lit area can also result from following a spontaneous event. There is a trade off between achieving good camerawork, good lighting and good sound matched against a production style that attempts to capture the vitality and energy generated by some forms of ad-lib programme content.

Change of shot

Invisible cuts

Continuous camera coverage of an event using a number of cameras relies on a stream of invisible shot changes in the sense that the transition between each shot does not distract the audience. The aim is to make the shot change unobtrusive to prevent the audience's attention switching from programme content to the programme production technique. Although individual camera operators frame up their own shots, the pictures they produce must fit the context of the programme and match what other camera operators are providing. No shot can be composed in isolation – its effect on the viewer will be related to the preceding and succeeding shot. The camera operator is directly involved in edit point decisions (see the use of the mixed viewfinder in Viewfinder, page 164).

Why use more than one camera?

If intercutting between cameras is potentially distracting to the viewer, why change the shot? Many football matches, for example, are covered by a single camera for news and sports reports but there are inherent problems with this technique. Close shots capture the excitement and personalities in the match whereas wide shots reveal tactics and the flow of the game. A single camera has to resort to zooming in and out continuously in order to provide both types of shots. If the game is shot continuously wide, then it lacks excitement. If it is shot too close, then there is the risk of missing vital action (like goals!). It is around the goal area that the single camera operator has to chance his/her arm. Zoom in for the expected goalkeeper save and the camera operator may miss the ball rebounding out to another player who scores from outside the frame.

Choice of shot

Multi-camera coverage of sport allows a director the option of choosing the size of shot and camera angle to match the action. With a five or six camera coverage of football, for example, as the action moves towards the goal area, each of the six cameras will have a designated role providing a range of close and wide shots which can be instantly cut to depending on the outcome of the attack. Many of the cameras will be isoed (their individual output continuously recorded) to provide instant replay in slow motion.

Editing decisions

Particularly in as-directed situations such as sport, discussion and many forms of music, etc., the camera operator must anticipate the shot structure and provide the right composition and choice of shot to satisfy standard

Multi-camera sports coverage
This type of sports coverage is fluent and flexible and should miss no important incident. In comparison, single camera coverage of similar events is at a considerable disadvantage.

editing requirements. Intercutting between cameras in multi-camera coverage occurs in real time without the benefit of the more extended decision-making time about edit points enjoyed in post-production. The timescale of the event covered dictates intercutting decisions and the shot rate (e.g. a 100 m race is covered in under 10 seconds, a 5000 m race in approximately 13 minutes).

Invisible cuts

What makes a shot change invisible?

Multi-camera coverage of an event involves intercutting between a variety of camera angles in order that different aspects of the event can be transmitted. If intercutting is badly done, then changes of shot are conspicuous and switch attention to the technique.

For a shot change to be unobtrusive:

- there must be an appropriate production reason to change the shot;
- the shots either side of the visual transition (cut, wipe, mix) must satisfy the editing requirements that link them.

Production reasons for a shot change

There are many production reasons for changing the shot. These include:

- following the action (e.g. coverage of horse racing: as the horses go out of range of one camera, they can be picked up by another);
- presenting new information (e.g. a wide shot of an event shows the general disposition, a close-up shows detail);
- emphasizing an element of the event (e.g. a close-up shot revealing tension in the face of a sports participant);
- telling a story (e.g. succeeding shots in a drama);
- providing pace, excitement and variety in order to engage and hold the attention of the audience (e.g. changing the camera angle and size of shot on a singer);
- structuring an event visually in order to explain (e.g. a variety of shots on a cooking demonstration that shows close-ups of ingredients and information shots of the cooking method).

In an as-directed camera coverage where the camera operator is finding and offering shots for the director to select, the nature of the shots must coincide with the specific programme format and include a reason to change the shot. For example, it is unlikely that a big close-up of the presenter's face that fills the screen would be required during a cookery demonstration whereas it might be entirely appropriate before match point in a Wimbledon final (see Assessing a shot, page 186).

What are the edit requirements for a good cut?

A good cut usually satisfies the audience's expectations. If someone speaks out of frame at some time, the audience will want to see them. For dramatic reasons, curiosity about the unseen voice can be intensified by delaying the cut, but this is not usually a requirement in a standard TV interview.

Editing conventions sometimes rely on everyone involved in the produc-

In general a change of shot will be unobtrusive

- if there is a significant change in shot size or camera angle (camera position relative to subject) when intercutting on the same subject;
- if there is a significant change in content (e.g. a cut from a tractor to someone opening a farm gate);
- when cutting on action – the flow of movement in the frame is carried over into the succeeding shot (e.g. a man in medium shot sitting behind a desk stands up and on his rise, a longer shot of the man and the desk is cut to);
- when intercutting between people if their individual shots are matched in size, have the same amount of headroom, have the same amount of looking space if in semi-profile, if the lens angle is similar (i.e. internal perspective is similar) and if the lens height is the same (see Cross shooting, page 158);
- if the intercut pictures are colour matched (e.g. skin tones, background brightness, etc.) and if in succeeding shots the same subject has a consistent colour (e.g. grass in a stadium);
- if there is continuity in action (e.g. body posture, attitude);
- if there is continuity in lighting, in sound, props and setting and continuity in performance or presentation.

tion having a knowledge of well-known shot patterns such as singles, two shots, over the shoulder two shots, etc. in the standard camera coverage of an interview. This speeds up programme production when matching shots of people in discussion either in factual or fictional dialogue and allows fast and flexible team working because everyone is aware of the conventions.

Intercutting

Matched shots on an interview

Multi-camera coverage of an interview is about the most widespread format on television after the straight-to-camera shot of a presenter. The staging of an interview usually involves placing the chairs for good camera angles, lighting, sound and for the ease and comfort of the guests and the presenter. The space between people should be a comfortable talking distance.

Eyeline

Eyeline is an imaginary line between an observer and the subject of their observation. In a discussion, the participants are usually reacting to each other and will switch their eyeline to whoever is speaking. The viewers, in a sense, are silent participants and they will have a greater involvement in the discussion if they feel that the speakers are including them in the conversation. This is achieved if both eyes of the speaker can be seen by the viewer rather than profile or semi-profile shots. The cameras should be able to take up positions in and around the set to achieve good eyeline shots of all the participants: both eyes of each speaker, when talking, can be seen on camera.

In addition, the relationship of the participants should enable a variety of shots to be obtained in order to provide visual variety during a long interview (e.g. over the shoulder two shots, alternative singles and two shots and group shots, etc.). The staging should also provide for a good establishment shot or relational shot of the participants and for opening or closing shots.

Standard shot sizes

Because so much of television programming involves people talking, a number of standard shot sizes have evolved centred on the human body. In general, these shot sizes avoid cutting people at natural joints of the body such as neck, elbows, knees. Normal interview shots include:

- CU (close-up) bottom of frame cuts where the knot of a tie would be;
- MCU (medium close-up) bottom of the frame cuts where the top of a breast pocket of a jacket would be;
- MS (medium shot or mid shot) bottom of frame cuts at the waist.

Other standard shot descriptions are:-

- BCU (big close-up). The whole face fills the screen. Top of frame cuts the forehead. Bottom of the frame cuts the edge of chin avoiding any part of the mouth going out of frame (rarely used in interviews).

- LS (long shot). The long shot includes the whole figure.
- WS (wide shot). A wide shot includes the figure in a landscape or setting.
- O/S 2s (over the shoulder two shot). Looking over the shoulder of a foreground figure framing part of the head and shoulders to another participant.
- two shot, three shots, etc., identifies the number of people in frame composed in different configurations.

Note: precise framing conventions for these standard shot descriptions vary with directors and camera operators. One man's MCU is another man's MS and can give rise to shot descriptions such as a 'loose MS' or a 'tight MS' etc. Check that your understanding of the position of the bottom frame line on any of these shots shares the same size convention for each description as the director with whom you are working.

Standard shot sizes

BCU (close-up)
Whole face fills screen. Top of frame cuts
forehead. Bottom of frame cuts chin

CU (close-up)
Bottom of frame cuts where
knot of tie would be

MCU (medium close-up)
Bottom of frame cuts where
top of breast pocket of a jacket would be

MS (medium shot)
Bottom of frame cuts at
the waist

LS (long shot)
Long shot includes whole
figure

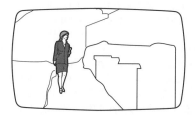

WS (wide shot)
Wide shot includes figure in
a landscape or setting

157

Cross-shooting

A standard cross-shooting arrangement is for the participants to be seated facing each other and for cameras to take up positions close to the shoulders of the participants (see opposite).

The usual method of finding the optimum camera position is to position the camera to provide a well-composed over the shoulder two shot then zoom in to check that a clean single can be obtained of the participant facing camera. A tight over the shoulder two shot always risks masking or a poorly composed shot if the foreground figure should lean left or right. To instantly compensate, if this should occur, set the pedestal steering wheel in a position to allow crabbing left or right for rapid repositioning on or off shot.

Crossing the line

There may be a number of variations in shots available depending on the number of participants and the method of staging the discussion/interview. All of these shot variations need to be one side of an imaginary line drawn between the participants.

To intercut between individual shots of two people to create the appearance of a normal conversation between them, three simple rules have to be observed. Firstly, if a speaker in a single is looking from left to right in the frame, then the single of the listener must look right to left. Secondly, the shot size and eyeline should match (i.e. they should individually be looking out of the frame at a point where the viewer anticipates the other speaker is standing). Finally, every shot of a sequence should stay the same side of an imaginary line drawn between the speakers (see diagram opposite) unless a shot is taken exactly on this imaginary line or a camera move crosses the line and allows a reorientation (and a repositioning of all cameras) on the opposite side of the old 'line'.

Matching to other cameras

In addition to setting up the optimum position for singles, two shots, etc., camera operators in a multi-camera intercutting situation need to match their shots with the other cameras. The medium close-ups (MCU), etc., should be the same size with the same amount of headroom. All cameras intercutting on singles should be the same height and if possible roughly the same lens angle (therefore the same distance from their respective subjects) especially when intercutting on over the shoulder two shots. This avoids a mismatch of the perspective of mass (i.e. the background figure is smaller or larger than the shot it is matching to). Other matching points are the same amount of looking room with semi-profile shots by placing the centre of the eyes (depending on size of shot) in the centre of frame.

The best method of matching shots is to use the mixed viewfinder facility or check with a monitor displaying studio out.

Camera positions for an interview

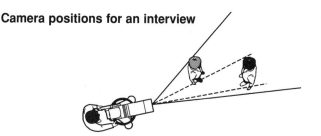

First set the camera position for a good over the shoulder two shot and then check that a clean MCU (i.e. the foreground head does not intrude into the MCU frame) can be obtained without repositioning the camera.

Crossing the line

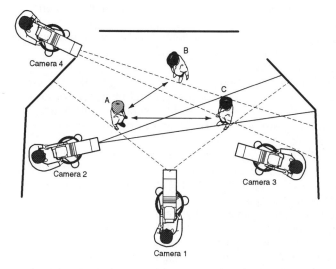

Because of the unrehearsed nature of a discussion, each camera takes up a position where it can match its shots to other cameras plus have the flexibility to offer more than one size of shot without repositioning. Constant camera repositioning during an interview can result in gaps in the camera coverage leading to participants talking in long shot because the camera that should be providing their closer shot is on the move.

Camera 4, looking for 'interesting shots', has gone upstage of the imaginary line(s) that connects the participants eyelines. When intercut with Camera 3, two people who, in the studio, are looking at each other (and therefore in opposite directions) will appear on screen to be both looking in the same direction. If cameras on both sides of the line are continually intercut, the viewer quickly loses the geographic relationship of the participants. Also, Camera 4 has created a problem for Camera 3 who is very close to being in Cameras 4's shot. By taking up such a position, Camera 4 has also pushed Camera 3 downstage to keep out of shot and forced Cameras 2 and 3 off their optimum eyeline position on the guests. Multi-camera camerawork is a team effort and any individual camera move or shot usually affects the work of the rest of the camera crew.

Interview/discussion

A production situation where matched shots and a shared understanding of the conventions of shot structure is required by camera operators is the television interview/discussion between two, three or many participants. Although the rehearsal procedure may vary, there is usually a requirement for the following production details to be agreed before transmission or recording.

The director uses the rehearsal time to check or inform the crew about the following:

■ Establish on which camera the presenter will introduce and wind up the interview and in what order he/she will introduce and question the guests.
■ Establish if there are any props or visual material that will be referred to. Agree on the cue words for their introduction of this material and decide which camera will cover the close-ups.
■ Check the range of shots available from all cameras and tell the cameramen which are likely to be used.
■ Match camera shot sizes.
■ Rehearse the beginning and end of the programme and any entrances and exits. It is usually unnecessary and unproductive to rehearse the interview. Voice levels are checked by sound and the guest's appearance and clothing are checked by lighting/vision control prior to recording or transmission.
■ It may be necessary for the camera crew and director to agree on standard shot size and abbreviation to avoid misunderstanding during transmission/recording. Abbreviation of shot descriptions (MCU, MS, etc.) are used so that shot size can be quickly changed.
■ There is often a convention by the director to state camera number first (e.g. 'Camera 3') and then the instruction ('two shot please').
■ During the rehearsal the camera operators will take the opportunity to look at all potential shots from their camera position and keep the director informed if he/she is requesting shots which cause problems or are more easily obtained on other cameras. They will also make certain, if they are on the 'live' side of the microphone, that they keep physical movement/noise to a minimum and that their camera position will not produce shadows on any part of the set in shot. Offer a two shot so that a lighting balance can be established.
■ A repositioning of a camera between shots which takes an appreciable time should be carefully considered on rehearsal as frequently, in a spontaneous event such as an interview, there is little or no time during transmission/recording to provide time for such a reposition. It can result in a participant talking out of shot as one or two cameras are taking up new positions. If asked by the director how long a reposition will take, estimate the time for the move and add ten seconds for safety.

Notes on intercutting

- The importance of offering different sized shots in order to get a good cut.
- The narrative 'weight' of a shot is dependent on the size of the shot and also on the composition. Emphasis can be strengthened or lightened depending on the reason for the shot.
- Decisions on the composition of a shot will have to consider how the shot relates in size, lens position, continuity (body posture, position, etc.), linked movement, crossing the line relationships, lighting, mood, atmosphere with the preceding and succeeding compositions.

Looking room

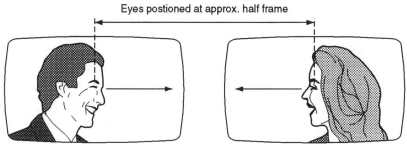

Eyes postioned at approx. half frame

Balanced 'looking room' on intercut shots

- During rehearsal, the floor manager will confirm with the presenter how he/she will signal when to move on to the next question (if needed), how he/she will signal the time to the end of the programme and the signal for any other instruction that the director may want to pass on. They will make certain that they stand in the presenter's eyeline so that the presenter can see their cues and signals. They should check that their arm movements do not produce shadows on the set. Frequently the presenter will be fitted with an ear-piece with direct talkback from the director and/or producer/editor. Either floor manager or presenter will brief the guests to ignore the cameras and studio and speak to the anchor person.
- The floor manager also checks that all studio doors are closed and everyone is present before recording or transmission commences.

161

Working in a camera crew

Camera crews

A feature of multi-camera productions since the earliest days of television production has been the contribution made by television camera operators working regularly together as a crew. The number of camera operators forming a crew varies depending on production requirements but it is generally agreed that the continuity of working regularly as a team has a positive influence on the quality of the combined effort.

Working many years together on a range of top quality programmes, a number of outstanding camera crews have not only taken a pride in their crew identity but have amassed a breadth of collective experience that is often used by the director to the benefit of the production.

Working as part of a camera crew on multi-camera productions requires a keen awareness of team work and a willingness to contribute. Apart from rehearsal/transmission, multi-camerawork also requires cooperation with other members of the crew when rigging and de-rigging, in the care and handling of equipment and in the sense of responsibility, if equipment is shared, to check that equipment is never passed on (even to an unknown camera operator or crew) that is faulty or has parts that are missing. The golden rule is that you always return with everything you took to a location.

Production team

Live and recorded-as-live production methods rely on every member of the production team perfecting their input into the programme at the moment of transmission. All the different skills employed – performance, lighting, sound, vision control, vision mixing, etc. – interact and the quality of the production is only as good as the weakest contribution. If one member of the team is badly prepared or lacks sufficient experience to resolve production problems, his/her incompetence will eventually affect the rest of the production team. The speed of multi-camera productions relies on everyone getting it right first time.

Everyone wants to work and achieve the highest possible standards in their particular craft area but television production is a group effort and good television techniques are working practices that enable other crafts to achieve a high standard of performance as well as the individual.

Perfect sound may be provided by a boom position that inhibits camera movement or a microphone position that casts shadows and intrudes into shot. This may be perfect sound but it is bad television production sound. A shot that is composed with so much headroom that there is no space for the boom microphone to get close to the performers may be a great shot in isolation but it is also bad television production practice.

An awareness of the day-to-day problems of the other skills within the production team and a willingness to reach a compromise on one's own

Your contribution to the team effort is by:

- being competent in your own job. This helps other craft skills to do theirs because they are not wrong footed by your operational errors and misjudgements
- being consistent in framing and shot structure and reproducing on transmission any part of the programme that was pre-rehearsed
- having an understanding and a respect for other people's skills and being willing to adjust your work to help resolve their production problems
- having a willingness to compromise from the ideal coupled with the judgement to assess the minimum standards that are acceptable.

Chain reaction

On transmission or recording watch out for the domino effect where one mistake ripples though the whole production forcing everyone into operational error. For example, a change in the running order of the programme results in the wrong pre-recorded insert being played out. This is abruptly cut away to a camera and a presenter who have yet to reposition to a new set-up. Sound meanwhile continues from the insert. Forget what has gone wrong. Concentrate on what has yet to come. Leave the post mortems until after the programme has ended.

production demands will improve the quality of the whole programme. Monopolizing rehearsal time to get your particular problems sorted out may possibly prevent someone else resolving their difficulties.

The viewfinder

A mixed viewfinder

The camera operator can usually switch his/her viewfinder feed from the camera output to a mixed feed of camera output and a designated source (e.g. another camera). The viewfinder feed can be switched either by a button on the pan bar or by a switch on or near the viewfinder. A 'mixed viewfinder' feed is also the common term applied to switching the viewfinder picture to a single (unmixed) video feed such as 'studio out' – the visual source that is currently being selected at the vision mixing panel – as opposed to 'station out' which is the programme currently being transmitted. 'Studio out' is useful when matching shots or identifying what other cameras are offering in an as-directed situation.

The mixed viewfinder facility is an invaluable aid in many production situations such as in motor racing coverage where a specific car or group of cars may have to be picked up immediately they come into the field of view of a camera. By monitoring the OB output via mixed viewfinder, a camera operator can identify lead cars or cars in shot on other cameras before they reach his/her position on the track. The speed of the event precludes identifying the cars in precise detail but, for example, the outline shape of two or three leading cars can be memorized and picked up and panned with as soon as they come into view.

The mixed output available at the viewfinder is usually selected in vision control/engineering although some models of cameras have a number of video sources that can be selected at the camera. Any video source can be mixed (depending on synchronization) with a camera output such as special effects and colour separation (see Chroma-key, page 255) but a check should be made that both video sources are combined at the viewfinder with correct timing. That is, one image is not displaced horizontally from the other due to taking a longer video path and therefore arriving later. This can cause problems when lining-up a precise match between the camera's picture and, for example, an electronic graphic.

The balance of the mix between the two sources can be adjusted to make one image brighter than another which sometimes helps when matching up the camera's output to another source (e.g. seeing the edge of a chroma key panel, etc.).

Another facility that is sometimes useful with mixed viewfinder working is a grid or a cursor that can be selected at the camera and superimposed over the camera's output to check horizontal lines. Although electronically generated text has superseded caption cards on cameras, occasionally there are situations when a visual element requires checking to see if it is horizontal or vertical.

Linear

The size of the scanned area in the viewfinder can be adjusted and it is obviously important that the whole of the picture area can be seen. It is

Setting up a viewfinder contrast and brightness

- To set the viewfinder contrast and brightness get the camera capped either electronically or by placing a lens cap on the lens and then reduce contrast and brightness to minimum.
- Increase brightness until the line structure of the viewfinder picture begins to show.
- Turn down the brightness until the lines just disappear.
- Uncap the camera and on a correctly exposed picture, increase the contrast until detail in the shadows and the highlights can be seen.
- During the rehearsal/transmission it may be necessary to adjust contrast due to ambient light or because of picture content (e.g. a scene that is mostly lit by red light will prompt a great deal of tweaking of viewfinder controls to get a picture that can be focused).

Peaking

As the camera operator must be the first person to see the loss of optical focus, it often helps to improve the definition of the viewfinder by adding an electronic edge enhancement to the image usually provided by a variable control on the viewfinder called 'peaking'. This does not affect the output of the camera.

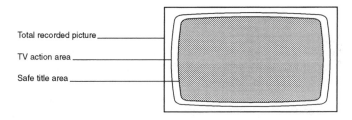

Total recorded picture

TV action area

Safe title area

Safety zone

Another viewfinder facility available on some cameras is the safety zone graticule which, when switched in, provides a white marker inside the frame showing the amount of cut-off (i.e. the edge of the picture not seen) on older TV receivers. When framing a shot, keep any vital information within the 'action area' to guarantee it being seen by the majority of viewers. Some cameras are also provided with a switchable 'centre screen' marker.

also important that the viewfinder picture is free from geometric distortion. Check the linearity of the viewfinder by framing up on a grid or a circle. If the squares of a grid vary in size across the frame (providing the camera is square to the caption) then there will be errors in framing and composition. Sometimes one side of the picture is non-linear which causes errors in framing.

Working with talkback

The lifeblood of multi-camera camerawork is talkback. Without talkback, a camera operator is cut off from the production process and can make little or no contribution unless a clearly rehearsed plan of action has been pre-arranged.

There are a number of working areas involved in a multi-camera pro-gramme and at some time in the production process they may individually need to speak to one or other of the team. Collectively they need the coor-dination of the director's talkback which knits the group effort together (see opposite).

Director's talkback

The director organizes the activity of the production team and coordinates changes or transitions during transmission or recording and keeps every-one informed about the progress of the production. He/she gives direct commands across a range of production decisions such as cueing of per-formers, intercutting between vision sources, shot size, details of up-com-ing action, etc. A number of other production decisions are the responsibil-ity of individuals such as the control of audio levels by the sound supervi-sor, the control of the lighting balance by the lighting director, the adjust-ment of framing and focus by the camera operator, the resetting of props or scenery controlled by the floor manger, etc.

Talkback on headset

The camera operator hears talkback on a headset plugged into the camera (or by radio talkback) and usually has the facility to communicate via a switched microphone attached to the headset. The director's talkback channel is usually shared by the production assistant (speaking on a sep-arate microphone) working alongside the director in the control room. Both talkback levels are adjusted by the same volume control on the camera.

As well as the talkback from the director, most camera channels have an engineering talkback facility which is often shared by vision control and light-ing. Their audio level is regulated by another volume control on the camera.

A direct feed of programme sound is usually provided and adjusted by a third volume control. These three basic talkback facilities are often aug-mented by omnibus talkback which allows other members of the production team (e.g. sound supervisor, technical manager, etc.) to 'switch in' and be heard on general talkback.

Sometimes talkback from a sub-mix director is put on the programme sound channel. The level between this talkback and programme sound is usually adjusted from Sound Control.

166

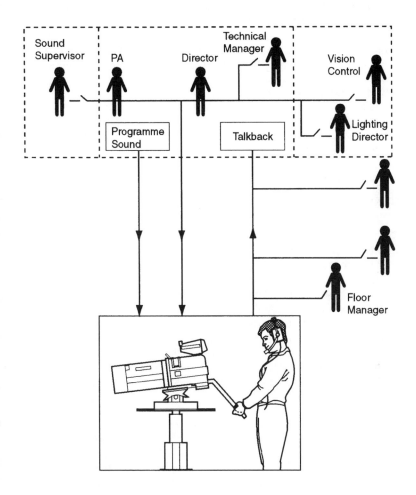

Some talkback systems also provide for inter-camera talkback which allows camera operators to talk to each other and to trackers/ grips.

New to talkback

Select what is meaningful

A camera operator new to wearing a headset and working with talkback might be overwhelmed by the amount of information received. With experience it is possible to ignore all but the information that affects camerawork. This is not simply camera direction. Any information that may affect future shots or shots that will be needed should be 'logged' by the camera operator and used when required.

Talkback discipline

With nearly all communication channelled through the control room, it is obviously important to choose the right time to talk to the director or control room. Do not interrupt an existing discussion or a briefing that will be addressed to the whole crew. Wait for a pause (and close to transmission or recording this never seems to occur) before opening your microphone and calling the control room. Keep the conversation brief and if questions from the director can be answered with a simple yes or no, nod the camera in the vertical direction for 'yes' and pan the camera in the horizontal direction for 'no'.

Programme sound

It is often important to listen to programme sound. During a discussion, sports commentary, etc., the camera shots offered will be directly related to the information supplied by programme sound. On OBs, 'clean commentary' is available on programme sound. This excludes the output of the effects microphones so that the commentary can be clearly heard. On other programmes, the spill from the sound monitor in the control room on to the director's microphone is usually adequate.

Many camera operators prefer to work with one of the headset earpieces on one ear and the other earpiece off the ear. Programme sound can then be heard directly and the uncovered ear is available in case of sotto-voce messages from other people such as floor managers, etc., during transmission.

Avoid talkback spillage

Another simple discipline connected with talkback is to always unplug your headset when you are not wearing it. If you hang the headset on the pan bar and leave the studio when an item is being recorded which does not involve your camera, the talkback spillage could easily cause a retake. If you are working on the live side of microphone, make certain you are working with the lowest talkback level that is required.

If you are new to wearing a headset, be careful that the reduction in local sound from wearing a headset does not cause you to raise your voice when speaking on talkback and disturb the rehearsal. Remember that the artistes cannot hear the director and it may be necessary when pointing out a problem caused by an artiste position or movement to choose your words with discretion. Ill-chosen comments can imply a performer is at fault when it is simply a small detail that requires attention.

High levels of ambient noise such as rock concerts or motor racing require special noise cancelling headsets otherwise talkback will be inaudible.

Cutting on action
Frequently cameras are intercut to follow action. It is important to know when to follow the action and when to hold a static frame and let the action leave the frame. For example, a camera framed on an MCU of someone sitting could pan with them when they stood up but this might spoil the cut to a wider shot. A camera tightening into MCU may prevent a planned cut to the same size shot from another camera. In an as-directed situation, use the mixed viewfinder to find out the shot pattern of the other cameras involved in the sequence.

Camera left, camera right
Camera left is the left hand side of the frame from the camera's viewpoint. For the presenter facing the lens, camera left will be their right hand side. Upstage is in the direction away from the lens and downstage is moving towards the lens.

Front of camera people are sometimes confused by the fact that a monitor is different from a mirror in that there is no horizontal reverse of the image. We are accustomed to mirror images reversing our reflection so that when for example we raise our right hand, the hand moving in the reflection is in fact the reflection's left hand. This can cause problems for artistes who are using a monitor to position a prop or to judge a performance such as puppeteers. This can be resolved by reversing the horizontal scans on a monitor.

Vision mixing terms

- A CUT: an instantaneous change between two visual sources.
- A MIX or DISSOLVE: a gradual transition between two visual sources.
- A WIPE: a geometric dissolve (with either a hard or soft edge at the transition between the two visual sources) such as line, circle or box travelling across the frame or as an overall pattern transition.
- A SUPER (abbreviation for superimposition): adding one visual source (usually text) on to another visual source.
- A FADE UP: when a visual source emerges from a blank screen.
- A FADE OUT: when a visual source fades into a blank (black) screen.
- A DVE: a digital video effect often combining two or more video sources in electronic movement such as spins and tumbles or contracting and inserting one video source into another.
- CHROMA KEY or CSO (colour separation overlay): technique of combining two or more separate images into one unified image.
- CAPTION GENERATOR: a piece of electronic equipment that produces a variety of text and identification logos/emblems.
- SCROLLING: moving the text across the screen.

Visual memory/camera cards

The ability to remember the precise framing of a shot comes with practice and experience. There are no visual memory rules or procedures to be learnt as visual memory appears to operate at the instinctive level. At the speed at which some shots are required, the reflex selection of lens angle and framing are completed in an instant. There is no time, for example, to check leisurely if the left-hand frame was exactly in line with a prominent edge. The shot is framed, focused and cut to. In these circumstances, visual memory is coordinating hand and eye to provide precisely the frame that is required. In general, however, it is always a good idea to make notes on the camera card as a reminder of a shot.

Camera cards

Most studio-based programmes and many OB programmes will have a pre-planned script which identifies which cameras cover specific action, dialogue or narration. Each shot is numbered in sequence with a relevant shot description if known. The shots applicable to each camera are listed on individual camera cards (called crib cards) attached to each camera.

The function of the shot cards on rehearsal is to provide sufficient information to set up each shot. The shot description needs to be abbreviated otherwise they would be unreadable when working at speed.

Camera cards therefore have two functions which sometimes conflict:

- During rehearsal, adequate information needs to be on the card in order that the camera operator can understand what shot is required plus any special requirement relating to the shot.
- During transmission/recording, the camera card provides a reminder of essential information and needs to be read at a glance while operating the camera. Anything superfluous to essentials or poor layout makes it difficult to 'snatch' information quickly from the card.

A camera card is an abbreviated script for the camera operator and the information is usually laid out in three columns detailing: shot number, camera position, shot description, with plenty of space for camera operators to add notes and alterations during rehearsal.

Shot number

Normally a script is divided into segments and itemized as shots. Any other change of visual source including VTR and electronic graphics is also assigned a shot number. The shot numbers are continuous and if during rehearsal an extra shot is added then it is given the previous shot number with an alphabet suffix (32, then new shot 32a followed by a second new shot 32b, and so forth). This avoids renumbering the whole script.

If the programme contains as-directed sequences such as a discussion then each camera will be given an indication on their individual cards such as two shot, MS, MCU, etc., followed by 'intercut' or 'as-directed'.

A portion of a Granada TV floor plan showing the set of 'The Rovers Return'

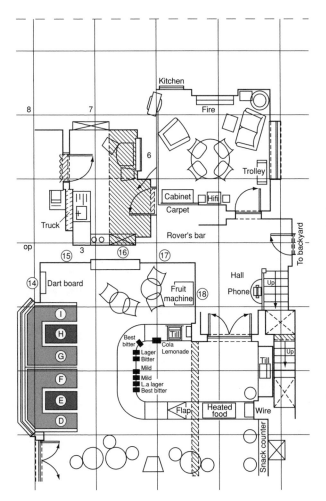

Camera position

If a programme has pre-planned camera positions marked on a floor plan, then each camera position will be lettered and this letter will appear against the appropriate shot number. Sometimes parts of the studio area or location will be identified by a name to indicate where a particular sequence will be staged. For example, 'cyc', which is the standard abbreviation for cyclorama, is the backcloth which is stretched in an arc around two or more sides of the studio.

MIKE:

I used to. The government give it
me to defend the British Empire.
Along with a pair of boots. They
can have the boots, but I wish
they'd left me the gun. World'd be
a safer place, I'm telling you.

DES:

371 1 A   Oh ah. /
     MS DEREK

     3 TIGHTEN FAST
                                      DEREK:

                                      I can't see 'em issuing every
                                      householder with a gun, Michael.

                                      MIKE:

372 3   It's coming, I tell you./ That's how
     MS MIKE
                                      they're going to save money on the
     1A LOOSEN FAST
                                      Police. Just give everybody a gun,

                                      say look after yourself. Twenty

373 2 A   years from now./ Mark my words.
     2/S MAUD/MAUREEN (REACTION)
374 3   / Burglar? Never mind nine nine nine.
     MS MIKE
375 1 A   Big Bang/and have done. I'm up for
     2/S DEREK/MAVIS (REACTION)
376 3   it./ And...And I'd have a law where
     MS MIKE
                                      the burglar's family'd have to pay

377 2 A   for cleaning the carpet./
     2/S A/B
     HOLD MAUREEN'S RISE ROF
                                      MAUREEN IS SITTING WITH MAUD AT A
     CLEAR 1 TO POS B   TABLE WITHIN EARSHOT. SUDDENLY SHE
                                      INTERRUPTS THEM.

**A page from a script of an episode of 'Coronation Street' set in the
Rovers Return**

SCENE 12   **ROVERS BAR**

357   2 / S JACK (ENTERING) / VERA

359   2 / S A / B

361   2 / S A / B

363   2 / S A / B

                    TAPE STOP AFTER SHOT 363

363   CLEAR TO POS A

365   4 / S MIKE / DES / DEREK / MAVIS   A
           FAV. DES

           (TIGHTEN)

367   3 / S DES / DEREK / MAVIS   A
           FAV. DES

           (PAN R. & RE-FRAME)
373   2 / S MAUD / MAUREEN (REACTION)   A

377   2 / S A / B
           HOLD MAUREEN'S RISE ROF   A

385   MS MAUREEN (REACTION)   A

                    TAPE STOP AFTER SHOT 385

A camera card detailing Camera 2's shots from the page of script on page 172

Camera card notes

Shot description

Shot descriptions are abbreviated as much as possible so that the information can be quickly scanned. In a complex show with many shot changes in a fast cutting sequence, the camera operator may have the briefest of time to look away from the viewfinder to check the next shot and camera position.

Marking up

Most camera operators prefer to scribble a few words against a complex shot description as additional information noted at rehearsal. These abbreviated reminders (which may be incomprehensible to anyone else) replace the typed shot description. The aim of any alteration to the card by the cameraman is to make instantly legible any essential camera movement and to link it to the action that cues it. During rehearsal, the camera operator will be marking up his/her card and marking the camera position, if necessary.

For example, if the camera is craned down on a tight shot of a performer and the shot requires the camera to hold the close shot as the artiste stands, the camera operator will have to crane up and keep a good framing, in focus, on the artiste. The essential point in this action is to know precisely when the stand occurs.

Watching during rehearsal, he/she may note that the performer will make one or two 'false' body movements as if he/she was going to stand but only actually make the move at the third indication. Although most performers rehearse and reproduce movement to dialogue, scribbling key words down does help, particularly if a number of camera movements are linked to actor movement during a scene. But there is a limit to this method. The camera card quickly fills up with dialogue lines that are difficult if not impossible to read at speed. As the camera operator is using a viewfinder it is often best to use visually observed movement as a cue to camera movement.

2 lean fwd stands

For example, a camera card may have the scribble '2 lean fwd stands' which translated by the camera operator means '*when he leans forward for the second time he will stand and I will need to crane up and focus forward*'. A well laid-out camera card will always have plenty of space for this type of rehearsal note. Some broadcast organizations, however, suggest that a camera card should be marked up so that another camera operator could take over the camera in an emergency and understand the rehearsal notes. It is also important that the changeover between two cards occurs during a sequence of slow shot change to avoid hastily scrabbling to get the top card flipped over while looking for the next shot.

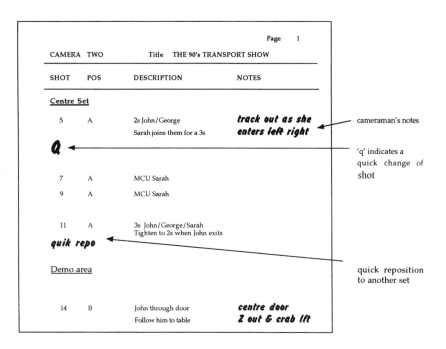

What you need to remember from the rehearsal

After rehearsal has finished, the camera card should provide the camera operator with all the information (plus his/her visual memory) that is required to complete the show. It is not unknown for camera operators to spend time before transmission/recording re-marking their cards or even completely rewriting a card in order to make the information instantly legible and able to be read at speed. A crib card should contain only essential information that can be read at a glance.

Reproduction

Many programmes require shots that have been set up in a rehearsal period to be accurately reproduced on transmission/recording. Marking up a camera card and marking up camera positions gives one set of parameters. The other essential component is the lens angle. Many zoom lenses can be controlled (in addition to the zoom demand control on the pan bar or lens) by a shot box (see Zooming, page 108).

If precise framing is required, either the shot box can be adjusted to give the required lens angle or the camera operator will have to rely on his/her visual memory to find the necessary framing.

Working to cue lights

The cue light system
All television cameras designed for multi-camera working are fitted with red lamps on the camera and in the viewfinder called cue lights or tally lamps. These are switched on when the camera is selected on the vision mixing panel. The cue light system is an essential part of multi-camera production technique as it identifies to the camera operator and all other production staff working alongside the cameras which camera is 'live' during rehearsal, recording or transmission.

Cue light position
A cue light is usually positioned on top of the camera and housed in a red cover that also displays the camera number. In this position, it can be seen by most people working on the production although it is often obscured when viewed from the front of the camera. As performers often have to be aware which camera is 'on', a duplicate of the light is positioned on the front of the camera and/or on the front of the lens housing. A prompter, if fitted, masks these lamps and therefore the front of the prompter is fitted with an additional cue light.

A cue light is also needed at the control point if the camera is remotely operated via a control panel in the studio/location or in a control room. When a camera is rigged on a crane or dolly, a cue light is often rigged in the eyeline of the trackers/riggers.

Viewfinder cue lights
A red cue light displayed in the viewfinder reminds the camera operator when his/her camera is on air. He/she should be aware from the director's instructions on talkback when his/her camera is going to be used (e.g. 'Coming to 2. Cut to 2') but sometimes on an ad-lib, fast cutting sequence, the shot he/she is providing may be taken without prior warning.

With experience, the cue light is used instinctively. There will be an automatic response to the cue light just as there will be instant adjustment in framing to compensate for subject movement. The tempo of intercutting between cameras requires the camera operator to develop the ability to work at two speeds. Off shot, there is often the need to find the required shot almost instantaneously. Once settled on the framing and the camera is cut to, there may be the need to develop the shot (zoom in or out, pan, track, etc.) at a tempo controlled by the subject matter. Frequently this will be a slow, unobtrusive movement. When the cue light goes off, the camera operator is again released to find the next shot in the fastest possible time.

The cue light is therefore a visual indicator that separates the two speeds of work. If, inadvertently, the camera is cut to while rapidly moving to a new shot, the cue light coming on should instantly change the

Page	Item	Pres.	Area	Vision	Sound	Dur	Total
	Ident	.	.	Beta 1	Sovt	05"	
	Titles	.	.	Beta 4		22"	27"
	Headlines	Ken	D	1		45"	1.12"
1		Sue		4			
	Link to	Ken	D	1			
	Shopping			Beta 3	Sovt	2.50"	4.02"
2	Spree						
	Shopping	Sue	A	1		3.15"	7.17"
	Interview	Guest		2			
3				3			

Running orders

Other types of information pinned to a crib card holder are **seating plans**, which give the names and positions of participants in discussion/interview programmes and **running orders**, which list programme items in an abbreviated manner.

camera movement to freezing on whatever composition is in the frame (if it is usable) or, as unobtrusively as possible, to adjust to an acceptable framing.

Cue light control

As soon as the fader on the vision mixing panel controlling a camera's output is moved off the end stop, the cue lights on that camera come on even though the output of that camera may not yet be visible on the transmission output monitor in the control room. When the cue light comes on at the beginning of a mix, any camera movement that may be required should be delayed until the mix has ended unless there is a production requirement to carry a movement though a mix.

Depending on the design of the vision mixing panel, a camera's cue lights may come on (even if not on transmission or recording) if the camera is previewed and selected for a digital effect. Conversely, some mixer designs allow a camera to be cut to 'line' through an effects bank without switching on the camera cue light. This can happen with some types of chroma key compositing and a check should be made during rehearsal (if available) if the camera is 'live' without showing a cue light and informing anyone who may be affected.

Green cue light working

With the growth of productions where a camera's output is fed to more than one production control room (e.g. golf coverage by two or more independent broadcasters) the red cue light in the viewfinder is lit when the master control room is using the shot and a second green cue light comes on when another control room has selected the camera's output for transmission. The camera operator can only work to one set of directions and therefore the red cue light takes precedence whenever there is a conflict of use.

Switchable cue lights

It is sometimes advantageous on location (or, for example, with a studio audience discussion) to switch off the external cue lights on the camera to avoid drawing attention to the use of the camera. The ability to switch off the cue lights can also help if unwanted reflections arise from glossy or polished surfaces. Alternatively, the cue lights are often blanked off using gaffer tape.

Other production staff's use of cue lights

Although the camera operator is continuously responding to the cue lights on the camera, other members of the production staff on the studio floor or location frequently need to know which camera is on air. The floor manager needs to be in a position alongside the taking camera to cue artists, etc., boom operators not only need to know which camera is on shot but also the size of shot they are taking. Other floor staff making scenery and props changes work to cue lights or, if graphic material is being used, when a caption can be replaced with succeeding material.

Covering football on a low angle dolly

Working on a crane

Development of the camera crane
The height of a standard camera mounting is controlled by the ability of the camera operator to see into the viewfinder. By mounting the camera and cameraman on a counter-weighted boom arm pivoted on a tracking base column, greater (and lower) camera heights can be achieved.

The introduction of small, lightweight cameras allows the remote control of pan, tilt, zoom and focus to be developed which removes the need for the camera operator to travel with the camera. Lightweight extending boom arms allow greater flexibility in the speed of movement and in the positioning of the camera.

The art of tracking
Working on a crane is essentially a team effort. It requires the ability to conceive visually what picture will occur wherever the lens is in space and the ability to compensate and react to whatever other members of the crane crew are doing.

It is an oft quoted cliché, but essentially true, that working as part of a crane crew will teach a newcomer to television more about the craft of camerawork than almost any other type of training.

Whereas a camera operator operating a pedestal is usually in full control of positioning the lens in space, when working on the front of a crane or operating the remote controls, a camera operator requires the full cooperation and attention of up to four or five people. The complexity of the camera moves that can be attempted depends on the ability of the trackers to coordinate their individual operations.

The camera operator when riding on a crane sometimes needs to use his/her feet to reposition the seat and camera while controlling framing and focus. He/she will also need to 'hand signal' to his/her trackers to cue movement and for small adjustments on shot to compensate for artistes' positions. Often this adjustment occurs when the camera is in close and focus becomes critical. The camera operator is therefore almost totally dependent on the skill and attentiveness of his/her trackers or grips.

Crane operation
There are basically four operations required on a manned crane. The cameraman seated behind the camera on the end of the boom arm controls framing and focus. The arm swinger positions the boom arm from the rear of the crane but often, due to the weight and size of the boom, is accompanied by another assisting at the back or, depending on the shot, working at the front of the boom near the camera. A tracker is needed to steer and adjust the speed and direction of movement on a motorized dolly. Lastly (and often essentially) someone is required to clear cables behind and in front of the dolly.

Tracking, steering and arm swinging all interact together to determine exactly where the lens is positioned in space. There can only be one decision maker on this position (working through the director) and that is the camera operator. Therefore the first priority is to put the lens exactly where the camera operator wants it. This requires the attention of the trackers on any possible adjustment hand signals from the camera operator.

The second priority is to duplicate exactly rehearsed crane moves matched to action. This requires a method of marking up the camera cards by the arm swinger and driver using a code or symbol to represent the position of the camera in space of the rehearsed moves. If a number of moves are from the same position, a tracking line will be chalked or taped on the floor marked like a ruler with different lettered gradations. The arm swingers will develop their own method of memorizing where the arm is positioned for different shots.

Remote control

Using a mini monitor

The camera operator's hand signals are frequently augmented by a mini monitor strapped to the back of the dolly fed with the output of the camera. Inexperienced trackers may become too preoccupied in watching this monitor and miss vital hand signals from the camera operator and/or ignore artiste movement.

Often arm movement is motivated by actor movement. Perfect synchronization of crane and actor can be achieved if the arm swinger watches for body posture signals from the artiste. Whether standing, walking or sitting, there are always body indicators of when this type of movement is going to occur. This may not be seen on a monitor and therefore it is essential to look at these activities during rehearsal and get an understanding of the specific artiste's characteristics.

Attention needs to be divided five ways: on the camera operator, on the action or artiste, on the monitor, on talkback and on the actions of the other trackers.

Technique

The advantages of a camera crane is that complex development shots can be achieved. A common technique is to set and mark the start and end of the shot and then work out who does what on the crane to move between these two set positions. Crane work requires the camera operator to select good pivot points and be able to hold these pivots while being swung and craned. He/she cannot achieve these transitions smoothly unless the swinger and the driver work together and have a feel for fluid and dynamic images.

Sometimes, high-speed movement of the camera through space appears on screen as less than dynamic because the shot has no design elements such as a patterned floor to indicate speed and movement.

Crane work on music and entertainment production numbers is often unmotivated in the normal sense by artistes' movement. For example, movement around a singer or a tracking shot along a church aisle may have no action movement within the frame to de-emphasize the camera movement. This lack of motivation requires perfect pivot points and smooth crane movements.

Remote control

By remoting all lens controls on the camera and by using a lightweight camera with servo pan and tilt, the camera operator can operate away from the front of the crane. Without the need to support the camera operator, the boom arm design can be lighter, longer, more flexible and therefore provide more operational permutations. It can be positioned in inaccessible situations for manned cameras and travel through small areas such as corridors, doorways, open windows, etc.

Trevor Wimlett (BBC OB London) on the Yorkshire moors shooting a children's drama

Remote head

The remote controlled camera is operated using a monitor fed with the camera's output to adjust pan/tilt, zoom and focus. Because the camera-man's attention may be fixed on the monitor during a camera move, it is important to be aware that cables are not being wound around the pan and tilt head or becoming snagged during movement.

To achieve movement on a remote controlled pan/tilt head in excess of 360°, there needs to be a method of supplying the camera controls and output through slip rings or by radio link. On some cranes the jib can be extended at different speeds by servo motor.

Usually a radio talkback system for inter-crew communication allows the coordination when setting up a shot and for instruction during camera movement.

Care should be taken when working and moving a crane above an audi-ence. A remotely controlled camera can be moved at speed on a lightweight boom arm and it should always work higher than the height of someone unexpectedly standing up in the audience.

Safety and crane work

With a manned crane (i.e. camera operator seated on the crane) one of the critical moments in safe working is when the cameraman gets on to and off the crane. There is usually a safety strap which holds down the crane when the camera operator is not on it. Check that this is in place before allowing the camera operator to leave the crane. Many cranes do not rely on safety bonds to restrain an imbalance between the weight tray at the back of the arm and front but require the weights to be removed to the equivalent weight of the camera operator before he/she leaves the front seat. When he/she remounts the crane, additional weights are added at the back until the arm is balanced.

Camera operators should wear a restraining harness or belt when seated on a crane and operators swinging a heavy boom arm should adopt safe body posture wherever possible to prevent back strain. When rigging a crane, check that there is sufficient slack in any cables that may be stretched by the jib-arm movement.

Personal assessment of risk
A crane moving at speed can injure or maim. If a fast move is required on shot, make certain everyone working in the vicinity of the crane is aware of its position and movement. The priority when working on a crane is first, personnel safety both on and off the crane, and second, safe handling so that equipment is not damaged. The third priority is achieving the required shot but this should never be promoted above other safe working considerations.

It is each tracker's responsibility to assess the potential risk of his/her actions and not endanger him/herself, colleagues and particularly the camera operators who may be exposed to collision while moving at speed though space.

Frequently check cable guards if fitted, especially if power is being fed to the crane via a cable, and do not allow bunches of cable to build up behind or in front of the dolly.

Jib arms, etc.
Jib arms are a smaller version of a crane and are often operated by a cameraman and a grip/tracker. Control of a remote head which is swung on a jib arm should have an observer of its position in space if the camera operator's view of the camera becomes obscured.

Check when first switching on a remote head that neither the camera nor persons standing close to the head will be harmed by a sudden reposition of the head as it responds to the controller setting.

184

Keith Salmon on a Tulip crane recording 'The Boys from the Blackstuff' (BBC TV)

Assessing a shot

Editorial priorities
Intercutting between different cameras provides an effective method of presenting information, telling a story or structuring an event. The pace, excitement and variety induced by a change of shot can potentially engage and hold the attention of the audience but shot change requires an underlying coherent structure if it is not to collapse into a succession of fleeting images. That overall structure is imposed by the director, assisted in an as-directed situation by the input from the camera crew.

Camera operators therefore need to have a grasp of the editorial priorities of the programme format they are involved in. In an interview situation involving a number of people, for example, they must be aware of the flow of the discussion to be able to respond and provide the appropriate shot of a participant at the moment they begin to speak. In sports coverage, they must follow the commentary, the flow of the game and know the rules of the game, as well as direction in order that the appropriate shot is framed and ready moments before it is required.

The ability to assess what shots are required and a feeling for the production style is the product of experience and concentration. Keeping up with the programme content allows time for the camera operator to anticipate what shots are needed and the speed of reflex to provide them. The cameramen in many situations are the eyes of the director but unless they share the same production values (i.e. they assume a certain shot structure is appropriate for the specific situation), a scrappy and often confusing treatment may result.

Variation in programme formats
Shot structure and production requirements vary with programme format. As we have already discussed, programmes that are tightly camera scripted (e.g. drama, orchestral music, etc.) will require little or no additional shots except when resolving production problems discovered during rehearsal. Other programme formats such as discussion, sports coverage, game shows and many live events require a constant flow of as-directed shots. These shots have to be appropriate to the specific programme and not simply a 'pretty' shot.

When to offer shots
One of the hardest techniques for camera operators to master in multi-camera camerawork on a fast-moving show is when to offer shots or when to wait for direction. A camera operator, for example, will often spot during a discussion a participant not on camera bursting to get their word in and may be tempted to offer up a shot of them. Many directors appreciate this sort of contribution and, providing there is the trust and experience devel-

oped in a long working relationship between camera crew, vision mixer and director, a variety of reaction shots can be offered and taken whilst still keeping up with the flow of the discussion.

Alternatively, many directors dislike being left without a cover shot and prefer to decide on all camera movement. In these circumstances the camera operator must stick on his/her last directed shot until directed to do otherwise. While this avoids any misunderstandings or the mistake of cutting to a camera just as it moves to a new shot, it can also limit the opportunity for visual variety and spontaneity in the coverage.

What shots are required?

A 'cut-in' shot will give more information or detail directly connected with the main content of the programme. A close-up of a golf ball going into the hole completes a sequence of shots starting with the golfer lining up his/her putt.

In the same golf coverage, a 'cutaway' to a seagull perched on a flag in an unplayed hole does not provide additional information about the match but it does provide variety and humour. This type of shot can only be offered when the tempo of the match allows. It is inappropriate, for example, at the moment of a critical putt.

Variation in camera angle and shot size are needed in most as-directed situations to give variety and pace to the presentation. The director will ask for a string of requirements and coordinate each camera but by listening to talkback and with the occasional use of the mixed viewfinder facility to see what shot has been selected, a camera operator will often be able to find an appropriate shot that matches the needs of the programme at that point. The judgement and ability to assess what shot is relevant is part of the skill needed to be developed by a camera operator. What shot is 'editorially' significant is part of the director's concept of the programme. Often, a cameraman will interpret that concept from experience or from deductions based on the production preferences of the director.

It is also important, especially on OBs, that the camera operator acts as 'the eyes' of the director and informs him/her by word or by showing on camera events or activities that the director may be unaware of in the scanner (e.g. if it begins to rain, personalities in the crowd, who is next to play, etc.).

Attitude and responsibility

Working in a mass medium

Television is the most popular form of mass entertainment worldwide and can exert an enormous influence on its audience. Everyone working in programme production has to take this into account when considering how their particular contribution can affect the audience.

On 11 May 1985, an OB unit was covering a football match in the North of England when a crowded stand caught fire. The match was abandoned as thousands of people struggled to leave the stadium. One camera operator close to the blaze managed to escape, other camera operators on the opposite side of the pitch turned their cameras on to the stand and became instantly 'news' cameramen. At first, no one knew the full horror of the situation but it became apparent as bodies were carried on to the pitch that many people had been killed. On realizing what was happening, some football fans turned their anger onto the TV camera operators and pelted them with missiles shouting 'ghouls – turn the cameras off'. The pictures the camera operators produced were seen worldwide and alerted many people to the dangers of stadium fires and provoked changes in stadium design.

Television is not the glitzy, glamorous business many newcomers to the industry imagine it to be and many people in their working career will face just as hard an ethical and professional decision as the camera operators covering that particular football match. It is advisable for every camera operator to review their professional attitudes and moral viewpoints before being confronted with such a situation.

We just work here

Only one or two individuals (usually the producer or director) in a production team are considered by commissioning organizations to be accountable for the programme content and its effects on an audience. The rest are paid to work on the programme and are expected to exercise a 'professional' approach detached from the subject matter. The inference is that although they enable the programme to be made, they are not publicly accountable for its effects. This ignores the fact that programme making is a team effort and to some extent, everyone involved is responsible for the impact of the programme.

News cameramen may be faced with the moral dilemma of choosing to continue to film people in distress or to put the camera down and attempt to offer them what aid and assistance they personally can provide. In order to carry out their job as news cameramen, they need the ability to stand outside the event and objectively report. In this sense, is 'professionalism' a mandate for non-involvement, a suspension of personal responsibility to act? Are you capable of demonstrating this degree of objectivity and detachment when required?

Professional conduct

As well as the qualities discussed in the previous topic on attitude, there are many important aspects of a being a professional camera operator that are sometimes overlooked.

Timekeeping
The transmission of television programmes is timed to the second. A train can be delayed for five minutes and affect hundreds of people. A television programme delayed for five minutes can affect millions of people and have a knock-on effect for the rest of an evening's schedule. Every member of the cast and crew is vital to the success of the production and their time-keeping should be as precise as the running time of the programme.

Make certain, as a courtesy to your colleagues and to the efficiency of the production, that you are always ready to begin rehearsal, recording or transmission at the required time. There are often large numbers of cast and crew involved in a multi-camera programme production and your two minutes' late arrival can keep every one of them waiting.

Chatting to the artistes
Most front of camera people appreciate a friendly camera crew to modify a working atmosphere that often appears cold, technical and high pressure. Before a recording or transmission, a presenter may be mentally running through his or her lines and moves and preparing for their performance. Avoid trying to engage them in informal talk which may distract and disturb their concentration at this crucial time.

Transmission lights
Check the warning lights above doors leading to operational areas and DO NOT ENTER if a red or amber light is flashing or is on. This means the area is engaged in a transmission or recording. Wait for a blue light signifying the area is in rehearsal or line-up before entering. Check with the appropriate person (floor manager or stage manager, etc.) that your presence will not disrupt the rehearsal/recording.

Working in front of an audience
Wear appropriate clothing for the programme format. For example, a church service is a solemn act of worship and people may easily be offended if a camera operator appears to show disrespect for their beliefs by lounging around the church in jeans and sweat-shirt. At formal events you may be required by the production company to wear formal clothes. At pop shoots and concerts you may appear conspicuous if you are not wearing informal clothes.

As well as appropriate dress, remember that the audience is there to

Tampering with equipment

Do not idly fiddle with equipment altering settings and twiddling controls. They may have been pre-set for transmission. Imagine your reaction if returning to your camera you found the viewfinder picture adjusted and the shot box presets altered. Likewise do not remove the covers of electrical equipment or otherwise tamper with potentially dangerous equipment.

watch the performance. If their attention is distracted by your behaviour their reaction and response to the programme will be diminished. As well as practising an invisible visual technique try to be inconspicuous when working in front of an audience and, whenever it is possible, move out of their sightline to the performers.

Eyelines and monitors

Do not stand in front of a monitor and obstruct other production staff who may need to look at the studio output for visual cues. Never stand on cables or distract artistes by standing in their eyelines. You may be privileged to work with talented and famous performers but you will not help their concentration by standing in their eyelines and staring at them. Wear soft soled shoes in a studio to avoid noise and do not walk between cameras and line-up charts when the cameras are being aligned.

Sitting on props

A studio set or location that has been dressed with furniture and props is not a shop for you to idly browse through when not operating. Do not touch or move props, musical instruments, books or any other programme production item. Their position may have been carefully set for a shot or they may be valuable and/or fragile. Do not, unless you have permission, sit on furniture or move or use it for your personal convenience.

Multi-camera productions

Live

Multi-camera live transmissions are planned and rehearsed on the basic requirement of providing continuous camera coverage of an event. Breaks from the main production location may include pre-recorded inserts or other non 'live' material. For example, a general election results programme that is anchored and presented in a studio will have provision for studio and location interviews and the display of results plus OB coverage of local announcement of results combined with regional opt-outs to update on local situations. The whole package will be planned to sustain a continuous transmission of many hours.

The advantages of live multi-camera camerawork include:

- topicality – national events, sporting activity, etc., can be seen as they happen often with the added interest for the viewer of progressing to an unknown final score or result;
- live multi-camera coverage is often experienced as more immediate because it follows an event in real time rather than the edited 'recreated' time of discontinuous recording;
- live television is usually more economic in time and money and requires no post-production.

The disadvantages include:

- camera position, composition, staging of performers, production style (change of costume, scenery, lighting set-ups, etc.) and change of location are controlled by the running time of the event covered, a mixture of live and pre-recorded material allows greater flexibility;
- all production decisions have to be made instantaneously 'against the clock' rather than in the extended time available to consider editing decisions in post-production;
- the transmission schedule is controlled by the timing of the event.

Continuous recording as live

Recording a programme as live with no recording breaks (e.g. some game shows, music, discussion and debate) shares many of the characteristics of live television with the added advantage, if necessary, of rectifying any serious production problem by selective retakes after the main recording before the programme is transmitted.

There are difficulties with retakes in programmes such as sitcoms, where the audience may have heard the material many times, and with some game shows where retakes may involve asking contestants the same questions to get the same scored result as in the original recording. Usually, in such situations, the recording is stopped immediately to retake a sequence to prevent further production problems escalating.

Discontinuous recording

The advantage of this recording method is that fewer compromises are required by all crafts involved and all operational and performance mistakes can be corrected, but there is the need for everyone involved in the production to sustain concentration over long periods.

With live television, a complicated camera development is required to be perfect at the instant it is needed on transmission. In discontinuous recording, the same move may have to be repeated many, many times and in each retake it has to be perfect.

Pre-recorded inserts

To allow greater production diversity in continuous multi-camera coverage, sections of the programme may be pre-recorded before transmission/recording. This allows:

- participants to appear who may not be available at transmission/recording time;
- performers, cameras, sound, lighting, scenery, etc., to reposition for sequences that would not be possible in the timescale of the recorded/transmitted event;
- complex costume or make-up changes which would take too long in front of an audience;
- complex special effects or shots that require space not available on recording/transmission;
- time for scenery changes or other re-positionings to happen on actual recording or transmission.

Pre-recorded sequences require the usual continuity in performance, lighting, camera matching, props, etc., plus the ability to cut into (and out of) the main body of the programme.

Repetition, retakes and continuity

A retake is a repetition of a pre-rehearsed and pre-recorded sequence. Frequently, because of a production problem or an operational/performer mistake, the material is reworked to resolve the difficulty. In such situations, there may be a tendency for the size and angle of the shot to evolve in a different way from its original concept. Beware that continuity and cutting points with the preceding and succeeding shot may be lost.

193

Transmission and recording (1)

Pre-transmission checks

On most programmes there is a period prior to transmission or recording for a facilities check, an engineering line-up and to establish communications, make-up and costume check for presenters, a 'confidence' brief or running order check by the director to the cast and crew. This period is also used by all crew members to review their individual role in the production and a last chance for camera operators to query any point on which they are uncertain.

Although it is the director's role to provide all relevant information, it is easy for someone who has worked closely with the programme content for several weeks to assume that other people will know the material as well as they do. It is up to each member of the production crew to extract the information they require to do their job.

If, to solve a problem, you require a production change after the rehearsal has ended, always make the alteration through the director so that everyone in the production team is aware of the change even if you imagine it will have no knock-on effect. For example, instead of a prop or similar item being cleared to one part of the studio, you have asked for it to be stored in another area. That resolves your problem by providing more floor space for a quick clear, but it might make it impossible for sound, for example, to reposition a boom.

There is often a point in rehearsal where confusion arises and a problem appears insoluble. If you have a bright idea to clear this log-jam then make your suggestion but the camera crew should avoid bombarding the director with numerous conflicting ideas. A production that is 'directed from the floor' soon loses coherence and efficiency.

Prior to transmission and recording

The usual procedure is that all the crew and cast will be in position at least five minutes before transmission or recording time or longer if additional rehearsal or briefing is required before transmission/recording. The floor manager checks that everyone is present and that the studio doors are closed or the location is ready. Recording/transmission lights are switched on over any door leading into the studio or production area.

Silence is established in the studio and the director will check that each section is standing by before the final 30 seconds is counted to transmission or recording. A VTR identification clock will be run before a recording.

If there has been adequate rehearsal, the recording should provide no problems with the director cueing action and prompting everyone of upcoming events (e.g. 'X is now going to stand up' 'Y is going to move over to the demonstration table').

Any engineering breakdowns or equipment failures require the director to state clear alternatives to the rehearsed programme. An experienced camera crew will also mentally anticipate how the breakdown will affect their individual operation. It is usually advisable to be positive in an emergency and stick with the decision.

Preparation and concentration

Operating a television camera with precision requires an equal measure of preparation, concentration and anticipation. Good preparation provides the camera operator with the right equipment and advance information about shot detail to allow the best operational technique.

The camera operator's concentration is split between director's talkback, programme sound or commentary and what is happening outside the viewfinder as well the viewfinder image. There is a balance between paying attention to the immediate shot (e.g. framing and movement) while anticipating the next shot sequence. Thinking ahead and mentally preparing for what is about to happen, in effect, expands time in which to act when a fast sequence arrives. Do not concentrate continuously on the viewfinder picture. Be aware, especially on live events, of what is happening around you.

Some people are in a panic as soon as the tempo of shots increases and they are unable to ad-lib and think fast enough. They have reached their ceiling of concentration and allow the excitement and confusion of a situation to get in the way of thinking clearly and reacting.

This need not happen as most events covered by television are not unique and original. The order in which activities happen may be unknown but an appropriate shot structure should be in place for any occurrence. The first law of unrehearsed live television is: 'Plan for the unexpected and have contingency plans for any eventuality.'

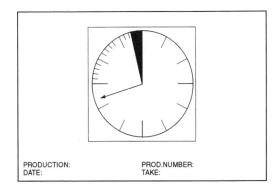

PRODUCTION: PROD.NUMBER:
DATE: TAKE:

VTR clock

The VTR clock is started 30 seconds (this varies depending on individual production company practice) before a recording. Three seconds before action the clock is faded out to provide 3 seconds of blank screen.

Transmission and recording (2)

As-directed procedures
As-directed procedures require fast reflexes and an awareness of the development in programme content. Sometimes a programme has sections which have a rehearsed shot structure interspersed with as-directed sequences. For a camera operator, the danger point is the junction between the two. It is easy to be caught in the as-directed mode of operation and therefore out of position for the scripted, numbered shot sequence.

Problems during the show
No live or 'recorded as live' programme will be without its problems or unexpected emergencies. Artistes miss their marks or are prevented from getting to a prearranged position and will need instant adjustment from the camera operator. Compensation will be needed for unexpected masking by people or structures. Sometimes flares, reflections or demonstration items held in the wrong position will throw a pre-rehearsed position or shot size. A cable trapped by a stage weight or a number of people standing on it can waste valuable time in repositioning and leave little or no time to get to a shot.

If a shot is missed, forget about it and make certain the next shot is there. Too often, a number of operational errors snowball because people spend time agonizing over their mistakes. If something is preventing you getting to a shot and you are unable to speak to the director, show on camera what the problem is. Help communicate other people's problems by showing on camera their circumstances (e.g. a stage manager who has lost talkback, equipment failure, etc.). If there is a production mistake on transmission, never spend time deciding on the cause. Get on with the next item and leave the post mortems until after the programme has finished.

Remember to follow up operational incidents (equipment malfunction, the wrong equipment, communication failures, operational procedures, etc.) that affected your work and check that they will not occur next time.

Making mistakes
Everyone makes mistakes including the director. Sometimes he/she will call for a shot that is obviously wrong. A camera operator in such circumstances will have to use his/her own individual initiative and a knowledge of the production to provide either the right shot or if they feel this will cause greater confusion, go to the directed shot.

A common example of this is when a camera is fitted with a prompter. The director clears the camera to the next shot while a presenter is still reading (as a voice-over) from the prompter even though they are no longer on shot on that camera. If the presenter has no script and the camera operator swings the camera away, the presenter will quite probably dry up and stop talking. If the camera operator sticks with the shot, the director will be concerned that the next sequence is in jeopardy. The solution in this case is to pull slowly away keeping the lens pointed at the presenter and hope it will become apparent to the floor manager or stage manager what the situation is and a script will be got to the artiste.

Silence
Reducing the amount of noise on recording/transmission can be achieved by:

- reducing cable noise – correctly wrapping other cables (e.g. lights, prompt, etc.) around the camera cable reduces the surface area of the cable dragging on the floor if no cable clearer is present;
- a well-maintained pedestal or other mounting to eliminate loose or rattly fixtures;
- wearing soft-soled shoes.

There is a trade-off between a fast move to achieve a specific shot against the amount of noise the move produces. If the noise is prohibitive then other ways must be found to achieve the shot.

VTR clearance
After a recording, there is a pause while VTR establish if they have a recording without fault or while the director decides if any section of the programme requires a retake. When the final clearance has been given, the de-rig can begin.

Outside broadcast preparation

Weather

Any pre-transmission or recording checks on an exterior OB must take into account potential changes in the weather. A check on the effects of any forecast of extreme weather must be assessed each day on exposed camera positions. If the programme is an extended coverage of an event, ensure that you have protective clothing for the worst conditions that could occur plus lens cloth and provision for creature comforts such as a drink of water, etc. You may be a long time up that hoist.

Check that any item you take to the camera position is securely anchored (especially when rigging a night cover) and will not be blown away if a wind should arise. Attach a harness, if working at a height, checking that the safety line is anchored. Take a quick look round on camera to see if any agreed shots are still available and are not masked by the unexpected arrival of people or vans, etc. Keep all equipment storage boxes dry.

Facilities check

Check out the standard production facilities on the camera – communications, mixed viewfinder, cue lights, 'clean' commentary (i.e. commentary with no crowd or atmosphere effects) and check the camera cover is secure and will not foul any part of the head or lens.

If the production involves reposition onto another cable or link during the programme, double check the radio talkback and agreed procedure when the repositions occur.

After the engineering checks are finished, the director will look over available shots if the programme format is largely as-directed. If you are new to the programme format, the camera supervisor and the director will have briefed you on your camera's role but never remain silent if you are unsure of the shots required.

It is also essential to check how cameras can cover for each other in the event of one camera becoming unserviceable. This is doubly important when cameras are widely scattered such as at sporting events like golf, horse-racing or motor-racing.

Coping with adverse weather

Wind buffeting the camera and causing an unsteady frame is unavoidable in many high camera positions. Either loosen off the shot or, if it is essential that it is shot on a long lens, the production will have to live with the subject being occasionally knocked out of optimum framing.

When to wipe rain off the front element is another problem faced in adverse weather. If the camera position provides a unique shot that must be used frequently, then at some time a wipe in-vision will occur. This distraction is preferable to a shot so degraded by rain droplets on the lens that it cannot be identified. Ask the director to 'cut away' from you so that you may clean the lens.

Operating a camera for a long period in cold weather requires gloves but frequently efficient warm gloves are too bulky for sensitive control of zoom and focus or for the adjustment of small 'needle' switches or controls that miniaturization has created. Some camera operators have found that battery-powered hand-warmers are a solution.

Offering shots

The balance between 'being directed' and offering shots is critical in many ad-lib situations. The camera operator at the point of action can frequently see much more than the director in the scanner but the director, previewing all the options, has a better overall view of shot structure. As we have discussed in developing the ability to assess the value of a shot, a camera operator must have a good grasp of the editorial priorities of the programme in order to offer an appropriate and useful shot. Often a camera operator can use talkback and show the director on camera what is available. When camera operators talking back to the control room can be picked up on programme sound (e.g. location interiors such as concerts, etc.) then shots can only be offered.

If possible, try to keep a framed shot at all times even though it may not be used. It allows camera faults to be quickly identified and if the shot is sufficiently 'non-descriptive' it may be a useful buffer shot in an emergency.

Single person camera operation

If operating a roving camera on a radio link, remember that you might have a restricted view of the immediate environment. With your eye glued to the monocular viewfinder, you may be unaware of potential hazards and should not attempt to walk backwards unassisted. Check that your operating position is not a danger to sports participants or spectators.

As-directed

Content

There are many programme formats where the broad outline of the content is known but where it is not feasible to rehearse the event. Sports events and audience discussion programmes, for example, have a known structure in which spontaneous and unknown incidents will occur. The camera coverage will have to be planned to cover all foreseeable eventualities. As we have discussed, there are a number of techniques that can be used and most of them can be illustrated by considering one genre of programme making – camera coverage of music.

Multi-camera music technique

Multi-camera music coverage on television covers a wide range of musical performances, production styles and visual preferences. At one end of the spectrum there are relays from concert halls of orchestral performances that are often tightly scripted and in general have an unobtrusive technique where the emphasis is on matching picture to content with the minimum of visual interpretation. In extreme contrast to this 'invisible' technique, there is multi-camera coverage of rock groups where an attempt is made to capture the atmosphere and excitement of a live event. Cutting rate and shots seek to reproduce the liveliness and frenzy of the rave.

Most of the following points are generalized and not all are applicable to the individual ways of presenting music on television within the wide range of production styles practised. They are an attempt to make the camera operator new to multi-camera music coverage aware of some aspects of production technique that he/she should consider when working on a continuous musical event.

The different methods of covering music continuously with multi-cameras without recording breaks or post-production can be grouped under the following headings:

- **Pre-scripted:** the whole performance is structured and shots assigned to each camera using a score or a break down of the number (e.g. the prom concerts or production numbers in variety shows). With complex music (e.g. an orchestral piece), the director, vision mixer and PA will be following the score with the PA calling shot numbers and bar numbers to allow camera moves such as pans, zooms and tracks to be precisely timed.
- **Camera scripted during rehearsal:** after looking on camera at the performance, shots are structured by the director and each shot numbered. This shot sequence is then exactly reproduced on the recording or transmission.
- **Top and tail:** the start and end of a musical piece is decided leaving the middle section to be as-directed.

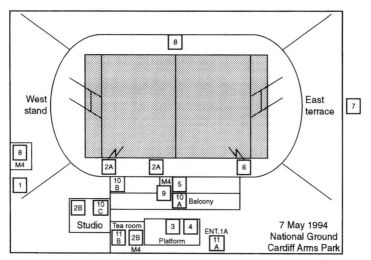

Camera positions

Camera 1	High W/A West Stand
Camera 2	Radio camera - touch line
Camera 3/4	Tight and wide cameras on gantry
Camera 5	Personality camera on commentary balcony
Camera 7	On 200ft hoist East Terrace
Camera 8	On North Terrace for reverse angle replays
Camera 9	Commentary balcony

ISO feeds

ISO 1	Cameras 2, 5, 6
ISO 2	Cameras 1 and 7
ISO 3	Camera 8 (reverse angle)
ISO 4	Main Mix
ISO 5	Camera 9 (Super Slo Mo)

Iso cameras

Sports multi-camera coverage developed the technique of continuously recording the output of individual cameras whilst the event was in progress as well as transmitting the normal intercut output of all cameras. The individually recorded cameras were available to be replayed into the broadcast in a slow motion mode at any time.

On some pop concert coverage one, two or all cameras are separately recorded and whilst the director may mix a rough cut during the performance, the final edited version will be compiled in post-production from the separate tapes of each camera's output (usually camcorders).

- **Assigned roles:** each camera is assigned one or two performers or instruments and offers a variety of shots connected with them. This gives the director a guaranteed appropriate shot at any time.
- **As-directed:** no shot structure is assigned and each camera operator is directed and/or offers a variety of shots checking that the shot they are offering is an alternative to the shot currently cut to line.

As-directed rehearsal

Pre-rehearsal
Check the following:

- Check that you have sufficient camera cable to allow movement to the limit of your designated floor area. Check that the cable is 'eighted' with nothing to impede its free run-out.
- Check your headset cable has the minimum length between headset and camera to avoid snagging the loop when working at speed.
- Check that you can be heard by the director and vision control on reverse talkback and that you can hear the director even when the group/orchestra is playing at maximum level. Use a headset that is designed to cut out ambient noise especially if you are positioned close to a sound monitor and turn down the programme sound feed on your headset.
- Check that your viewfinder is set correctly and that you have available a mixed feed of programme out.
- Check that you have something to mark up your crib card if specific shots are to be scripted.
- If there are no pre-scripted shots and the number is to be rehearsed and recorded as-directed, take the opportunity during the sound check to find all the possible permutations of shots available from your camera position. Practise any camera moves that may be possible and check that there is sufficient space to reposition and that the floor is free from sound/lighting cables that could prevent access.

In rehearsal
Check the following:

- If 'top and tail' shots are decided or a sequence is roughly blocked out, make easily readable shot descriptions on your crib card with any shot numbers that may be assigned.
- If a shot requires a very precise framing in a hurry, set the lens angle on the shot box (if fitted) and mark the camera position with lo-tack tape in the studio. Check that you will not constantly 'bump' over the tape on other shot development.
- If a number is to be shot as-directed, make a note of any individual solos and the order in which the solos occur so that you can offer appropriate shots *before* the event occurs. For example, '*the number opens on keyboard then vocal, then lead guitar, vocal ends on keyboard*'.
- Note where you are liable to cross another camera's shot when repositioning particularly at the opening and closing which may be wide.
- Check if the production convention on this recording is to accept cameras in shot or, as in standard orchestral concert coverage, shots are framed to avoid including them. Hand-held cameras working close to a

group can be especially intrusive (even wearing dark clothing) unless thought is given to the 'on-stage' camera repositioning in the performing area. A handheld position on the downstage end of a keyboard blocks out nearly every other shot of that artiste.

■ Check that you can recognize and know the standard position of every musical instrument in the orchestra.

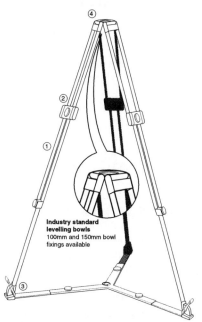

Industry standard
levelling bowls
100mm and 150mm bowl
fixings available

Lightweight tripod design requirements
1 rigid but light construction
2 positive safe clamping
3 secure (and long lasting) connection between tripod and   spreader
4 standard levelling bowl of 100 mm or 150 mm
5 compact foldaway of tripod with spreader attached

Other mounts
There are a number of foldaway light portable dollies which can be packed and transported in a car. They consist of track and a wheeled base on which a tripod can be securely mounted. They require a tracker and sufficient time to level the track before shooting.

Steadicam EFP is composed of a harness worn around the torso supporting the camera and detached viewfinder. When the operator walks, the device eliminates any roll or shake in the picture.

Clamps, gimbals and helicopter mounts provide stability when the camera is required to be mounted in moving vehicles, etc.

As-directed transmission

Recording/transmission
Check the following:

- Do not continually work so close to performers that you mask and inhibit other camera shots.
- Use your mixed viewfinder feed to monitor occasionally what shot is on air to avoid duplication.
- Do not hold and stick on the same shot if the director gives no indication that it will be taken – it is probably inappropriate, not wanted or available on another camera. Find another shot.
- Avoid continually offering 'abstract' shots (e.g. reflections, large defocused areas). Provide a proportion of information shots that clearly present the performers.
- Check out the potential for a move on shot before you are cut to and give a quick nod with the camera if the director asks if you have a move available.
- Whenever you can, pre-set the zoom focus for a zoom in.
- Do not risk injuring yourself, the public or production staff by reckless movement. Be aware of the distance between your lens and the performers especially on a wide-angle movement.
- Watch out for changes in the music. The end of a chorus or section may catch you offering the wrong shot (e.g. an instrumentalist may end just as you are cut to).
- Disguise a 'flat' zoom out by combining it with a pan, track or crab to give movement across the frame and a change in perspective.
- Match the speed of the shot development to the tempo or duration of the phrase or chorus.
- In very quiet music (quartets, piano recitals, etc.) be aware of camera and cable noise.
- In very up-tempo numbers, the cutting rate will increase. You may be directed to hold your shot for a fast intercut sequence. Wait to be released before repositioning.
- Never get between the conductor and the performers.
- When working close on a wide-angle lens, watch out for significant camera shadows on performers and instruments.
- If you frame up a close shot of hands on a keyboard, remember they may instantly spread or even move to another keyboard.
- Watch out for a sudden end to a number on rehearsal. You could be halfway through a move on transmission when you run out of music.
- If you are cut to when repositioning, freeze the shot if it is half usable. This is usually less obtrusive than trying to reframe.
- On many types of pop presentations, cameras will be cut to on the move

and cut away from on the move. Other multi-camera presentations (orchestral, etc.) require the camera to be steady at the end of a phrase or solo to allow mixes or cuts.

- On slow numbers, the director may only use mixes between cameras. The cue light will come on before your picture is fully faded up. Delay any camera movement until the mix has ended unless the director has requested the camera movement to be carried across the mix.
- During slow mixes, try to match your framing (use viewfinder mix) to the shot that is being mixed away from. For example, if the previous shot is framed left with space right, put your performer in the right of frame and try to leave space on the left.
- As in any other type of ad-lib camerawork try to position your body and viewfinder so that you end a camera move in a comfortable operating position even if this means starting the move awkwardly.
- Check that you are not winding or snagging the camera cable around the pedestal by continually panning or repositioning the same way.

And finally
- Listen to the director (even if the ambient noise level makes this difficult).
- Keep an eye on your crib card if you have marked shots.
- Watch your cue light before repositioning.
- Use your mixed viewfinder feed to check what other cameras are doing.
- Give way to (and get out of the way of) any camera that is on shot and moving.
- Listen to the music and anticipate changes in mood and content.
- On fast numbers, settle your framing as quickly a possible.

As in all good multi-camera camerawork, the appropriate shot can only be achieved by intelligent anticipation and a feeling for the performance.

It's a wrap

When is it a wrap?
Clearance for the de-rig will be given after a transmission or when all retakes of a recording have been cleared or the main recording has been checked by the VTR engineers. A 'spot check' of a video recording is a random replay at different points in the recording to check for technical quality. Sometimes this involves replaying sequences to check content for production purposes. This may trigger further retakes so it is never a wrap until all the technical and production content has been finally judged acceptable.

The importance of the de-rig
Although everyone wants to get away as fast as possible, the de-rig should be carried out in a safe and orderly way protecting members of the public, colleagues and equipment. Secondly, equipment should be carefully boxed, stored and checked that it is complete, serviceable and undamaged. Do not box or wrap wet equipment unless a label is attached which warns of its condition so that it can be dried out at base.

Equipment should be stored for easy access for the next programme or crew. Sorting out gear at the beginning of the day and finding that items are missing, in the wrong place or stored in a mess possibly causes more negative feelings in a camera crew than anything else that is going to occur that day.

Safety
Do not start a de-rig in areas where members of the public are still present. Cables being pulled can easily trip up people. Be especially careful in overhead de-rigs. Keep the area clear beneath the equipment to be de-rigged and policed before starting to dismantle.

Check that exit doors are unlocked and open to allow heavy equipment to be carried through and, if it is feasible, coordinate the use of trolleys to shift equipment back to stores. It is at de-rig time that the greatest cooperation is required between all concerned if safety and efficiency is not to be jeopardized. Your own safety as well as the safety of other production staff should not be endangered by the urge to get the de-rig over as quickly as possible.

Equipment
Often camera accessories and parts of the camera mountings have been rigged over several days. During the de-rig, they are rapidly dismantled and boxed. Make certain each item is replaced in its correct storage area and that nothing is missing when a box is closed. De-rigging at night on location is a particular problem but it should be remembered that the same equipment being hurriedly packed away tonight may be carried to a remote camera position tomorrow where a vital part may be found to be missing.

Hoisting equipment at a football ground

Although equipment may be protected from wet weather, storage boxes are often left out in exposed situations. On the de-rig, if cameras or lenses are packed away in wet boxes, the equipment will become damp and condensation build up in a lens. If this is the situation, the equipment should be returned to base or hirer with a label which indicates that 'this has been packed wet'. Attempt to keep equipment cases dry as well equipment.

Check that all components taken to a location or to a studio are returned. Someone on the crew should go round the site doing a last minute check to ensure that nothing has been left. Looking after the interests of the next user of the equipment may possibly ensure that you will not be cursing a missing lens cable when rigging.

Fault reporting

If a piece of equipment is found to be damaged or unserviceable, attach a label to the equipment (and to the outside of its storage box) and return it to the appropriate person for repair. Protect camera cable ends by fixing cable covers and coil monitor and power cables and tie off so that they can easily be run out on the next job. Check that cameras are switched off before using camera covers to avoid a build up of heat.

Television is a team activity and the de-rig time is traditionally the moment when the director thanks the crew. If anyone has helped you during the production, have the courtesy to acknowledge their contribution. Everyone appreciates encouragement and television cannot be made unless there is an input from a wide range of crafts and skills.

Finally

The word 'wrap' is apparently an old film term used at the end of the day to confirm that the film could be taken out of the camera. It is an abbreviation for 'wind, reel and print'. Wrap confirms that the day's work has finished.

Composition

What is composition?

Composition is commonly defined as arranging all the visual elements in the frame in a way that makes the image a satisfactory and complete whole. Integration of the image is obtained by the positioning of line, mass, colour and light in the most pleasing arrangement.

This definition is a start in the examination of composition but it does prompt further questions. What counts as 'satisfactory and complete' and is 'pleasing arrangement' an objective or subjective judgement?

Many television camera operators know, through many years of experience, exactly how to position the lens in space or choose a different lens angle in order to improve the appearance of the shot. They are either working to inherited craft values of what is good composition or they are repositioning and juggling with the camera until they intuitively feel that they have solved that particular visual problem.

Frequently there is no time to analyse a situation and the only thing to fall back on is experience. Compositional experience is the result of many years of solving visual problems. Good visual communication is not a gift from heaven but is learnt from finding out in practice what does and does not work.

Visual communication

Effective communication can be carried out in many languages. The very basic requirement for communication between individuals is their need to speak in the same language. Using a visual medium is choosing to communicate through pictures and ultimately the visual language used must be compatible with human perception. Although aesthetic fashion influences composition, good visual communication rests on an understanding of the psychology of perception.

Man has specific ways of visually understanding the world. If a composition is arranged to work in accord with those underlying visual principles, then there is more chance of the visual information being understood and enjoyed. If the composition conflicts with the pattern of visual expectation, then confusion and rejection of the message may occur.

These perceptual phenomena have been intuitively understood and employed by painters of great works of art for centuries. Their work engages our attention and is visually satisfying. These masterpieces still communicate and satisfy because they are structured for visual understanding and their viewers respond intuitively to the underlying reinforcement of the visual system.

Visual coherence is related to the inherent characteristics of perception. Seeing is not simply a mechanical recording by the eye. Understanding the nature of an image is initially accomplished by the perceptual grouping of

Place de la Concorde (Vicomte Ludovic Lepic and his Daughters) (1875) Degas.
For many centuries the aim of composition in Western painting was to weld all the elements of the painting into a pictorial unity – to achieve balance. The concept of dissonance – to deliberately offset compositional elements in order to create visual tension – only entered composition technique to any extent in the nineteenth century.

significant structural patterns. One of the aims of good composition is to find and emphasize structural patterns that the mind/eye can easily grasp.

Seeing an image as the camera sees it requires training the eye and brain. Understanding how we see is the first step in controlling visual communication.

Perception

How the mind responds to visual information
Much of the theory of perceptual characteristics has been influenced by Gestalt psychologists. Gestalt is the German word for 'form' and these psychologists held the view that it is the overall form of an image that we respond to and not the isolated visual elements it contains. In general, we do not attempt to perceive accurately every detail of the shapes and objects perceived but select only as much as will enable us to identify what we see.

Characteristics of perception
There have been many experiments and many theories about perception, some of which appear to be contradictory. Most agree that perception is instantaneous and not subject to extended judgement. It is an active exploration rather than a passive recording of the visual elements in the field of view and is selective and personal.

The mind makes sense of visual elements by grouping elements into patterns. Any stimulus pattern tends to be seen in such a way that the resulting structure is as simple as the given conditions permit. Making sense of visual stimuli involves testing by hypothesis. An unfamiliar or ambiguous image may be assigned a tentative definition until further information becomes available (see opposite 'duck or rabbit?').

In searching for the best interpretation of the available visual data we utilize a number of perceptual shorthand techniques which include organization of similar shapes and similar size. Shapes that are similar are grouped and form a pattern that creates eye motion. A 'good' form to be striking and easy to perceive is simple, regular, symmetrical and may have continuity in time. A 'bad' form without these qualities is modified by the perceiver to conform to 'good' form qualities.

Good composition reinforces the manner in which the mind organizes information. It emphasizes those elements such as grouping, pattern, shape and form that provide the viewer with the best method of 'reading' the image smoothly and efficiently. If there is friction in visual movement of the eye across the frame, if there are areas of the image which stop the eye dead, then an unsatisfactory feeling is unconsciously experienced and in an extreme form will end the attention of the viewer. There is a fine dividing line between teasing the eye with visual ambiguities and losing the interest of the audience.

Summary
The mind tends to group objects together into one single comprehensive image. The mind sees patterns; composition can enhance or facilitate this

Perception is making sense of an image – searching for the best interpretation of the available data. The mind sees patterns and searches for the best interpretation. A perceived object is therefore an hypothesis to be tested against previous experience. If it looks like a duck then it is a duck. That is, until we see it as a rabbit.

tendency or it can prevent it. A knowledge of how the mind groups visual elements is therefore a valuable tool for good communication.

Visual design

Control of composition

Control of composition is achieved by the ability to choose the appropriate camera technique such as viewpoint, focal length of lens, lighting and exposure in addition to employing a range of visual design elements such as balance, colour contrast, perspective of mass/line, etc.

A well-designed composition is one in which the visual elements have either been selectively included or excluded. The visual components of the composition must be organized to engage the viewer's attention. A starting point is often to follow the old advice to simplify by elimination, and to reduce to essentials in order to create an image that has strength and clarity.

Emphasizing the most important element

Composition involves drawing attention to the main subject and then making it meaningful, but often a shot can be selected on a visual decision which ignores all but one part of the image. The poor compositional relationship between this area and the total frame may only become apparent after the event has been recorded. One of the more obvious mistakes therefore is not to see the whole picture but only that part which has initially attracted interest.

There is a puzzling piece of advice about camerawork that urges all students to 'Look before you see'. In essence this simply means to look at the overall image and at its underlying pattern before concentrating too much on the main subject. Developing a photographic eye is giving attention to all visual elements within the field of view and not simply selecting those elements that initially attract attention. With experience comes the ability to visualize the appearance of a shot wherever the lens is positioned, without the need to continually move the camera in order to look through the viewfinder to find out what the shot will look like.

Before deciding camera position, lens angle, framing, etc., it is worth considering the following questions.

- What is the purpose of the shot?
- Is the shot fact or feeling? Will the image attempt to be factual and objective and allow the viewers to draw their own conclusions or is it the intention to persuade or create an atmosphere by careful selection?
- In what context will the shot be seen? What precedes, what follows?
- What will be the most important visual element in the shot?

The best viewpoint is that lens position in space which emphasizes the main subject. Make certain that the eye is attracted to the part of the frame that is significant and avoid conflict with other elements in the frame.

A balanced composition

The aim of a balanced composition is to integrate all the visual factors such as shape, colour and location so that no change seems possible. The image achieves unity as a result of all its essential elements.

An unbalanced composition appears accidental and transitory. There is no organizational pattern and any part of the frame could be masked with no loss of communication. There is insufficient arrangement of shapes to assist in grasping the reason for the image. It is ambiguous and unable to hold any visual attention beyond the initial search for understanding.

Emphasis

To emphasize the most important element, use subject size, position, selective focus, colour, brightness and relationship to background to focus attention. Use either contrast of tone, colour and form to stress the differences between visual elements in the shot and to balance out active relationships between opposed elements.

Check the following:

- The purpose of the shot is understood.
- The main subject is identified.
- Arrange the camera parameters (lens position, angle, height, etc.) to emphasize the principal interest.
- Use leading lines to point to the main subject.
- Examine supporting visual interest within the frame and use framing and lens position to maximize their support for the main subject and to eliminate or subdue competing areas of interest. Offset the dominant interest and balance this with a less important element.
- Avoid corners for principal information and keep the attention within the picture space.
- Simplify the image if possible by reducing to essentials.

Reading an image

Taking the eye for a walk

Although perceptually we have an awareness of a large field of view, only a small segment can receive our full attention. It is necessary for the eye to make small eye movements continuously called 'saccades' in order to scan an object. It is similar to the eye movement necessary to examine each word of text on a page.

In the West, a page of text has a structure to allow the information to be read out in the correct sequence. Starting from the top left of the page to bottom right there is no misunderstanding the path the eye must traverse. There is no similar learnt procedure for scanning an object or image unless a deliberate perceptual route is built in which channels the eye movement along a pre-planned path.

Emphasizing the main subject involves control of the eye movement across the frame. The eye travels the line of least resistance and in its movement around the frame it is similar to a pin-ball bouncing off different obstacles before being forced by the designer of the composition to end up at the main subject of interest. An interesting composition allows the eye movement moments of repose and this stop/start journey creates visual rhythm. The strongest rhythms occur in patterns. Organization of the image requires the eye to be shown new unsuspected spatial relationships between similar shapes, similar tone, texture or colour.

Fill the frame if possible with interest and avoid large plain areas that are there simply because of the aspect ratio of the screen. If necessary, mask off part of the frame with a feature in the shot to give a more interesting composition and to emphasize the most important element in the frame.

The normal scanning of an image from left to right appears to give less weight to an object on the left than if it is placed on the right of the frame.

Scale

A great deal of our understanding of the physical nature of the world around us is achieved by comparison of size. We often achieve recognition of an object by its proportions and its normal size relationship with other objects. A 3 m high shirt button would require a moment to categorize before we had established a new frame of reference, whereas it would be instantly recognized as a button if it was at a normal size.

The human figure is the most easily recognised and most often used in size comparisons. An over-used technique is the familiar zoom out from a presenter to reveal that he or she is located at the top of an enormous bridge, building or natural feature. This shows scale but requires a great deal of 'dead' visual between the start and the end of the shot, the only two images that are being compared. This is shown in the bottom figure opposite.

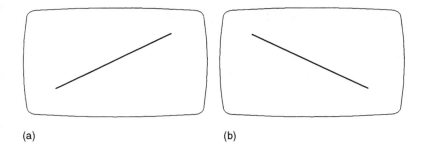

(a) (b)

Reading an image left to right
Because of the Western tradition of scanning text from left to right, the movement of the line in (a) appears to be travelling uphill whereas the movement of the line in (b) appears to be going downhill.

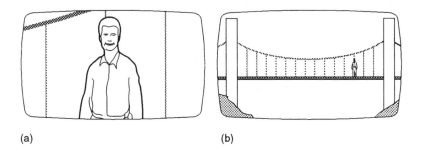

(a) (b)

The proximity of one subject to another allows a frame of reference to be established and associations and comparisons to be made. The same factors are at work with adjacent shots allowing development of new information or continuity in story telling. Proximity of subject allows judgements of scale and connections. Proximity in time allows continuity and the relationship between visual references which constructs an argument.

A frame around an image seals off most of its frame of reference and can cause problems in recognition unless it is a very familiar object such as the human face or figure. Most people have been visually tricked by a close shot of a model replica when the camera pulls back to reveal it is as a fraction of the size of the original. Some objects need to be set in context in order to communicate clearly without any confusion of their identity.

A composition can achieve an impact by introducing an indication of scale or size comparison. It may be simply contrasting one subject with another – a small child in a large space or an ocean liner being pulled by a small tug. Viewers unfamiliar with the subject depicted may need some indication of size by comparison with a known object.

215

Grouping and organization

Perceptual response
There is a perceptual tendency to group and organize items together to form a cluster of shapes to make up a total image that can be fully comprehended in one attentive act. Some elements are grouped together because they are close to each other. Others are bound together because they are similar in size, direction or shape. Composition must therefore aim to create a unifying relationship between the visual elements of an image in order to feed the perceptual system with patterns that can be easily assimilated by the viewer.

Similarity by proximity
Grouping objects together because they are near to each other in the frame is the simplest method of visual organization. One of mankind's oldest examples of perceptual grouping is probably the patterns imposed on isolated and unconnected stars to form the signs of the Zodiac. Grouping a foreground and a background object by proximity can achieve a coherent design in a composition.

Proximity of objects in the frame can also create relationships that are unwanted (e.g. the example of objects behind people's heads which appear on the screen as head-wear).

Similarity of size
Same size objects in a frame will be grouped together to form one shape or pattern. The most common example of this principle is the grouping and staging of crowd scenes.

This grouping by size and proximity can be used in a reverse way to emphasize one person in a crowd scene by isolating the individual so that they cannot be visually grouped with the crowd (see opposite).

Because of the assumed similarity of size between individual people, staging people in the foreground and in the background of a shot allows visual unity in the perception of similar shapes and also an effective impression of depth indicated by the diminished image size of the background figure.

Similarity by closure
Searching for coherent shapes in a complex image, human perception will look for, and if necessary, create simple shapes. The more consistent the shape of a group of visual elements, the more easily it can be detached from a confusing background. Straight lines will be continued by visual projection, curved lines that almost form a circle will be mentally completed.

A popular use of this principle is the high angle shot looking down on a seething crowd moving in one direction while the principal figure makes a desperate journey through the crowd in the opposite direction. We are able to keep our attention on the figure because of the opposing movements and also because we mentally project their straight-line movement through the crowd. The principal figure would soon be absorbed within the crowd if they frequently changed direction.

Similarity of colour
Objects grouped by colour is another effective method of compositional organization. Uniforms and team sports wear are linked together even if they are scattered across the frame. Identically coloured dance costumes for the chorus in musicals are used to structure movement and to empha- size the principals dressed in a contrasting colour scheme.

The eye is instantly attracted to the 'odd one out'

Spatial organization

Sp ati l org anizati on isthe vit alfacto rin a noptic alm essage
Spatial organization is the vital factor in an optical message

- Understanding the nature of an image is initially accomplished by the perceptual grouping of significant structural patterns.
- Grouping objects together because they are near to each other in the frame is the simplest method of visual organization.
- Same size objects in a frame will be grouped together to form one shape or pattern.
- Searching for coherent shapes in a complex image, human percep- tion will look for, and if necessary, create simple shapes.
- Objects grouped by colour is another effective method of composi- tional organization.

The edge of the frame

Frame – an invisible focus of power
At the same moment that we perceive the identity of an object within a frame, we are also aware of the spatial relationship between the object and the frame. Perceptual psychologists have established that observers unconsciously imply potential motion to a static object depending on its position within the frame. A single object will either be 'pulling' towards the centre or to the corners and/or edge of the frame. The edge of the frame and also the shape of the frame have therefore a strong influence on composition.

The pattern of a shot is more than the relationship between size, shape, brightness differences and colour contrast of the visual elements; there is also a hidden structural pattern created by the frame. An image contains more than the visible elements that make up the shot, and these 'unseen' aspects can exert a powerful influence on the composition.

The frame's 'field of forces' exerts pressure on the objects contained within the frame and any adjustment to the composition of a group of visual elements will be arranged with reference to these pressures. This strong perceptual awareness of the invisible reference points of the frame can be demonstrated by examining a simple medium close-up shot framed with normal headroom. If the camera is panned up, a point is reached, with a large amount of headroom, where the subject appears to be slipping out of the bottom of the frame. Panning down to create a shot with no headroom produces the feeling that the subject is leaving through the top of the frame.

Different placement of the subject within the frame's field of forces can therefore induce a perceptual feeling of equilibrium, of motion or of ambiguity.

Viewfinder as an editing tool
The viewfinder is selective – it excludes as well as includes visual material. The frame of a shot creates an 'enclosure', a fence that separates the image from its environment – a bright rectangle surrounded by blackness. A video viewfinder image is seen by the camera operator in very different conditions to the television viewer. Viewfinders display images that deviate in significant ways to our normal experience of perception (see Monochrome viewfinders, page 250).

Static viewpoint
Human perception is unable to be static and as continuously focused and attentive on a selected portion of a field of view as a camera (see bottom figure on page 217). Attention, after a short period of time, will inevitably be captured by movement or noise from visual subjects outside the selected zone of view. The camera can continue its static unblinking gaze until altered by the camera operator.

The influence of the frame

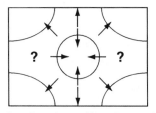

A field of forces can be plotted to show the position of rest or balance (centre and mid-point on the diagonal between corner and centre) and positions of ambiguity where the observer cannot predict the potential motion of the object and therefore an element of perceptual unease is created. Whether the object is passively attracted by centre or edge or whether the object actively moved on its own volition depends on content.

The awareness of motion of a static visual element with relation to the frame is an intrinsic part of perception. It is not an intellectual judgement tacked on to the content of an image based on previous experience, but an integral part of perception.

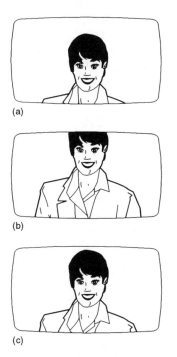

There is a strong perceptual awareness of the invisible reference points of the frame. (a) If the camera is panned up, a point is reached, with a large amount of headroom, where the subject appears to be slipping out of the bottom of the frame. (b) Panning down to create a shot with no headroom produces the feeling that the subject is leaving through the top of the frame. (c) There is a point of equilibrium where the subject is balanced against the invisible forces of the frame.

219

Frames within frames

The aspect ratio of the frame and the relationship of the subject to the edge of frame has a considerable impact on the composition of a shot. Historically, in print photography, there have been two preferred aspect ratios – the landscape format, which has a predominantly horizontal shape, and the portrait format, which has the shortest side of the rectangle as the base.

Standard TV aspect ratio is 4:3 which is gradually being replaced by a 16:9 shape (see Aspect ratio, page 224) which retains the same frame shape whatever the subject. One simple way of breaking up the repetition of the same projected shape and of adjusting the aspect ratio to suit the content is to create compositions that involve frames within frames. The simplest device is to frame a shot through a doorway or arch which emphasizes the enclosed view and plays down the enclosing frame and wall. Another popular convention is to include in the top of the frame of a wide shot a bit of 'dingle dangle' – a tree branch often supported out of vision by a gallows arm or a similar wooden structure.

By using foreground masking, an irregular 'new' frame can be created which gives variety to the constant repetition of the screen shape. A frame within a frame breaks the monotony and also provides the opportunity for compositional diversity. The familiar over-the-shoulder two shot is in effect a frame within a frame image as the back of the foreground head is redundant information and is there to allow greater attention on the speaker and the curve of the head into the shoulder gives a more visually attractive shape to the side of the frame.

A second frame

A frame within a frame emphasizes the principal subject by enclosing it with a secondary frame and often gives added depth to the shot. There are a number of ways of creating a secondary frame including the use of semi-silhouette foreground objects, or windows or mirrors that divide the frame into a smaller rectangle. If this is badly done, there is the risk of creating a divided frame with equal and competing areas of interest. Strong vertical and horizontal elements can create two images which are unconnected and provide no visual direction and allow ambiguity in the viewer's mind as to which image is dominant.

The other compositional problem occurs with the relationship between the edge of frame and the frame within a frame shape. If these are similar and the inside shape follows the frame line then there is simply a contraction of the screen size. Divided interest in a frame can be created by the over-emphasis of visual elements that are not the principal subject or there may be indecision as to what is the principal subject.

Frame within a frame

The 'over-the-shoulder two shot' was in use as early as 1914 and still appears in most narrative films. The back of the artiste is redundant information and is there to allow greater attention to be focused on the speaker. The curve of the foreground head gives a more visually attractive shape to the side of the frame.

Divided interest

NEWS-O RAMA

The most common example of divided interest is the newsreader/presenter shot framed in one half of the shot and 'balanced' by a logo or generic graphic enclosed in a 'window' in the other half of the shot. The two images are usually not visually integrated and fight each other for attention. Often the newsreader appears to be uncomfortably near one edge of the frame being pushed out by the dominant position of the graphic.

It is almost impossible to achieve visual unity with a combination of presenter plus a strong graphic 'window' unless the presenter occupies at least three quarters of the frame and can overlap the graphics window. A 50/50 split in the frame is often seen in news bulletins reflecting journalistic preferences formed by experiences of text page newspaper layouts.

Electronic graphics have a generous surround of 'non-action' area which was once required because some domestic television sets were overscanned and the margins of the transmitted picture were not seen. Essential information such as text (name supers, telephone numbers, etc.) was automatically kept out of this border. Pictures derived from cameras have no such automatic control and can and do produce images that overlap the action area boundary. Consequently many factual programmes allow electronic graphic material to push presenters off the screen or squeeze them to the edge of the frame in composite shots.

221

Closed and open frames

Closed frame

One of the early Hollywood conventions was to compose the shot so that it contained the action within the frame and then, by cutting, followed the action in distinct, complete shots. Each shot is self-contained and refers only to what is seen and shuts out or excludes anything outside of the frame. This is the closed frame technique and it is structured to keep the attention only on the information that is contained in the shot. If there is any significant reference to a subject outside of the frame, then there is a cut or a camera move to bring the referred subject into frame.

This convention is still followed in many different types of programme format. For example, in a television cooking demonstration, the demonstrator in medium close-up (MCU) may refer to some ingredient they are about to use which is outside the frame. Either the MCU is immediately loosened to reveal the ingredient or there is a cutaway to a close-up of the ingredient.

Open frame

The open frame convention allows action to move in and out of the frame. An example would be a character in a hallway who would be held on screen while in dialogue with someone who is moving in and out of frame entering and leaving various rooms which are unseen. Their movement while they are out of frame is implied and not cut to as separate shots. The open frame does not disguise the fact that the shot is only a partial viewpoint of a much larger environment. This technique considers that it is not necessary for the audience to see the reality beyond the shot in order to be convinced that it exists.

Limited depth and perspective indicators

The viewfinder image has limited depth indicators of overlap, size changed by movement, mass and line perspective and aerial perspective. Human perception with binocular vision allows depth and size judgements to be made by head and body movement. The perspective of the viewfinder picture can be entirely different from the impression of depth experienced by an observer beside the camera.

Frame and subject size

Filling the frame with the principal subject appears to be, at first sight, an efficient way of eliminating irrelevant detail. A close shot concentrates the attention and avoids the complications of integrating other visual elements into a cohesive composition. The closer you get to the main subject, the easier it is for the viewer to understand the priorities of the shot and the quicker it is for the camera operator to find the optimum framing. The close

Levelling up the head

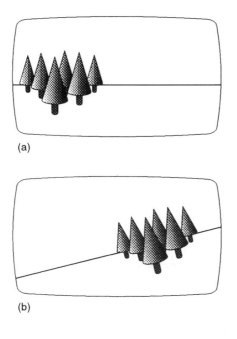

(a)

(b)

The edge of frame as a reference
Because of the strong influence of the frame edges, they tend to act as an immediate perceptual reference point to horizontal and vertical lines in the image. The camera needs to be levelled to produce horizon or equivalent lines parallel to the bottom of the frame and vertical lines parallel to the side of the frame unless a canted picture is required (a Dutch tilt). If this does not happen, any camera movement will produce greater or lesser distortion of the vertical and horizontal elements.

A tripod and camera can be set up on uneven ground so that it appears in the viewfinder as if the horizon is level but a canted horizon may be produced if the camera is panned left or right. When first setting up the camera on a tripod always level up using the spirit level in the pan/tilt head as a reference.

shot is efficient in communication and often, because it only requires a small area to be designed and lit, economical in production.

Aspect ratio

The ratio of the longest side of a rectangle to the shortest side is called the aspect ratio of the image. The aspect ratio of the frame and the relationship of the subject to the edge of frame has a considerable impact on the composition of a shot. Historically, as film progressed from the Academy aspect ratio of 1.33:1 (a 4:3 rectangle) to the advent of digital production and reception, the opportunity was taken to convert to a TV widescreen ratio of 1.78:1 (a 16:9 rectangle).

Screen size and resolution

Dr Takashi Fujio at the NHK research laboratories carried out research on viewers' preference for screen size and aspect ratio and his findings largely formed the justification for the NHK HDTV parameters. The research suggests that the majority of viewers preferred a wider aspect ratio than 4:3 plus a larger screen with a corresponding increase in resolution, brightness and colour rendition. His conclusion was that maximum involvement by the viewer was achieved with a 5:3 aspect ratio viewed at 3 to 4 picture height distance. Normal viewing distance (in Japan) was 2 to 2.5 m, which suggested an ideal screen size of between 1 m × 60 cm and 1.5 m × 90 cm. Sitting closer to a smaller screen did not involve the viewer in the action in the same way.

Screen size

Someone sitting in a front-row cinema seat may have as much as 58° of their field of view taken up by the screen image where the viewing distance is 0.9 times the picture height. This can be reduced to as little as 9.5° when the same screen is viewed from the back row of the cinema at a viewing distance of 6.0 times the picture height. The average television viewer typically sees a picture on a 51 cm diagonal tube (21 inches) no wider than 9.2° at a viewing distance of 6.3 times the picture height. Human vision is aware of about 200° in the horizontal plane (although only fully concentrating on a small proportion of this) and therefore the proportion of the visual area of a 51 cm screen in the home occupies only 0.4% of the maximum field of view of the viewer.

TV or cinema pictures with rapid movement produce no visual fatigue if viewed at a distance equal to about 4 times picture height although the resolution of the viewed image should be good enough to allow a viewing distance of 3 times the picture height. As the screen image and resolution is increased, most people prefer a 5:3 aspect ratio, although when viewing landscapes and sport many people favoured a 2:1 ratio.

Film and TV aspect ratios

There are compositional advantages and disadvantages in using different aspect ratios. Widescreen is good at showing relationships between people

Aspect ratios of film and television frames

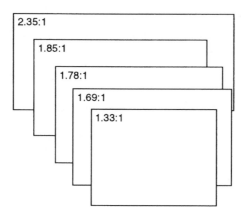

and location. Sports coverage benefits from the extra width in following live events. Composing closer shots of faces is usually easier in the 4:3 aspect ratio but, as in film during the transition to widescreen framing during the 1950s, new framing conventions are being developed and old 4:3 compositional conventions that do not work are abandoned. The shared priority in working in any aspect ratio is knowing under what conditions the audience will view the image. The current mixture of formats is transmitted and viewed with a variety of smaller or larger black bands around the image depending on the format of the receiver.

Transfer between film and television

Many television productions are shot on film and there is a continuous search for a worldwide video standard to allow a transparent transfer of film to video and video to film. There have also been many proposals for a high definition television format and international pressure for agreement on a standard HDTV system. One solution suggested is to have a HDTV acquisition format of 24 frame, 1080 line, progressive scanning video system that would allow high definition video productions suitable for transfer to film for cinema presentation. It would be the video equivalent of 35 mm film and allow a seamless translation to all other standard definition (SD) video formats.

Transitional period

The worldwide changeover period from mass viewing on 4:3 analogue sets to mass viewing on 16:9 digital monitors, and therefore mass programme production for 16:9 television, will take many years. The transition period will require a compromise composition (see Widescreen composition, page 230) and many broadcasters are adopting an interim format of 14:9 to smooth the transition from 4:3 to full 16:9. But the compositional problems do not end there. The back library of 4:3 programmes and films is enormous and valuable and will continue to be transmitted across a wide range of channels in the future. The complete image can be viewed on a 16:9 screen if black bars are displayed either side of the frame. They can be viewed by filling the full width of the 16:9 display at the cost of cutting part of the top and bottom of the frame or, at the viewer's discretion, they can be viewed by a non-linear expansion of picture width, progressively distorting the edges of the frame to fill the screen.

The same size camera viewfinder used for 4:3 aspect ratio is often switched to a 16:9 display. This in effect gives a smaller picture area if the 14:9 'shoot and protect' centre of frame framing is used and makes focusing and following distant action more difficult. Also, the majority of video camera operators are probably the only viewers still watching colour TV pictures in monochrome. Colour is not only essential to pick up individuals in sports events such as football, where opposing team shirts may look identical in monochrome, but in all forms of programme production colour plays a dominant role in composition.

Compromise composition

From a camera operator's point of view, the biggest difficulty during the transition period is attempting to find a compositional compromise between the two aspect ratios. If a 16:9 image is transmitted in a letter-box format (i.e. a black band at the top and bottom of the frame when viewed on a 4:3 TV set) then all shots can be framed with respect to the 16:9 border. Some companies, however, have adopted a half-way stage of transmitting the 16:9 format in a cropped format of 14:9 in an effort to make the letter-box effect less intrusive for 4:3 viewers. This technique loses a portion of the left and right hand edge of the frame and may destroy the balance of a 16:9 image. It is an experience that viewers, watching widescreen films shown on TV, have been subject to for many years, modified by the limited remedial efforts of the widescreen image being panned and reframed via telecine on transmission. There is very little satisfactory compromise that can be made in an attempt to compose for both formats at the same time if they are viewed full screen on different aspect ratio screens.

Composition problems will continue while 16:9 and 4:3 simultaneous productions are being shot during the analogue/digital changeover. They neither take full advantage of the width of 16:9 nor do they fit comfortably with the old 4:3 shape. Possibly ten years of dual format compromise production will then join the back library and be transmitted from then on. The only safe solution is the 'protect and save' advice (see page 231) of putting essential information in the centre of frame, but that is a sad limitation on the compositional potential of the widescreen shape.

Dual format CCDs

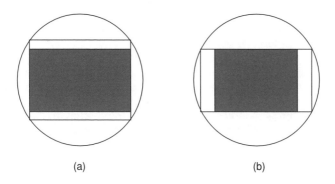

(a)   (b)

The transition between 4:3 aspect ratio television and the conversion to 16:9 has produced an interim generation of dual format cameras. Different techniques are employed to use the same CCD for both formats. If a CCD block design is optimized for the 4:3 shape and is then switched to the 16:9 format, lines are discarded at the top and bottom of the frame in order to convert the image area to a 16:9 shape (a). As 4:3 working occupies the same area of the CCD as a standard 4:3 camera there is no change in angle of view or resolution. When switched to 16:9, however, there is a reduction in resolution and a decrease in vertical angle of view. If the CCD block is optimized for 16:9 format working (b), and is then switched to a 4:3 aspect ratio, the image area now occupies a smaller area than a standard 4:3 CCD image (a), and therefore has a reduced resolution and a reduction in horizontal lens angle. Some dual format camera manufacturers claim that it is not possible to satisfy the competing demands of both formats; one of the formats will be compromised in resolution or change in lens angle. Other camera manufacturers claim that they can offer a switchable camera that retains the same number of pixels in both formats.

227

Why conversion is needed

Viewers will be watching a mixture of aspect ratios on different aspect ratio receivers for the foreseeable future. 16:9 programme material could be transmitted to fill the screen of a 16:9 receiver and presented in a 'letterbox' format (black bands top and bottom of frame) on a 4:3 receiver. 4:3 programmes could be transmitted to fill the 4:3 screen of receivers and presented with black bands left and right of the frame on a 16:9 receiver. In the UK, however, there is a great deal of audience resistance to watching pictures with black borders. To avoid this, Cinemascope films for many years have been panned and scanned so that although the vertical information fits the 4:3 screen, the horizontal information is reframed to include any vital aspects of the composition. French TV viewers accept Cinemascope films transmitted in their original aspect ratio with the corresponding large black borders at top and bottom of the frame.

Electronically, a picture could be cropped or expanded to fit any shape, but this would lead to loss of information, loss of resolution and possibly picture distortion when images are stretched to fit a different shape to their production aspect ratio.

Some type of aspect ratio conversion has to be employed either before the programme is transmitted or at the receiver. Several countries utilize a compromise aspect ratio of 14:9 to bridge the gap between 16:9 production demands and 4:3 receivers. The ratio converter chops out portions of the left and right of the frame for 4:3 viewers who watch with a small black border top and bottom of the frame.

16:9 set-top aspect ratio conversion is under the control of the viewer who can select full frame with black side curtains left and right of the image when watching a 4:3 transmission or partial expansion of the 4:3 frame to a 14:9 shape when information is equally lost at top and bottom of frame. Another set-top aspect ratio conversion option is for the viewer to 'zoom' in on a portion of the 4:3 frame so that it fills the 16:9 frame. Part of the 4:3 picture will now be lost at the top or bottom of the screen or the picture can be positioned to distribute the lost parts of the image. Note that essential parts of the 4:3 image will vary depending on shot content. Picture content of course changes with each shot. Some set-top aspect ratio converters also provide for non-linear distortion of the horizontal part of the 4:3 frame to fit a 16:9 TV set.

This mixture of aspect ratio formats will always need conversion unless the unlikely step is taken to scrap all 4:3 programme material when everyone has converted to 16:9 reception. Black and white movies continue to be popular forty years after the introduction of colour television. The decision to change the TV aspect ratio was not simply a technological change, it has and will have continuous programme making and programme watching implications.

Aspect ratio conversion at the receiver

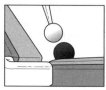

(a) 4:3
Original framing

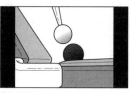

(b) 4:3
Picture on 16:9 receiver

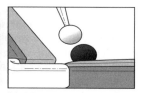

(c) 4:3
Stretched to fill 16:9 receiver
screen

(d) 4:3
Centre of frame zoomed to
fill 16:9 receiver

(e) 4:3
Centre of frame zoomed to
fill 16:9 receiver

It is a paradox that in some countries, viewers actively dislike the black band side curtains (b) when watching a 4:3 picture on a 16:9 receiver and appear to prefer either the distortion introduced when stretching the 4:3 picture to fit the 16:9 screen (c) or to crop the top and bottom of the transmitted image (d). Unless the viewer constantly monitors and adjusts this last option (zooming), subsequent shots may suffer loss of essential information (e).

Some 16:9 TV receivers have a progressive distortion (anamorphic) facility to stretch a 4:3 transmitted image. This progressive rate of expansion across the screen results in the snooker example above of the shape of the ball changing as it travels across the frame. It is ironic that decades of research and development expended on producing perfect electronic images that are free from geometric distortion can be negated by the touch of a button on a channel changer. Weather presenters change shape from fat to thin as they walk across the frame, or shoot out their arm to double its apparent length when this aspect ratio conversion option is selected.

Aspect ratio conversion decisions are taken out of the viewer's control when 4:3 material is integrated into 16:9 productions. The director of the programme then has the choice either to show the inserted 4:3 material with black side curtains or force the 4:3 image to fit the 16:9 format by stretching or cropping the original framing.

The intention is that eventually there will only be 16:9 receivers, but the back library of 4:3 programmes and films is enormous and valuable and will continue to be transmitted across a wide range of channels in the future. Aspect ratio conversion problems are now built into the television industry.

Widescreen composition

The growth of the cinema widescreen format in the 1950s provoked discussion on what changes were required in the standard 4:3 visual framing conventions that had developed in cinema since its beginnings. The initial concern was that the decrease in frame height meant that shots had to be looser and therefore had less dramatic tension. Another problem was that if artistes were staged at either side of the screen, the intervening setting became more prominent. Compositional solutions were found but the same learning curve is being experienced in television as the move is made to widescreen images. If anything, television is more of a 'talking heads' medium than cinema but the advent of the large, wider aspect screen has tended to emphasize the improvement in depicting place and setting.

One of the main compositional conventions with 4:3 television framing is the search for ways of tightening up the overall composition. This is partly due to fashion but also because viewing a TV picture occupies a much smaller zone of the human field of view compared to cinema viewing. Wide shots on television with small detail are not easily perceived on an average size receiver. Tight compositions eliminating all but the essential information have traditionally been preferred.

If people are split at either end of the frame, either they are restaged or the camera is repositioned to 'lose' the space between them. Cinema widescreen compositions relied less on the previous fashion for tight, diagonal, dynamic groupings in favour of seeing the participants in a setting. Initially, Cinemascope directors lined the actors up across the frame but this was quickly abandoned in favour of masking off portions of the frame with unimportant bland areas in order to emphasize the main subject. Others simply grouped the participants in the centre of the frame and allowed the edges to look after themselves – in effect 'protect and save' (see opposite). There were other directors who balanced an off-centre artiste with a small area of colour or highlight on the opposite side of the frame. This type of widescreen composition is destroyed if the whole frame is not seen.

Many film directors exploited the compositional potential of the new shape. They made big bold compositional widescreen designs knowing that they would be seen in the cinema as they were framed. Their adventurous widescreen compositions were later massacred on TV with pan and scan or simply being shown in 4:3 with the sides chopped off. The problem with the video compositional transition to widescreen is the inhibition to use the full potential of 16:9 shape because the composition has to be all things to all viewers. It must fit the 14:9 shape but also satisfy the 4:3 viewer. It is difficult to know when the full potential of the widescreen shape can be utilized because even if the majority of countries switch off analogue transmissions at some time in the first decades of the century, there will probably be billions of TV sets worldwide that will still be analogue.

230

A conventional TV single can cause problems in staging and bits of people tend to intrude into the edge of frame. Headroom has tended to be smaller than 4:3 framing and there are some problems in editing, particularly if the cut is motivated by action on the edge of a 16:9 frame which may not be visible to 14:9 viewers.

Protect and save

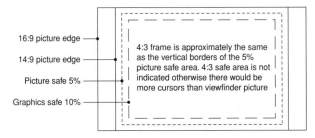

16:9 picture edge

14:9 picture edge

Picture safe 5%

Graphics safe 10%

4:3 frame is approximately the same as the vertical borders of the 5% picture safe area. 4:3 safe area is not indicated otherwise there would be more cursors than viewfinder picture

As many broadcast organizations have adopted the 14:9 aspect ratio as an interim standard, camera operators shooting in 16:9 follow a 'shoot and protect' framing policy. The viewfinder is set to display the full 16:9 picture with a graticule superimposed showing the border of a 14:9 frame and a 4:3 frame. Significant subject matter is kept within the 14:9 border or, if there is a likelihood of the production being transmitted in 4:3, within the smaller 4:3 frame. The area between 16:9 and 14:9 must be still usable for future full digital transmissions and therefore must be kept clear of unwanted subject matter. Feature film productions that were shot in 4:3 but were intended to be projected in the cinema with a hard matte in widescreen can sometimes be seen in a TV transmission with booms etc., in the top of the frame that would not have been seen in the cinema. 'Shoot and protect' attempts to avoid the hazards of multi-aspect viewing by centring most of the essential information. This does of course negate the claimed advantages of the widescreen shape because for the transitional period the full widescreen potential cannot be used.

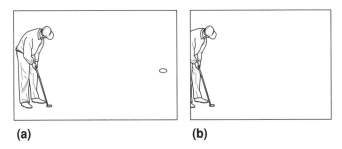

(a)   **(b)**

If the 'protect and save' viewfinder indicators are ignored when framing, for example, a golf shot in 16:9 aspect ratio (a), viewers watching a 4:3 picture will have a poorly composed picture (b) and no indication when the ball exits right on their viewed picture if the ball has entered the hole. With this framing, it is likely that even if the programme is transmitted in 14:9 aspect ratio, many viewers (with over-scanned TV receivers) will not be able to see the hole on the right of the frame present in the original 16:9 framing.

THE LIBRARY
GUILDFORD COLLEGE
of Further and Higher Education

Ratio and proportion

Greek and Renaissance ideals
The concept of proportion and ratio in composition played an important part in Greek/Roman art and architecture and reappears in some contemporary discussion in the 'format' war concerning the 'ideal' shape of a television frame.

The ancient Greeks were also interested in the ideal proportions of rectangles and discovered that a ratio where the value of the longest side divided by the shortest side equalled 1.618, had remarkable arithmetic, algebraic and geometric properties. Renaissance scholars and painters rediscovered this ratio and Leonardo dubbed it 'the divine proportion'. It subsequently became known as the golden section. Television widescreen ratio of 16:9 comes close to this preferred ratio.

Compositional balance using this ratio revolves around positioning the main visual elements on the subdivisions obtained by dividing the golden section according to a prescribed formula.

The rule of thirds
The academic emphasis on proportion and ratio was probably the precursor to a popular compositional convention called the rule of thirds. This 'rule' proposes that a useful starting point for any compositional grouping is to place the main subject of interest on any one of the four intersections made by two equally spaced horizontal and vertical lines.

The ratio of dividing the frame into areas of one third and two thirds is close to the approximation of a golden section division. These ratios occur so often in Western art, architecture and design that they became almost a visual convention.

The influence of photography
In the latter part of the nineteenth century, the evolution of faster film allowed snapshot street scenes to be captured. People were captured on the move, entering and leaving frame, which resulted in quite different images from the carefully posed groups of the long exposure film. The accidental quality of these snapshot compositions was considered by many to be more realistic and lifelike than the immobile studio set-ups. Painters were attracted by the sense of movement that could be suggested by allowing subjects to hover on the edge of frame (see Dissonance, page 238).

When the frame cuts a figure there is the implication that the frame position is arbitrary, that the scene is endless and a portion of the event just happened to be cut by the frame at that point by chance. The accidental character of the boundary was indeed arbitrary in many snapshots, but as a conscious compositional device it had been used for centuries.

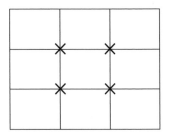

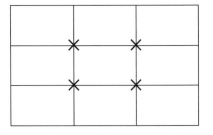

Rule of thirds
4:3 aspect ratio

Golden rectangle: 16:9 aspect ratio
The rule of thirds proposes that a useful starting point for any compositional grouping is to place the main subject on any one of the four intersections made by two equally spaced horizontal and vertical lines.

In an outside broadcast event the viewer may be aware that they are being shown selected 'portions' of the event and that the frame can be instantly adjusted by zooming in, to provide more detailed information, or by zooming out, to include more of the televised event.

Lines and curves

Line

Line is a powerful picture making design component and can be used to structure the attention of the observer. Within the frame, any visual elements that can be perceptually grouped into lines can be used to direct the eye around the image from one part of the picture to another to end, preferably, on the main subject of interest. Attention is attracted to where two lines cross or one line abruptly changes direction. The eye is attracted to the point of convergence of lines or the implied point of crossing. In practice, a line need not be visible to act as a strong compositional element, but it can be implied, such as the line of a person's gaze.

The vertical line: An isolated vertical subject such as a tree or a tower has directness and rigidity. It is immediately seen and takes visual precedence over any horizontal or other lines in the frame. The human figure in a landscape immediately attracts attention not only because of its psychological importance but because of this vertical aspect.

The leaning line: Diagonal arrangements of lines in a composition produce a greater impression of vitality than either vertical or horizontal lines. A line is most active when it runs from corner to corner. Compositions with a strong diagonal element imply movement or vitality.

Convergence of lines: As we have discussed, the distance from lens to subject, lens angle and camera height are a decisive influence on the convergence of lines within a frame. Lines of convergence can be placed to have as their focus the dominant subject in the frame. Strong pictorial lines can be controlled by lens position to lead to and emphasize the main subject.

Curves: One of the useful compositional uses of curved lines in an image is to guide the eye to the main point of interest. A straight line takes the eye immediately from point A to point B. A curve can move the eye around the frame in a less direct movement and knit disparate elements together on the way. A curve has the advantage of being a progressive change of direction, which allows a softer visual movement around an image compared to the zigzag pinball movement of straight lines. Also, unlike straight lines, curves do not interact with the edge of frame either in direction or by comparison.

Shape: The outside boundary, the shape of an object, plays a significant part in visual composition because of the ease and speed of grasping its simple pattern and relationships. Shape is a simple, visually easily 'digestible' element in a composition and, when setting up a shot, a few similar shapes should be looked for which can be grouped to reinforce the overall impact of the image.

Triangle: The triangle is a very flexible shape as a design element in a composition. The camera operator can control the shape and impact of a triangle by choice of lens angle, camera distance and height. The line convergence forming the boundary of a triangle within a composition can be altered and arranged to provide the precise control of the compositional elements.

Using shapes: The ability to analyse shapes in an image rather than simply seeing the content is an essential step in developing an eye for composition. If there appears to be a lack of unity in the image, if the main subject appears to be fighting the background then it is more than likely that an overall leading shape line around the frame is missing. Search for background shapes or re-light for background shapes that will connect and relate to foreground.

A curved lead-in line to the main subject of interest has always been one of the most common techniques to get the observer into the frame and then out again. There is often an inclination to try to avoid such a clichéd technique but the perceptual experience is that it is effective, that it holds and guides the attention of the viewer and that alternative 'lead-in' devices can just as quickly become visually devalued and stale.

Light/dark relationships: Every element in an image has a specific brightness. One area will be seen as bright, another will be perceived as dark. The visual 'weight' of different brightness levels will depend on proximity, area and contrast. The eye is naturally attracted to the highlight areas in a frame but the contrast and impact of an object's brightness in the frame will depend on the adjacent brightness levels. A shot of a polar bear against snow will require different compositional treatment than a polar bear in a zoo enclosure. A small bright object against a dark background will have as much visual weight in attracting the eye as a large bright object against a bright background. The relationship between different brightness levels in the frame plays an important part in balancing the composition.

Figure and ground: The relationship between figure and ground is fundamental to an understanding of perception and composition. Figure describes the shape that is immediately observable whilst ground defines that shape by giving it a context in which to exist. Figure is the prime visual element that is being communicated but can only be transmitted in a relationship with a ground. Any visual element in the frame that stands out and achieves prominence will be considered by the observer as figure, even if this object has been assessed as being of no visual importance by the camera operator. Hence the infamous background object that sits neatly on a subject's head totally ignored by the snapshotter whose concentration is wholly centred on what he/she considers is the only 'figure' in frame. When two or more objects are grouped together they are perceived as one 'figure' even though the camera operator may have mentally marked out one of them as 'background'.

Control: Controlling figure/ground relationship requires emphasizing the importance of the selected figure by light, brightness, colour, differential focus, texture, position etc. whilst removing sufficient visual detail from the ground to avoid it competing with the figure. It is easy to overestimate the psychological or narrative importance of one element when setting up a shot and underestimate its actual visual dominance within the frame. It may well have strong narrative importance but does it look visually significant? Many snapshots fail because the attention, when the photograph was taken, was wholly concentrated on the one element in the frame that had strong personal significance.

235

Balance

Visual reorganization

Due to the effect of perceptual 'reorganization', no visual element can exist in isolation within the frame. Within the act of perception, the eye/mind groups and forms relationships of the shapes it has organized.

One relationship is balance: the relative visual weight of one clump of visual elements compared to another and their individual relationships to the whole.

A technological definition of balance is the state of a body in which the forces that act upon it compensate each other. Camera operators will know that when they mount a large lens on the camera there is the need to pull the body of the camera back on the pan/tilt head until the point of balance has been achieved – the seesaw principle where a small child at the extreme end can be balanced by an adult sitting opposite but much closer to the pivot point. There is also another aspect of balance connected with a combined group of objects such as lens, matte box, camera, pan bar, viewfinder, etc., which is connected to their overall centre of gravity and the physical position of that point of balance. This is the centre of balance of the combined mass.

Balance in a composition is distributing the visual elements across the frame so that a state of equilibrium is achieved for the whole. Equilibrium need not mean at rest for, as in the seesaw analogy, balance can still allow movement and therefore visual interest.

As with a camera mass, a visual pattern has a centre around which the visual elements are grouped. The pivot point need not be and frequently is not the centre of the frame. Balance can be achieved by visual weight determined by size, shape (regular shape is heavier than an irregular shape), colour, light/dark relationships, isolation of a pictorial element, direction and the intrinsic interest of content. For example, the observer's wishes and fears induced by the image may outweigh any perceptual considerations of balance. For many people, a snake moving in any part of the frame will capture their attention irrespective of any other compositional design.

The content or intention of the image will determine which type of visual weight will be chosen to be pictorially reorganized in the process of composition. Balance helps meaning to be made visible.

Only the content can determine which pattern can be created by balancing out colour, mass, direction, etc., and which aspect of visual design is to be chosen and subjected to the business of pictorial organization. The function of visual design can be shown only by pointing out the meaning it helps to make visible.

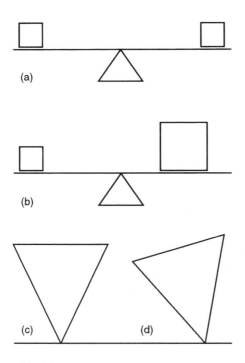

The resolution of balance

The two factors that determine balance are visual weight and the direction of movement of the visual pattern. Visual weight is conditioned by its position in the frame. A visual element at the centre or close to the centre vertical axis has less weight than one at the edge of the composition. An object higher in the frame is heavier than the same size object in the lower part of the frame. An object in the right of the frame (for most Western observers) will have less compositional weight than if it was positioned in the left of the frame.

Similar to the seesaw principle (a), visual weight increases proportionally the further it is from its point of balance. A small significant object in the background will balance out a larger object in foreground.

The resolution of balance in a composition therefore requires small to be weighted against large with reference to the centre and outside edges of the frame in order to achieve unity of the total image. A small 'weight' in the composition can be placed a long way from the centre if a balancing 'large weight' is placed close to the centre (b).

'Weight' need not only be differences in the physical size of balancing visual elements. Balance can be resolved with line, mass, light/dark, colour, etc.

Dynamic balancing

Finding a dynamic balance requires not only positioning small with large or light with dark, etc., but also finding linking patterns to the main balancing duality.

Our experience of the physical properties of objects provides us with the knowledge that an object that is very large at the top and tapers to a very small base is likely to be unstable and easily toppled (c). The equivalent visual weight is attached to a large object at the top of the frame and a smaller object at the base. The composition appears to be unstable and transient (d).

Dissonance

Whereas a balanced composition aims to promote a sense of equilibrium or stability, dissonance in a compositional grouping induces a feeling of discord or of resolution still to be realized.

Effective dissonance in music is not created (except by accident) by a non-musician aimlessly pressing groups of notes on a piano. It is based on the application of the theory of harmony. Dissonance in visual composition requires the same understanding of technique in order to achieve controlled disharmony.

For many centuries, the aim of composition in Western painting was to weld all the elements of the painting into a pictorial unity to achieve balance. The concept of dissonance – compositional elements deliberately offset in order to create visual tension – only entered compositional technique to any extent in the nineteenth century.

With the advent of 'snapshot' photography in the 1860s when exposures of 1/50 second were possible, many artists were influenced by the random photographic compositions created by people in motion. Degas was one of the first artists to use decentralized compositions with the main subject offset to the edge of the frame (see the Degas reproduction opposite Composition, page 209).

A new pictorial convention emerged of cutting off part of an object by the frame to imply that the action continued outside the frame. If the observer is led out of the picture frame, there is set up an expectation or curiosity in the viewer which is not satisfied by the framed image. The composition is unresolved (see Closed and open frames, page 222).

Dissonant compositions are therefore deliberately structured to evoke a sense of incompleteness. Just as there is a strong wish to straighten a picture hung crookedly on a wall, a well-structured dissonant shot will evoke the same feeling of a composition seeking to achieve balance. The friction and conflict that is set up can convey a strong sense of unresolved tension as well as creating interest and involvement.

Dissonant arrangement of subject matter creates a dynamic tension. But increasing the degree of unbalance to an extreme might collapse into visual anarchy and produce a composition of random items that have no relationship.

A shelf with a central object such as a clock flanked by two candlesticks can be arranged symmetrically and provide a balanced but stale arrangement. If the clock is moved towards one of the candlesticks, a dissonance is set up which may make the image stronger and more interesting because of the visual inclination to return to a symmetrical balance.

Dissonance is as necessary to good composition as balance. Offsetting balance creates interest. Achieving balance can satisfy the urge for symmetry but quickly becomes uninteresting. If balance is a full stomach, then dissonance is an appetite that needs to be satisfied.

Formal balance

Many examples are seen in religious art of figures grouped either side of the main subject (see below). Balance is achieved by equal weighting of both sides of the frame. Although formal balance emphasizes the main central subject's importance, its symmetrical solemnity precludes visual excitement. Another form of classical balance is by the use of the golden section (see Ratio and proportion, page 232).

To hold visual attention, it is necessary to provide greater visual complexity. A formal central grouping of figures balanced around the centre of the frame, although assimilated instantly, fails to provoke further curiosity. Once the eye has swept around the central shape it has visually 'consumed' everything provided. To entice the eye to take a second tour, less obvious visual relationships need to be discovered. The eye and mind must be fed with visual variations embedded within the basic dominant pattern although it must always be remembered that the eye takes the visual path of least resistance. Unravelling a very complex set of visual variations may mean a 'switch off' for the majority until easier shots come along. But visual variety provides the stimulation necessary for holding the attention.

'The Martyrdom of San Sebastion' Pollaivols (c.1475). (Reproduced by courtesy of the Trustees, The National Gallery, London).

239

Divided interest

The viewfinder and composition
An electronic viewfinder will produce a monochrome image with a much smaller contrast range than that experienced by human sight. This tends to provide a much simpler image than the original, eliminating colour contrasts and the emotional effect of colour and emphasizing tone, mass and the perspective of line.

A stronger sense of pattern is usually displayed by a two-dimensional viewfinder picture than is seen by human perception unless an individual has trained himself to 'see' like a camera. The viewfinder image therefore helps in composing a picture because to some extent it accentuates certain compositional elements.

Divided interest
A composition with divided interest, where the eye flicks back and forth between two equal subjects, is a composition without balance. One subject must be made subservient to the other by placement, size, focus, colour, or contrast.

Sound is another design element to restore balance as viewer attention will always be directed to the source of dialogue or other sound produced by one of the competing subjects within the frame.

Visual attention can always be captured by movement. Independent of the usual compositional controlling visual elements such as brightness, mass or colour, human perception is invariably attracted by movement. At one stage in human history, survival may have relied on instantly being aware of change in the environment and movement indicates change. It may have tilted the balance between successfully gathering food or being gathered as food. Movement within the frame usually takes precedence over all other compositional devices in attracting attention.

Intrinsic interest
Possibly the strongest design element that can be used in a composition to capture attention is for the content to have a strong emotional or psychological connection with the viewer. Either the subject of the shot has a personal association or it features a familiar human experience.

Millions of snapshots are treasured not for any intrinsic photographic values but because of the innate interest of their subject. This does not prevent a photo having a strong subjective interest and also having qualities which would appeal to a 'disinterested' observer with no involvement with the subject. Home videos of domestic or holiday topics can be shot so that they have a much wider appeal beyond their participants or their friends. The usual weakness of home movies is their inability to separate subjec-

240

tive interest from the considerations of structure and design. The content of the video dominates its form.

The personal significance of the content of a shot will always be the most powerful design element in attracting attention but by its presentation (compositional design) its appeal can be broadened to involve and engage a much wider audience.

Divided interest
The eye constantly flips between weather board and weather presenter whilst attempting to listen to the weather forecast and pay attention to the constantly changing graphics.

Border incidents
A well-designed image has information included but also information that has been excluded. The frame acts as a controller of attention by limiting what is to be in shot. The edge of the frame is a frontier checkpoint and the basic advice often given to trainee cameramen is to always check the edge of the frame for unnecessary detail. With a small viewfinder image, it is not always easy to see 'border incidents' of items creeping into the frame and others sliding out. When observing a large projected image or colour picture, these fringe visual activities are immediately obvious and distracting and shift the emphasis from the main subject of the shot.

Natural perspective

Normal perspective
If an observer looks at a field of view through an empty picture frame held at arm's length, he/she will require the frame to be progressively increased in size the greater the distance the frame is positioned away from him/her in order that the same field of view is contained within the frame at all times.

As we have discussed, the perspective of mass and the perspective of line are created by the distance of the subjects from the observer. Size relationships and convergence of line in his/her field of view will depend on their distance from him/her. Therefore if the observer does not change his/her position, the perspective appearance of the 'image' within the frame will remain unchanged. The frame will simply get larger and larger the further it is from the observer's position.

If a photograph was substituted for the frame and increasingly enlarged to match frame size, the two factors which control the exact replication of perspective characteristics in an image are revealed as image size and the distance of the image from the observer.

No lens produces a 'wrong' perspective provided the viewer views the correct size image at the taking distance. A wide angle shot taken close to the principal subject would require the viewer to almost press their nose to the screen in order to experience perspective characteristics of the image that they would have experienced if they had been the camera.

The calculation of what lens angle provides 'correct' perspective (i.e. equivalent to an observer replacing the camera) must include image size of reproduction and the distance the viewer is to the screen. A person sitting in the back row of a cinema may be viewing a screen size that is a tenth of the size the audience in the front is experiencing. There is no lens angle that can provide both viewing distances with correct perspective. The audience in the front row will experience wide angle shots as having correct perspective while the audience in the back row may judge narrower angle shots as having more correct perspective.

Often the requirements of a script require interpretation rather than precise replication of correct perspective. Interpretative compositions can therefore be created using perspective characteristics which expand or flatten space.

Estimating distance
There are a number of perceptual clues that are used to estimate distance or space. The depth indicators include binocular vision which allows convergent and divergent movement to be estimated by the use of 'two' viewpoints. Subjects moving towards or away from the observer alter the size of the image focused on the retina of the eye. Colour change due to atmospheric haze and hazy outline at long distance also aid depth perception.

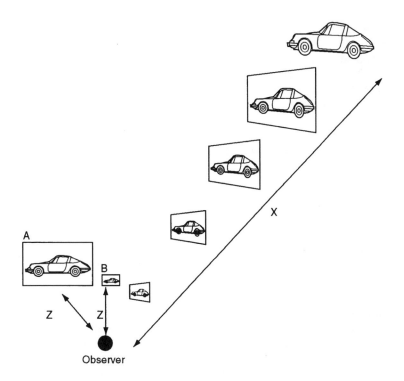

Natural perspective

The screen size of the reproduced image will increase proportionally to the viewing distance if the original perspective experienced by the observer at distance z from the subject is to be duplicated.

The viewing distance z of screen A is too close to reproduce a 'natural' perspective and would simulate a 'wide angle' look at that viewing distance.

Screen B would simulate a 'narrow angle' viewpoint because the screen size is too small for viewing distance z.

All these depth indicators can be used in film and television composition not only to replicate normal perceptual experiences but also to create atmosphere or to interpret narrative requirements.

Harmony and contrast

Resolving visual confusions
There is a continuous perceptual quest to resolve visual confusions, to reduce visual ambiguities and to rationalize and explain. In effect this is a continuing drive towards equilibrium – that is, towards no visual uncertainties. The way we achieve understanding in a composition is to group and organize diversity, to simplify complex images into regular patterns, to eliminate, where possible, conflicting readings of an image.

Visual puzzles
There is an equal and opposite force at work in this human disposition towards visual simplicity. Continuous perceptual attention requires continuous challenges. Perception requires visual puzzles to unravel and decode. But if the challenge of the visual puzzle is too great, if the viewer is supplied with images that make no sense, perceptual attention will be discarded once one or two clues have proved unsolvable.

If there is no ambiguity in a visual image, no uncertainty in the act of perception, if there is a surfeit of simplicity and symmetry, attention will drift and a visual condition close to sleep will be induced. Attention often requires unbalance, visual shock, stimulation and arresting images.

Contrast to aid meaning
Although perception seeks visual unity, a detailed visual communication requires contrast to articulate its meaning. Morse Code can be understood if the distinction between dot and dash is accentuated. A visual message requires the same accentuation of contrast in order to achieve coherent meaning. Light, by supplying contrast of tones, can remove visual ambiguity in a muddle of competing subjects but the wrong tonal contrast can produce a confused and misleading 'message' – the dots and the dashes come close to the same duration and are misread.

Communication is achieved by contrast. The communication carrier – sound or light – provides a message by modulation. There is a need for polarities whether loud or soft, dark or light; meaning is made clear by comparison.

The choice between harmony and contrast
These two competing systems – **harmony**, which tends to balance out conflict of mass and **contrast**, which stresses differences and therefore makes meaning clear – are referred to in Gestalt terminology as tendencies towards **levelling and sharpening.**

Levelling is the weakening or toning down of irregularity. It is epitomized by the perfect distribution of ratio and balance accomplished in classical art. There are no visual ambiguities or uncertainties of what is displayed either in the objectives of the visual designer or in the perception of the viewer. But perceptual attention demands stimulation whereas harmony tends towards the elimination of visual conflict. There is a visual design need to introduce tension through contrast.

Sharpening allows clarity of communication through contrast. In its most extreme form the middle tones are eliminated to provide a simplification of the image to the bare essentials. If the main purpose of a visual statement is to convey ideas, information and feeling, then contrast is required to articulate the image and to focus on the meaning of the message.

A dynamic image is one where a visual conflict or tension has been set up and then resolved. The yin/yang of visual design is harmony and contrast. Harmony appeases the perceptual system and therefore facilitates the delivery of the message. Contrast grabs the attention and ensures the perceptual system stays switched on to receive the message.

A dynamic image is one where a visual conflict or tension has been set up and then resolved. The yin/yang of visual design is harmony and contrast. Harmony appeases the perceptual system and therefore facilitates the delivery of the message. Contrast grabs the attention and ensures the perceptual system stays switched on to receive the message. (Reproduced by kind permission of Richard L. Rosenfeld.)

Light

Lighting and composition
The most important element in the visual design of television images is light. Apart from its fundamental role of illuminating the subject, light determines tonal differences, outline, shape, colour, texture and depth. It can create compositional relationships, provide balance, harmony and contrast. It provides mood, atmosphere and visual continuity. Light is the key visual force and is therefore central to any consideration of visual composition.

Hard and soft
Within a broad generalization, two qualities of light that are used in television production – hard and soft – have a similarity with the sharpening and levelling previously discussed.

Usually hard light produces the greatest contrast, modelling and texture. It creates depth, shape and relationships. All light, hard or soft, can reveal modelling, texture, contrast – it is a matter of shadow structure which determines the 'sharpness' of the effects.

Diffused light is often applied to reduce the contrast introduced by a hard light source and to create an integrated harmony of tones.

Lighting and visual communication
Contrast makes meaning clear. Generally lighting for contrast involves using hard light sources which are often easier to control than diffuse sources. This enables light to be directed and controlled to provide light exactly where it is required and to keep light away from where it is not required. An image with strong contrasts which only emphasizes the required visual elements may appear mannered and artificial because in everyday situations subjects are not lit in such a precise and controlled way.

'Found' lighting
Naturally occurring light sources do not discriminate between important and unimportant visual elements ascribed to them by individuals. It is the human mind in the act of perception that attaches relevance to one image as opposed to another. The quest to replicate naturally occurring lighting effects is at odds with most visual communications such as scripted drama, information, etc., which aim, by selective production techniques, to focus on one aspect in order to communicate a specific message.

'Realistic' lighting (i.e. everyday random and haphazard illumination) may require modification not only to conform to the technical requirements of the medium (e.g. contrast range, minimum exposure) but also as part of the overall production strategy to be selective in the message produced.

Realism

'Realistic' lighting aims to replicate naturally occurring light sources whether sunlight or light naturally found in interiors or exteriors. As an objective, it is nearly always compromised because of the technical considerations of the recording medium. Intercutting between a subject in full frontal sunlight facing a subject who has only naturally occurring reflected light will produce an obvious mismatch. Nearly all subjects illuminated by naturally occurring light sources will need some lighting modification even if it is simply restaging their positions to reduce the worst excesses of uncontrolled light.

Elimination of strong modelling

Diffused light technique was used in a move away from what many saw as the 'unrealistic' contrast introduced by hard light sources. These selectively lit aspects of a subject and setting, especially in what was considered the artificial and mannered three point portrait lighting system where every face had a key, fill and backlight.

Diffused light often eliminates strong modelling and the separation of planes which indicate depth. It may be difficult to separate foreground/background without some form of backlight or hard light emphasis on selective areas of the frame and therefore the illusion of depth is diminished. The direction and selective coverage of soft light is more difficult to control and therefore inevitably there is less control of tone and mass in a composition.

Controlled lighting and composition

One of the main values of light in relation to composition is the ability to accentuate tonal differences and provide balance or visual unity. Compositional design using light sources relies on control of light direction. Keeping light off surfaces in the field of view can be as important for the composition of the shot as controlling where the light will fall.

Modulating the light pattern of a shot is achieved by introducing selective contrast and this is best achieved by a hard light source. But the degree and extent of the artificial contrast or range of tonal values in an image that is introduced by the selective positioning of lamps gives rise to arguments about styles of lighting.

Colour

Colour and composition

Balance in a composition depends on the distribution of visual weight. Colour can be used to balance and to unify an image in many ways. If the weight of colour elements is ignored (or unseen), it can frequently unbalance the considered monochrome composition of tone and line. A composition framed in monochrome may result in over-reliance on tone, mass and linear design as the main ingredient of the composition. Colour not only has a profound influence on composition, in many forms of image making, it is the *subject* of the composition.

The relative quality of colour

The faithful reproduction of colour requires techniques to ensure that the specific colours of a scene are reproduced accurately and colour continuity requires that the same colours are identically reproduced in succeeding shots. This is often a basic requirement in most types of camerawork but colour, as an emotional influence in establishing atmosphere or in structuring a composition, also plays a vital role in visual communication.

The perception of the apparent hue of any coloured object is likely to vary depending on the colour of its background and the colour temperature of the light illuminating it. Staging someone in a yellow jacket against green foliage will produce a different contrast relationship to staging the same person against a blue sky.

The perceptual impact of a coloured object is not consistent but is modified by the quality of the light illuminating it, by reflection, shadow and by its relationship with surrounding colours.

Balancing a composition with colour

Balance in a composition depends on the distribution of visual weight. Mass, relative brightness, line and the psychological importance of a visual element can all be structured to provide visual unity in an image and to provide a route for the eye to travel in order to emphasize the most important element. Colour can be used to balance and to unify an image in many ways.

An out-of-focus single hued object within the frame (e.g. red) often exerts a strong influence in the composition and may distract attention from the main subject.

Light/dark relationships

As we have seen, the eye is attracted to the lightest part of an image or that part of the image that has the greatest contrast, and if colour is reproduced as a grey scale, yellow, after white, is the brightest colour. Depending on their backgrounds, a small area of yellow, for example, will carry more visual weight than a small area of blue. When balancing out a composition, attention should be paid to the relative brightness of colour and its location within the frame.

Viewfinder adjustment

The monocular viewfinder is the first and often the only method of checking picture composition for the camera operator. It is essential, if the relative compositional weight of different tones is to be correctly assessed, that the brightness and contrast of the viewfinder display is correctly set up (see The viewfinder, page 164). The action of the brightness and contrast controls therefore needs to be clearly understood.

Brightness: This control alters the viewfinder tube bias control and needs precise adjustment. Cap up the camera or place a lens cap over the lens and get the exposure set for black. Increase the viewfinder brightness control and check that the viewfinder image becomes increasingly grey and then white. This obviously does not represent the black image produced by the camera. If the brightness is now turned down, the image will gradually darken until the line structure of the picture is no longer visible. The correct setting of the brightness control is at the point when the line structure just disappears and there is no visible distinction between the outside edge of the display and the surrounding tube face. If the brightness control is decreased beyond this point, the viewfinder will be unable to display the darker tones just above black and distort the tonal range of the image. There is therefore only one correct setting of the brightness control, which, once set, should not be altered.

Contrast: The contrast control is in effect a gain control. As the contrast is increased the black level of the display remains unchanged (set by the brightness control) whilst the rest of the tones become brighter. This is where confusion over the function of the two viewfinder controls may arise. Increasing the contrast of the image increases the brightness of the image to a point where the electron beam increases in diameter and the resolution of the display is reduced. Unlike the brightness control, there is no one correct setting for the contrast control other than to say that an 'over-contrasted' image may lack definition and accurate focusing becomes difficult. Contrast is therefore adjusted for an optimum displayed image which will depend on picture content and the amount of ambient light falling on the viewfinder display.

Monochrome viewfinders

The last monochrome viewers

Nearly all broadcast television cameras are fitted, as standard, with monochrome viewfinders. There are significant exceptions, but the majority of cameras in daily use, up to and including the introduction of high definition equipment, use monochrome viewfinders to acquire the basic material for colour television.

One of the most common misconceptions with this situation is the myth that there is no need for a colour viewfinder except where colour differentiation is necessary, for example sports coverage, snooker etc. The camera manufacturers believe that the viewfinder is simply there to be used for focus and what they term 'the adjustment of the picture angle'.

The fact that colour plays a significant part in picture composition is either ignored or conveniently becomes the responsibility of other technicians in the television production chain.

Problems associated with monochrome viewfinders

The result of framing a composition in monochrome is often an over-reliance on tone, mass and linear design as the main ingredient of the composition. If a colour monitor is accessible, then adjustment can be made for the colour component of the shot, but only too often the frame of reference for the composition is the monochrome viewfinder or a small portable low quality colour monitor. Colours of similar brightness such as red and the darker shades of green merge and may be indistinguishable in the monochrome viewfinder and yet, as separate hues, they exercise a strong influence on the composition. Saturated red and blue appear much darker in a monochrome viewfinder than their brightness value in colour. A small saturated colour against a complementary background has a much greater impact in colour than its viewfinder reproduction.

Compositions based on mass and line

A flat-lit scene viewed in black and white gives the impression of lack of contrast and punch whereas the same scene in colour may be much more acceptable than the monochrome rendering suggests. A shot lit with predominantly red light has very little contrast and low modulation when viewed through a monochrome viewfinder. This often provokes an unnecessary struggle by the camera operator using a monochrome viewfinder to provide dynamic compositions using mass and line, which is quite unnecessary when the same shot is viewed in colour.

Composing with a monochrome viewfinder results in emphasizing contrast, mass and usually the convergence of lines. Colour becomes simply the accidental effect of individual objects within the frame rather than the conscious grouping and locating of colour within the frame. The weight of

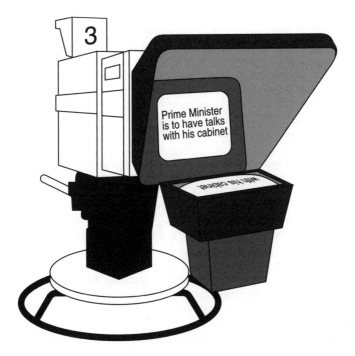

After a prompt has been rigged, check that it does not appear on the edge of frame in the widest angle of the zoom, that it does not foul the rig steering wheel when the camera is panned down, that the glass is clean and does not produce spurious flares when the camera is repositioned and that the cue light on the front of the prompter is working. Check also that the junction between the back of the prompter and camera is covered by black cloth to form a 'light seal'. Problems with flares on the prompter glass preventing a presenter reading the prompt can be resolved by altering the camera height or by a small reposition and/or by adjustment of lamps.

colour elements is not used to balance the composition and can frequently unbalance the considered monochrome composition of tone and line.

251

Working at speed

Quick compositional decisions

Most actuality camerawork – working live or recording as live – requires a stream of continuous pictures involving each camera operator framing up their shots at speed. Occasionally they may have time to reframe without haste and to take time out to consider the precise framing of the shot. This is a rare and infrequent luxury. Most productions require a constant variety of shots often linked to the timescale of a specific event.

The live, multi-camera coverage of an orchestral concert, for example, will be camera scripted in sympathy with the piece performed. Depending on the nature of the music and television treatment decided on by the director, there may be in excess of 300 shots shared between five or more cameras.

Each shot has its designated function in the score and must be ready and framed at the precise bar that it is required. The speed of the camerawork will therefore be synchronized with the music and at times this will entail rapid and continuous shot change. The tempo of the camerawork varies between extremely quick reactions off shot to find the next instrument, to slow camera movement on shot that reflects the mood of the music. Panning movements have to be synchronized with the number of bars allocated to that shot and must finish exactly on the instrument or group of instruments agreed because possibly, at that point in time, a solo or change of tempo may occur.

Reflex framing

Reflex framing, with no time to consider composition consciously, is achieved by relying on habit and the developed feeling for a good picture that instantly oversees eye/hand coordination. If there is no time to consider the image, the only thing to do is to rely on experience and training. Live television continually requires quick compositional decisions.

Camerawork that is carried out in the real time of the event covered often allows no time for any thoughtful considerations about the precise framing. There is no time to re-order the visual elements. The most that can be done in the time available is to trim the shot by way of zoom angle and a slight adjustment of the framing points.

An example of the instinctive response to movement can often be seen in slow motion replays of fast sporting action. The square-on 'slo-mo' camera operator in cricket coverage is required to follow the ball as soon as it leaves the bat. Sometimes even the batsman does not know which way the ball went. Continuously during the game, the slow motion replay reveals that the camera operator has instinctively followed the ball to a fielder who has gathered the ball and aimed back at the stumps in one fluid movement. The framing seen in slow motion belied the real speed and technique required to follow this 'blink of an eye' action and keep the ball and the players involved in the frame.

During the match, it is sometimes judged that the action of bat, ball and player is too fast for the umpires on the field to assess what has happened and they call upon a third umpire in the stadium to adjudicate. The third umpire can only do this by relying on the slow motion replay of the debated incident. It is somehow inferred that this is a 'high-tech' solution to an event that is too fast for the eye to see when in fact it relies on the fast reflexes of the camera operator.

Compositing

Compositing has become the umbrella description of one of the oldest techniques in film and television production, namely, the combining of two or more separate images into one unified image. The aim of the technique is to eliminate any indication in the final composite image of the join between the separate images that have been combined.

Electronic keying, using a luminance key (off black or white), was superseded by colour separation – chroma keying using a saturated colour, usually blue. Later variants such as linear keying allowed realistic semi-transparent effects such as transparent shadows and partial reflections.

The growth of digital post-production allowed enormous flexibility in re-arranging, combining and manipulating the structure of an image. Modern techniques allow digital keying, matting, painting, retouching, rotoscoping, image repair of keying and the combining of real and computer-generated backgrounds.

In all these techniques, a 'seamless' technique is the target. The aim is an invisible join between two or more images.

Electronic keying

Combining two images requires a switch to be inserted in the signal chain which will electronically select the appropriate image. Blue is commonly chosen as the colour to be used as the separation key but other colours can be employed. When the chroma key switch is in use, any blue in the selected image (foreground) is switched out and replaced with the corresponding area of a chosen background scene.

Linear keying is similar to a film travelling matte system and does not switch between foreground and background. It suppresses the unwanted colour of the foreground (e.g. blue) and turns on the background image in proportion (linearly) to the brightness of the blue of the foreground image. Shadows cast by foreground objects can therefore be semi-transparent rather than black silhouettes.

Invisible keying of one image into another requires the application of a perfect electronic switch obtained by appropriate lighting of foreground and background, correct setting up and operation of the keying equipment, a match between foreground and background mood and atmosphere which is achieved by lighting and design, appropriate costume and make-up of foreground artistes, a match between foreground artiste's size, position and movement and background perspective achieved by camera position, lens and staging.

The following pages will centre on compositional techniques to achieve a match between foreground artiste's size, position, movement and background perspective and staging for live action that can be employed to persuade the viewer that no technique has been employed.

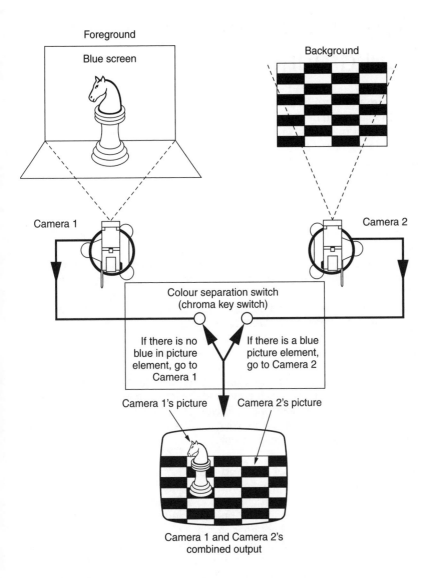

Foreground

Blue screen

Background

Camera 1

Camera 2

Colour separation switch
(chroma key switch)

If there is no
blue in picture
element, go to
Camera 1

If there is a blue
picture element,
go to Camera 2

Camera 1's picture

Camera 2's picture

Camera 1 and Camera 2's
combined output

Chroma key

Combining two images requires a switch to be inserted in the signal chain which will electronically select the appropriate image. Blue is commonly chosen as the colour to be used as the separation key but other colours can be employed.

When the chroma key switch is in use, any blue in the selected image (foreground) is switched out and that part of the frame which contained blue is replaced with the background image.

255

Two- and three-dimensional backgrounds

Two-dimensional backgrounds

The simplest type of chroma or linear key camerawork is placing a presenter beside a primary colour panel and keying in a logo or a diagram such as a weather chart. As the infill image only exists in two dimensions, there is no problem with matching the perspective of the presenter (foreground) with the perspective of the keyed-in image (background). The foreground camera will shoot all or part of the blue screen and any person or object placed in front of the screen will overlap or be 'in front' of the image that is keyed into the panel. The background weather chart can be generated by another camera simultaneously with the foreground camera. Combining the two images simply involves the foreground camera adjusting the framing to contain any artiste movement. The background camera then adjusts its framing so that the required information fits the keyed area in the foreground shot.

Obviously, once this match has been achieved, neither camera can move without revealing that what appears to be a single image is in fact a composite of two different shots. Usually the weather chart will have been generated by computer graphics and keyed into the blue screen 'window' direct.

Any visual source – camera, frame store, computer graphics, VTR, film – can be used for a key background and the image can be moving or static. The production intention with this type of composite is to persuade the viewer that the presenter is standing beside the weather chart and can point and touch any relevant part of it.

Matching perspective of line and mass

The problems associated with keying a two-dimensional graphic into a picture are fairly straightforward compared to trying to achieve a realistic composite of two separate images. A pre-recorded background is often used either because of lack of floor space or lack of budget.

A typical example of compositing occurred in a production based on the life of a politician. The story required the statesman at one point to be in a deserted House of Commons. Because of the width of shot required, it would have been too expensive to build a replica of the Commons so therefore a recording of the Commons interior was made and then keyed into the blue screen in front of which the actor made the required movement.

The problem is exacerbated if there is actor movement towards or away from the foreground camera. If the match is incorrect, then it appears as if he inhabits a different space from his background. Which of course in real-

The composite image combined the space recorded by the location camera with the space occupied by the actor in the studio. The problem is to get the actor's studio space to be identical to the location space. If the resultant composite seeks to convince the viewer that both background and foreground are contiguous – that is, that they are adjacent and are observed from the same viewpoint, then the line perspective of both images will have to match in every particular. It is matching the line and mass perspective of two images, especially if the background is pre-recorded and not subject to adjustment, that often causes the most problems in shooting on blue screen.

ity is the case. Matching line perspective and the perspective of mass is the essential requirement for a seamless join between the foreground and background image.

Camera height and chroma key

Background/foreground camera height

Our normal perceptual experience of someone of our own size moving on flat ground towards us is that the horizon line will always intersect them at eye level. We have to duplicate this condition in the studio when the horizon line will be a separate image to an actor moving towards the lens. We have to ensure that our everyday experience of a three-dimensional world is convincingly reproduced when the three dimensions are recorded as two separate two-dimensional images and then combined.

In terms of a perspective match on blue screen, the lens axis height and tilt becomes as important in achieving an invisible join as the 'crossing the line' conventions of picture editing. A jump cut across the line will register just as the wrong lens height may show up when actor movement is involved.

If the lens height of the level background camera was at eye level, say 1.5 m, then everyone in the foreground studio shot needs to be intersected at eye level by the keyed or matted horizon line so they may move naturally towards and away from the camera.

Their position in the frame, relative to the background horizon line, follows our normal expectations of people walking on level ground. They must appear to grow progressively larger commensurate with their walking speed and their head must stay in the same relation to background horizon line. It must follow the horizontally parallel line from our eye (the lens) to the horizon. They must not cross the line.

If the foreground camera lens is higher than the background lens then a figure moving towards the camera will appear to be walking downhill and conflict with our expectations. Their head will start in frame above the horizon line and the end of their movement will take their head below the horizon line. This is identical with our perception of a person walking downhill even though the actor will be walking on a flat studio floor.

Likewise if the foreground camera is set too low then an approaching figure to camera will appear to be walking uphill. It is important to realize that it is not a differing lens angle or subject distance that is causing this mismatch but lens height. Tracking the camera in or out, zooming in or out or tilting will not improve the perspective match until the foreground camera is at the same height as the camera that recorded the horizon.

Camera height and blue screen

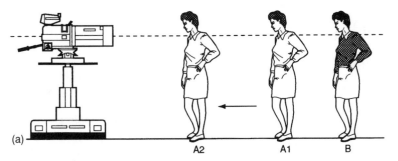

(a) With level camera and lens at eye height, person A, walking to camera on level ground, will always have their eyes at the same height in the frame as person B (assuming A and B are of the same height).

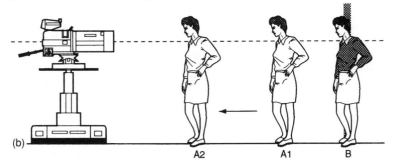

(b) The same shot is now duplicated on blue screen with A on the foreground camera and B is keyed into the background. If the foreground camera's height, lens tilt, subject distance and lens angle match the background camera's, A's walk will be appropriate to the space depicted in the keyed-in background.

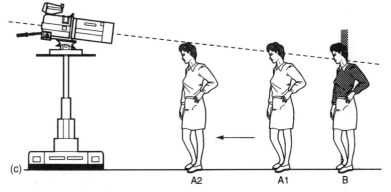

(c) The same blue screen set-up as in (b) but the foreground camera lens height is too high and therefore the height of the projected line between A and B changes during A's walk. This produces the impression that A is walking downhill. Her head moves progressively lower in the frame as she approaches the lens in relation to the position of B's head.

Matching foreground to background

Working with illustrations

The castle and its surrounding countryside is a perfectly convincing representation of a landscape, see (a) opposite. But keying the boy walking in this 'illustrated' space requires the boy to follow the drawn perspective.

It is a matter of determining the lens height and lens angle and staging the boy's walk so that it follows the drawn path. A speedy way of finding the path on the studio floor is to first determine the camera height. Then have a similar size stand-in positioned at the start of the walk and at the end of the walk to find camera distance. You will remember this determines size relationships. Then adjust the final overall framing with the zoom.

If he walks on the path with giant strides, then the camera is too close. Track out and zoom in. If he covers too little space for the length of his stride, then the camera is too far away. Track in and zoom out. If he floats across the path, then the camera is too high – crane down. If his feet sink into the path – crane up.

It is worth repeating that size relationships within the frame are the product of camera distance from the subject not the lens angle. If a two shot was taken on a wide angle lens and, without moving the camera, the same two people were taken on a narrow angle lens, their relative size relationship would be the same in both shots.

Confusion arises with this simple point because in attempting to match the foreground figure size on opposite ends of the zoom it is necessary to move the camera close to the subject to fill the frame when using the wide angle lens. It is the simple fact of moving the camera closer to the subject which changes the size relationship *not* the lens angle.

The important point to remember is that subject size relationship is a product of camera distance. How the subject fills the frame is a product of lens angle.

The need to quote lens angle vs focal length

Foreground and background cameras should attempt to use the same lens angle but this need not necessarily be the same focal length. Lens angle or angle of view is related to the focal length of the lens and the *format* size of the pick-up sensor whether it be tube, chip or film gate. A 50 mm lens on a 35 mm stills camera will not produce the same angle of view as a 50 mm zoom lens setting on a Betacam, whereas the lens angle of a 50 mm lens on a 16 mm film camera will match the 32 mm focal length setting on a ½ inch CCD camera and provide similar perspective of mass, assuming all other factors are equal.

Angle of view is therefore best stated in degrees rather than the dimension of the focal length of a lens when matching two different formats.

(a) Background with a drawn path

(b) Boy in studio walking against blue screen with no line showing between floor and background. His walk must follow the drawn path in the illustration above (a). The second figure is a stand-in to find the end position of the boy's walk. The size of background figure will be determined by camera distance/height and must match the perspective of background. As the boy walks towards this second position his change in size and his position in the frame must match the drawn background.

(a) and (b) combined into a single shot with the boy appearing to follow the drawn path with the appropriate reduction in size as he walks away from camera.

Camera movement on blue screen

Camera movement

When a foreground artiste is composited with a background image, any camera movement by the foreground camera will displace the artiste in relation to the background, unless the camera providing the background image also duplicates the foreground movement, and vice versa.

Panning on the background image will 'fly' the foreground figure through space. To achieve natural movement of a combined image both foreground and background movement have to be in perfect synchronization. The synchronization must provide not only for the same ratio of change in picture size in background and foreground image but a perfect match in perspective change.

Synchronization of perspective change is therefore almost impossible to achieve with manually operated cameras but can be guaranteed with a motion control rig which is a motorized crane where all movement of its lens in space is computer controlled.

Memory heads

Precise duplication of movement of background and foreground images to ensure that the combined image stays in register during camera movement can also be achieved by using a special pan and tilt head that records each movement on a computer disk.

The background scene can be pre-recorded using a memory head and all the essential data that we have talked about, namely lens height, lens angle, tilt, distance from subject, speed of pan, tilt, zoom movement, speed of zoom and focus, can be memorized on a floppy disk which can then be used to program the foreground camera to duplicate camera moves on the foreground subject on blue. It can also be used to synchronize two camera movements so that there is no image slip between the composited shots.

Virtual studios

As the cost of computing power decreases, more and more facilities utilizing enormous amounts of computer memory are available for production. Virtual scene construction allows an artiste moving on a blue screen background to be composited into a background electronically created or based on a still.

The foreground camera capturing the artiste on blue can pan, track and move with the subject and the computer software will automatically alter the background accordingly. The distance from camera to presenter is continuously calculated and fed to the computer. This allows them to appear to walk behind and in front of computer-generated graphic 'objects' (such as simulated furniture), which is composited into the shot.

The claim for the virtual reality studio is that it can exist simply as a blue screen studio whilst its keyed 'scenery' will be held in the computer to be changed, depending on programme format, at the touch of a button. The system allows more than one camera to be used and to be routed as normal through a mixing panel for intercutting. Each shot will have the appropriate section of the computer-generated set as background.

Differential focus

A simple technique for creating depth on a composite sequence is differential focus. By throwing the background out of focus a better foreground to background match can be achieved. This simulates the depth of field that is normally available on close ups. Throwing the background out of focus also helps for better edits using portions of the same illustration. Another point to bear in mind with depth of field is the need to create a believable focus-zone gradation between background and foreground. It might be necessary to pre-record the background slightly out of focus to match the foreground action depending on size of shot on foreground actor. An everyday example of this is the newsreader in front of blue with a keyed-in picture of a defocused newsroom.

Background problems

If the foreground camera is limited in its framing by the restraints of matching both the linear perspective and mass perspective there are situations where a difficult or unacceptable framing arises.

A foreground figure will be either too high or too low in the frame and the camera is unable to tilt or crane to compensate because this will destroy the perspective match. Typically this happens if there is a high horizon and low lens height on the background camera and an artiste walks towards the foreground camera. The result is crushed headroom on foreground with no way of compensating.

The reverse produces the opposite problem. A low horizon and above eye line lens height on the background camera will create excessive headroom in foreground as the subject moves towards camera. Little or nothing can be done by the foreground camera to provide a more acceptable framing. The solution lies in changing the background to fit the required foreground framing and/or restaging the foreground action. This may cause a serious problem that could be avoided by production pre-planning.

It is important to remember that the lens height, lens angle, camera distance from subject and camera tilt recording the background will control and constrain any subsequent foreground movement on chroma key.

Further reading

Ray, S.F. (1994) *Applied Photographic Optics*. Butterworth-Heinemann, Oxford.

Ward, P. (1996) *Composition for Film & TV*. Butterworth-Heinemann, Oxford.

Ward, P., Bermingham, A. and Wherry, C. (1999) *Multiskilling for Television Production*. Butterworth-Heinemann, Oxford.

Ward, P. (2000) *TV Technical Operations: An Introduction*. Butterworth-Heinemann, Oxford.

Ward, P. (2000) *Digital Video Camerawork*. Butterworth-Heinemann, Oxford.

Ward, P. (2001) *Basic Betacam Camerawork*, 3rd edition. Butterworth-Heinemann, Oxford.

Glossary

Many of the jargon words associated with multi-camera production have already been discussed. The following expressions may also be encountered.

actuality event: any event that is not specifically staged for television that exists in its own timescale

ad-lib shooting: impromptu and unrehearsed camera coverage

angle of view: the horizontal angle of view of a specific focal length lens. A zoom lens has a variable angle of view

as-directed: unrehearsed camera coverage controlled at any moment by the director

aspect ratio: the proportion of the picture width to its height

back focus: see flange-back

barndoors: hinged metal flaps on the front of a lamp used to control the spread of light

big close-up (BCU): a description of the size of a shot. When applied to the face, the frame includes only the point of the chin to mid-forehead

black level: the amplitude of the television video signal representing the darkest part of the picture

BNC: a twist-lock cable connector often used on monitor video cables

camera angle: the position of the camera relative to the main subject in the shot

camera left: left of frame as opposed to the artiste's left when facing camera

camera right: right of frame as opposed to the artiste's right when facing camera

caption generator: electronic equipment that allows text to be created and manipulated on screen via a keyboard

CCD: a charge-coupled device; it converts light into electrical impulses which are compiled into the TV picture format

chroma key: an electronic process for inserting an artiste (foreground) into a background picture; also known as colour separation overlay (CSO) in the BBC

close-up (CU): shot size. When applied to the face, the top of the frame rests on the top of the head and the bottom of the frame cuts at the position of a knotted tie if worn

coaxial cable: cable with a central conductor surrounded by a sheath of screening

coloration: unpleasant effect where sound is repeated with a small time delay. This may occur where two microphones pick up the same sound

colour bars: a special test signal used in colour television

colour temperature: a convenient way to describe the colour of a light source by relating it to a black body radiator, e.g. heated poker, measured in kelvin (K) after Lord Kelvin (physicist)

component: the individual or difference signals from the red, blue and green channels and luminance signal

composite: the colour signals encoded (combined) with the luminance signal. Also, old definition for luminance signal plus synchronizing pulses

compression: the process of reducing the amount of signal data that are required to be passed through a finite channel whilst endeavouring to maintain the quality of the originating signal. Also a method of reducing the range of audio levels

contrast ratio: The ratio between the brightest part of the subject and the darkest part

crash zoom: either an intentionally maximum speed zoom or zoom to re-compose on shot

crib card: camera card attached to the side of the camera describing the planned shots and production information connected with that camera

crossing the line: moving the camera to the opposite side of an imaginary line drawn between two or more subjects after recording a shot of one of the subjects. This results in intercut faces looking out of the same side of frame and the impression that they are not in conversation with each other.

cue: a particular lighting condition or an indication for action to start, i.e. actor to start performing or lighting change to start

cursor/graticule: a vertical or horizontal line that can be positioned by the cameraman in the viewfinder as a reminder of a precise frame position or to check a vertical or horizontal visual element

cut to line: the video source selected as the output of the vision mixing panel

cyclorama: a general purpose background curtain, usually off-white

decibels (dB): a logarithmic ratio of changes in sound intensity similar to the ear's logarithmic response to changes in sound intensity

depth of field: the zone of acceptable focus in the field of view

dingle: branches placed in front of a luminaire to create a dapple effect or in front of a lens to create a foreground feature

Dolby: a noise reduction process used in audio recording and playback

down stage: moving towards the camera or audience

effects (FX): visual or audio effects

EFP: electronic field production is the term used to describe single camera location video programme making other than news

electronic shutter: an electronic method of varying the length of exposure time of the CCD. Can be used to improve the slow motion reproduction of motion

encode: the technique of combining colour information with a luminance (monochrome) signal

ENG: electronic news gathering describes the single camera video recording of news events

establishing shot: the master shot which gives the maximum information about the subject

extender: an additional lens which can be switched internally in the zoom lens to extend the zoom range of focal lengths

eyeline: the direction the subject is looking in the frame

f-number: a method of indicating how much light is being allowed to pass through the aperture of the lens

field: one top-to-bottom scanning of an image. Two fields interlaced make up one frame

filter wheels: filter holders of colour correction, neutral density or effects filters that are arranged within the camera to allow for the quick selection, by rotating the wheel, of the required filter combination

first generation: the acquisition medium on which the video signal was first recorded

flange-back: the distance from the flange surface of the lens mount to the image plane of the pick-up sensor commonly known as the back focus

focal length of a compound lens: is the distance from the principal point of a compound lens (e.g. a zoom lens), to the point at which rays from an object at infinity form the most sharply defined image

focus pull: moving the zone of sharpest focus to another subject

foldback: a feed to allow artists to hear selected sound sources on loudspeakers or headphones

format: the method of recording the image (e.g. DVCPRO; S-VHS; Betacam, etc.)

frame store: an electronic device for storing individual video frames

frame: one complete television picture comprising two interlaced fields or a single film image

fresnel: stepped lens used in the fresnel spotlight

gain: the degree of amplification of a video or audio signal

gallery: production control room

gamma: a measure of the degree of linearity between a scene and its reproduction

gobo: stainless steel stencil used in profile projectors to create effects, e.g. windows, abstract pattern, moon, etc.

grads: an abbreviation of graduated applied to front of lens filters which progressively filter or colour the picture vertically

grid area: the structure above a studio floor

GV: general view; this is a long shot of the subject

hand-held: operating a portable camera without a camera mounting
hard light: any light source that casts a well defined shadow
Hertz: unit of frequency, 1 Hertz = 1 cycle/second
high angle: any lens height above eye height
high key: picture with predominance of light tones and thin shadows
HMI: a discharge lamp producing light by ionizing a gas contained in the bulb
hot head: a remotely controlled camera pan/tilt head often on the end of a jib arm

image size: the image formed by the lens on the face of the CCD
interlace: a method of scanning separate parts of an image in two passes (fields) in order to reduce the bandwidth required for transmission
invisible technique: production method which emphasizes the content of the shot rather than the production technique
iris: variable circular aperture in the camera used to control exposure, calculated in f-stops
isoed: recording the (isolated) output of an individual camera or cameras in a multi-camera shoot in addition to the main recording

kelvin (K): a unit measurement of heat used to describe colour temperature
key: mood of a picture, i.e. high key/low key
keylight or key: the main source of light illuminating the subject
kicker: light used at eye level from upstage, at eye level to 'kick' the side of the artiste's head
knee: modified part of the transfer characteristic of a camera designed to progressively compress highlights

linear matrix: involves cross-coupling between R, G and B to help obtain the desirable analysis characteristics essential for faithful colour reproduction
live: the transmission of an event as it takes place
locked-off: applying the locks on a pan and tilt head to ensure that the camera setting remains in a pre-selected position
long lens: a lens with a large focal length
low angle: a lens height below eye height
low key: picture with a predominance of dark tones and strong shadows
long shot (LS): a description of a shot when the full length human figure fills the frame
luminaire: name given to a complete lighting unit, i.e. light source or lamp plus its casing

macro: a switchable facility on a lens that allows focusing on an object placed closer to the lens than the normal minimum object distance (see MOD)

matte box: a filter holder and bellows extension for the control of flare, fitted to the front of the lens

medium close shot (MCU): a shot description usually describing a framing of a person with the bottom of the frame cutting where a suit breast pocket would normally be

medium shot (MS): a description of shot size with the bottom of the frame cutting at the waist when applied to the human figure

megahertz (MHz): one million cycles per second

mired: micro reciprocal degree value allows the relationship between a correction filter and the colour temperature shift to be calculated

minimum object distance (MOD): the closest distance a subject in acceptable focus can be to the lens

modelling: the action of light revealing contour and texture of a subject

monitor termination: a switchable electronic 'load' (usually 75 ohms) on the back of a monitor inserted at the end of a video cable feed to prevent the signal 'bouncing back'. If several monitors are looped together, termination only occurs at the last monitor

movement blur: the degradation of the image related to the speed of subject movement during the exposure time of a single picture

multi-generation: numerous re-recordings of the original recording

neutral density filter: a filter which reduces the amount of light transmitted without altering the colour temperature

noddies: television jargon for cutaway shots recorded for editing purposes after an interview showing the interviewer listening and 'nodding' at the interviewee's comments

OB: abbreviation for outside broadcast (remote)

off shot: describes the camera when its output is not selected at the vision mixing panel to be fed 'to line'

on shot: describes the camera when its output is selected at the vision mixing panel to be fed 'to line'

PAL (phase alternating line): A European development of the American NTSC system of encoding colour

peak white clipper: A 'gain limiting' circuit set to the same level in each colour channel of the camera that restricts any signal to a maximum level

peak white: either 100% video signal level or 60% reflectance neutral grey surface

ped: abbreviation for pedestal – a camera mounting

pixel: abbreviation for picture cell – a single point in an electronic image

planning meetings: a meeting of some members of the production staff held for the exchange of information and planning decisions concerning a future programme

playback: replaying a recorded shot or sequence of shots or audio

PLUGE (picture line-up generating equipment): test signal used for alignment of monitor contrast and brightness

point-of-view shot: a shot from a lens position that seeks to duplicate the viewpoint of a subject depicted on screen

post-production: editing and other work carried out on pre-recorded material

practical: an in-shot light source, e.g. wall light

prime lens: a fixed focal length lens

production control rooms: production areas on outside broadcasts (see Scanner), or adjacent to studios used by production staff, lighting and audio

prompters: a semi-silvered mirror attached to the front of the lens reflecting text displayed on a TV monitor below the lens

PSC: the production method of recording material on a portable single video camera

real time: the actual running time of an event as opposed to 'screen time' – the compression of time achievable by editing

recces: the inspection of a location by production staff to assess the practicalities involved in its use as a setting for a programme or programme insert

recorded-as-live: a continuous recording with no recording breaks

reverse angle: when applied to a standard two-person interview, a camera repositioned 180° to the immediate shot being recorded to provide a complementary shot of the opposite subject

robotic camera: a camera with a remotely controlled camera head, e.g. pan/tilt, zoom and focus. May also include camera position and height

rocking focus: moving the focus zone in front of and behind the selected subject in order to determine sharpest focus

scanner: the production control rooms of an outside broadcast production

shooting off: including in the shot more than the planned setting or scenery

shot number: a number assigned to a specific shot as detailed in a camera script or camera rehearsal

single shot technique: the single camera discontinuous recording of a number of shots that are later edited in post-production

slo-mo replay: replaying a pre-recording at a slower speed than normal transmission

vision mixer: the person who switches between video sources. Also applied to the equipment they use to perform this function

white balance: the electronic process of defining a reference white lit by a light source of a specific colour temperature

wide shot (WS): a description of shot size which includes objects greater than the size of the human figure

working-as-live: continuous recording with no opportunity for recording breaks or retakes

zoom ratio: the ratio of the longest focal length to the shortest focal length a specific zoom lens can achieve

zoom tracking: a lens pre-focused on a distant subject will stay in focus for the whole of its zoom movement towards (or away) from that subject providing the back focus (flange-back) has been correctly aligned

zoom: a variable focal length lens achieved by internally moving elements of the lens

ⓕ Focal Press

www.focalpress.com

Join Focal Press on-line
As a member you will enjoy the following benefits:
- an email bulletin with **information on new books**
- a regular **Focal Press Newsletter**
  - featuring a selection of new titles
  - keeps you informed of **special offers, discounts and freebies**
  - alerts you to **Focal Press news and events**such as author signings and seminars
- complete access to **free content**and reference material on the focalpress site, such as the focalXtra articles and commentary from our authors
- a **Sneak Preview**of selected titles (sample chapters) *before* they publish
- a chance to have your say on our **discussion boards**and **review books**for other Focal readers

Focal Club Members are invited to give us feedback on our products and services.
Email: worldmarketing@focalpress.com – we want to hear your views!

Membership is FREE. To join, visit our website and register. If you require any further information regarding the on-line club please contact:

Emma Hales, Marketing Manager
Email: emma.hales@repp.co.uk
Tel: +44 (0) 1865 314556
Fax: +44 (0)1865 315472
Address: Focal Press, Linacre House,
Jordan Hill, Oxford, UK, OX2 8DP

Catalogue
For information on all Focal Press titles, our full catalogue is available online at www.focalpress.com and all titles can be purchased here via secure online ordering, or contact us for a free printed version:

USA
Email: christine.degon@bhusa.com

Europe and rest of world
Email: jo.coleman@repp.co.uk
Tel: +44 (0)1865 314220

Potential authors
If you have an idea for a book, please get in touch:

USA
Lilly Roberts, Editorial Assistant
Email: lilly.roberts@bhusa.com
Tel: +1 781 904 2639
Fax: +1 781 904 2640

Europe and rest of world
Christina Donaldson, Editorial Assistant
Email: christina.donaldson@repp.co.uk
Tel: +44 (0)1865 314027
Fax: +44 (0)1865 314572